Adam Wierzbicki

Web Content Credibility

 Springer

Adam Wierzbicki
Polish-Japanese Institute of Information Technology
Warsaw, Poland

ISBN 978-3-030-08542-1   ISBN 978-3-319-77794-8   (eBook)
https://doi.org/10.1007/978-3-319-77794-8

This Springer imprint is published by the registered company Springer International Publishing AG part
of Springer Nature.
The registered company address is: Gewerbestrasse 11, 6330 Cham, Switzerland

*To all participants of the **Reconcile project**.
Thank you for a rewarding and inspiring
collaboration.*

***To my mother and father**, with love and
respect.*

***To my wife Małgosia**, who is my best friend,
partner, and my better half.*

***To my son Tomek** and his sisters Asia, Róża,
and Ania. The future belongs to them.*

Preface

The lack of support for credibility evaluation is one of the major weaknesses of the Web today. Despite mature search services, as well as advanced content filtering and recommendation methods, only a few services attempt to support credibility evaluation on the Web. This situation allows the spread of fake news, rumors, and factually incorrect Web content. The increasing reliance of our society on the Web makes solving this problem an important goal for informatics.

This book has been written for an audience of researchers and developers who wish to design and implement credibility evaluation support systems for the Web. I hope that the book can serve as a basis to accelerate the research in this area.

The study of Web content credibility evaluation is an interdisciplinary area. The book attempts to bridge the gap between research on credibility evaluation in media science, social science, psychology, and informatics. The book contributes operational definitions, as well as models, of source and message credibility that base on theoretical work in disciplines other than informatics.

Supporting better Web content credibility evaluation is an important social goal. Because of this, the book falls into the broader discipline of social informatics: *a discipline of informatics that studies how information systems can realize social goals, use social concepts, or become sources of information about social phenomena.*

This book is based on research supported by the grant "Reconcile: Robust Online Credibility Evaluation of Web Content" from Switzerland through the Swiss Contribution to the enlarged European Union (http://reconcile.pja.edu.pl).

Warsaw, Poland
Adam Wierzbicki
May 2018

Contents

Chapter 1
Introduction

Lying only works if there is first a mutual assumption of cooperation and trust: you only lie because you know that I will trust your information as truthful and act accordingly.
Michael Tomasello

Credibility has recently become a hot topic in Web content research. Companies such as Google aim to discern the veracity of statements of fact contained in webpages.[1] Crowdsourced services striving to filter out non-credible information have been subject to research and are applied in practice. Among systems using that approach are the Article Feedback Tool on Wikipedia, the TweetCred[2] system for Twitter, or the WOT system for evaluating Web portal credibility.[3] Content evaluation can also be supported by machine classification approaches that attempt to learn quality ratings and predict the ratings of new content.

Diverse techniques have been applied to address the problem of supporting Web content credibility evaluation. They range from Crowdsourcing, machine classification, reputation systems, to Natural Language Processing. The domains of application also vary: credibility evaluation has been applied in the domain of health information on the Web (Health on the Net (HON)[4]) as well as in the domain of politics and media (PolitiFact[5]). The first goal of this book is to provide a sound theoretical foundation for research on Web content credibility and present an overview of the state of the art. This goal is achieved in part by presenting openly available datasets (such as the Web Content Credibility Corpus produced

---

[1]http://www.newscientist.com/article/mg22530102.600-google-wants-to-rank-websites-based-on-facts-not-links.html.

[2]http://twitdigest.iiitd.edu.in/TweetCred/.

[3]http://www.mywot.com/.

[4]http://www.hon.ch/.

[5]http://politifact.com/.

© Springer International Publishing AG, part of Springer Nature 2018
A. Wierzbicki, *Web Content Credibility*,
https://doi.org/10.1007/978-3-319-77794-8_1

as a result of the Reconcile project[6]) for reproducible evaluation of algorithms for Web content credibility evaluation, as well as methodologies for carrying out experimental evaluations of systems for supporting Web content credibility evaluation of users. The book contributes to theory by formulating a new definition of credibility (Chap. 2) and theoretical models of credibility based on game theory (Chap. 5). Another goal of the book is to provide reference models and designs of Web content credibility evaluation support methods, taking into account the diversity of these methods for various types of Web content. This goal is achieved in Chaps. 3 and 4.

1.1   Credibility and Relevance of Web Content

The enormous utility and ubiquity of the Web are due not merely to the Web's information content, but rather to the increasingly intelligent functions of the Web that enable the discovery of the most useful Web content. Among these functions, Web information retrieval (Web search) plays a central role. Web search is an unquestionable success of information and computer science, as well as one of the most prolific research areas in these disciplines. There are widely used and highly effective practical Web search systems, but even today there are ongoing projects to develop new search engines (such as Wikipedia's new search engine project, the Knowledge Engine,[7] or continuous commercial efforts).

This striking success of Web information retrieval is in contrast to the current state of the art of research on Web content credibility evaluation support. While research on credibility is very active, it has a long way to go before reaching the mature state of research on Web searching. In order to try to understand the reasons for this difference, one must first consider the reasons for success of Web information retrieval.

Research on Web information retrieval has a very long history when compared to other research areas concerning the Web (semantic Web, Web intelligence, or Web content credibility evaluation). First, large-scale information retrieval systems have been developed in the early 1970s. It can be said that the commercialization of the Web in the early 1990s merely gave a new application domain to an already mature research area. Later research that resulted in breakthroughs, such as the invention of PageRank in 1996, may have been inspired by earlier results on the use of eigenvalues in scientometrics for ranking scientific journals, published 20 years before.

Another important factor in the successful development of Web information retrieval is the research methodology. In 1992, the US Department of Defense along with the National Institute of Standards and Technology (NIST) organized

---

[6]http://reconcile.pjwstk.edu.pl/.

[7]https://en.wikipedia.org/wiki/Knowledge_Engine_(Wikimedia_Foundation).

the Text REtrieval Conference (TREC) that became a series of annual conferences, continuing until today. TREC allow for evaluation and comparison of competing Web search systems and algorithms on the same, public datasets. According to the organizers (NIST), in the first 6 years of the TREC organization, the effectiveness of Web information retrieval systems approximately doubled. TREC today present challenges for the research community in various areas of Web information retrieval, including the newer discipline of Human-Computer Information Retrieval (HCIR) which tackles issues such as automatic query reformulation, faceted search, lookahead, or relevance feedback.

Time and a good methodology brought about the development of sophisticated algorithms and some of the most advanced information systems practically used today (such as the Google search engine). Web search algorithms use diverse mathematical models, such as set-theoretic models, algebraic models, and probabilistic models. These models can take into account term interdependencies, as well as contextual information.

A final, and perhaps most important, reason for the success of research on Web information retrieval is the good understanding of basic concepts involved in an evaluation of search results by computer scientists. In Web information retrieval, the notion of quality of retrieved documents is called relevance. Relevance is understood by computer scientists as a measure of how well retrieved Web content matches the information need of the user. While it is understood that ultimately relevance judgments are made by humans, the success of currently used algorithms suggests that there is little inherent difficulty in predicting human relevance judgments based on available data.

The state of research on Web content credibility evaluation is far different. From the beginning, the concept of credibility has been considered by computer scientists as difficult to understand, fuzzy, and uncertain. One of the reasons for this difference in understanding of the two concepts of relevance and credibility may lie in the origin of early credibility research: media science and social science. The goals of these two fields of science are different from the goals of computer science or information science, which are applied sciences. Media science and social science aim to achieve an in-depth understanding of studied social phenomena or concepts, taking into account all possible aspects. On the other hand, informatics requires an operational understanding of the concept of credibility, because this is a prerequisite for developing information systems and algorithms that may be used in practice.

The difficulty of understanding credibility of information, as well as the late start of research on Web content credibility in computer and information science—which dates back to the 1990s—results in the current state of the Web that can successfully support search, but has little functions or tools for supporting Web content credibility evaluation. This does not mean that credibility is less important than relevance on the Web. In fact, research on the nature of human communication and human thought suggests the opposite, as explained in the next section.

1.1.1   Credibility and Relevance in Human Communication

The human condition has been subject to inquiry since the ancient times, as the entire discipline of philosophy has aimed to understand what makes us human. Recently, however, this question has become a subject of empirical sciences such as anthropology, evolutionary psychology, or evolutionary linguistics, and significant progress has been made. Scientists seek to understand what makes us human by experimentally investigating primate behavior and comparing the results to human behavior (especially child behavior). Seminal research by Michael Tomasello [192], as well as by Robin Dunbar, has shed new insight on the human condition and highlighted the importance of two specifically human concepts: credibility and relevance.

Tomasello argues that human cognition is special due to its focus on collaborative communication and emergent states of the mind called joint attention and joint intentionality. In short, humans are able to understand not just the received communication but also the intentions of the communicating partner and to act accordingly based on this understanding.[8] This process is, in fact, recursive, as a communicating human is able to anticipate the understanding of their intentions by the receiver, and can take this knowledge into account. However, human communication is essentially collaborative: its goal is a joint action that should reach a joint goal. This is why it is so important that this communication should be true. To quote Tomasello,

> The notion of truth entered the human psyche not with the advent of individual rationality (...), but, rather, with the advent of joint intentionality and its focus on communicating cooperatively with others.
> A Natural History of Human Thinking. Michael Tomasello

While Tomasello does not explicitly use the term, evaluating credibility (or believability) of communicated information is an essential part of his theory of what makes us human. Humans do not merely communicate informative facts; rather, they commit to the truth of a statement and back up this commitment with reasons and justifications as necessary. This kind of cooperative argumentation is another important human characteristic, requiring a special way of thinking, which Tomasello refers to as the "Web of beliefs":

> The ability to connect thoughts to other thoughts (both those of others and one's own) by various inferential relations (prototypically by providing reasons and justifications) is key to human reason in general, and it leads to a kind of interconnection among all of an individual's potential thoughts in a kind of holistic "web of beliefs."
> A Natural History of Human Thinking. Michael Tomasello

---

[8]Other neuroscientists, such as Graziano, go even further and hypothesize that perceiving and understanding the intentions, emotions, and minds of others is the basis of perception of our own consciousness, as well as the basis of spiritual and religious beliefs [53].

Tomasello's idea of recursive credibility evaluations points out the fact that not just the receiver but also the sender of information evaluates the information's credibility. Furthermore, the goal of the sender's evaluation is different from the receiver's. The receiver wishes to know whether the received information is true (or sufficiently reliable). The sender's credibility evaluation of his own information, however, has the goal of predicting whether the information will be judged as credible by the receiver. These two (often conflicting) goals point out the essential difference between truth and credibility: the receiver wishes for information that is true, while the sender wishes to produce information that is credible. Further, it becomes clear that the sender has many means to modify his information in order to persuade the receiver that it is credible. In fact, humans' invention of truth also resulted in the invention of lying, as succinctly expressed by Tomasello in the motto of this chapter. The differences between truth and credibility leads to a new definition of credibility, discussed in Sect. 2.3.

Another basic characteristic of human thinking is an evaluation of relevance. However, according to Tomasello, relevance evaluations are actually secondary to credibility evaluations: they can only be made once the receiver is assured (or assumes) that the received information is credible. Then, it becomes important to understand why the information is relevant for the receiver:

> The second important consequence of this new cooperative way of communicating was that it created a new kind of inference, namely, a relevance inference. The recipient of a cooperative communicative act asks him or herself: given that we know together that he is trying to help me, why does he think that I will find the situation that he is pointing out to me relevant to my concerns.
> A *Natural History of Human Thinking*. Michael Tomasello

The relevance judgment is another human ability that requires the establishment of a common (joint) basis of facts and attention between the receiver and the communicating partner: the Web of beliefs is therefore also fundamentally important for relevance evaluations. Tomasello's view on the fundamental role of credibility also points out an underlying assumption on Web information retrieval that is so obvious that one usually forgets about it. Obviously, retrieving the most relevant document will result in the best satisfactions of a user's information needs, *assuming that the retrieved document is credible*.

Tomasello's theory on what makes human thinking special shows that the two concepts of credibility and relevance are inherently connected. They are also two important, basic human concepts, similar to trust and fairness. Since much, if not the majority, of human communication occurs on the Web today, a solid understanding of credibility and relevance should therefore be the basis of any technological solutions that support communication or information retrieval on the Web. The concept of relevance is the basis of Web information retrieval, and has been studied in computer and information sciences for several decades, resulting in enormously successful technologies such as contemporary search engines. On the other hand, the equally important concept of credibility has not yet reached a similar understanding. The aim of this book is to make a first step towards changing this situation.

1.1.2   Epistemic Similarities of Credibility and Relevance
Judgments of Web Content

The predominant view on the main reasons (besides lack of time) for the less advanced state of the art of research on Web content credibility evaluation support is that it's a result of lacking understanding of credibility in computer science. What follows is the comparison of the concepts of credibility and relevance from a methodological point of view. The goal is to understand whether credibility is inherently more difficult to investigate than relevance.

To compare the difficulty of researching credibility and relevance, it is possible to start by comparing the methodologies currently used to further this research. Credibility is the first issue to be addressed. Here, the main methodology is empirical: researchers conduct experiments during which human users evaluate Web content from specially prepared corpora. These experiments are used to gather datasets of human credibility evaluations, which are then used to study factors affecting human evaluations, or to train and evaluate machine learning algorithms that aim to predict credibility evaluations. Several such experiments will be described in detail in the second chapter of this book.

The research methodology used in Web information retrieval is best described by the methodology of the TREC. First, large corpora of Web content are prepared by the conference organizers. These corpora depend on the track; however, for simple Web search, the corpora are usually real webpages or documents, chosen to reproduce topical diversity. Next, the organizers prepare search topics that represent a user's information needs. The description of the topics is quite detailed, for example [60]:

> A relevant document will either report an impending rail strike, describing the conditions which may lead to a strike, or will provide an update on an ongoing strike. To be relevant, the document will identify the location of the strike or potential strike. For an impending strike, the document will report the status of negotiations, contract talks, etc. to enable an assessment of the probability of a strike. For an ongoing strike, the document will report the length of the strike to the current date and the status of negotiations or mediation.

Finally, TREC participants devised algorithms for searching that took as input the document corpora and the search topics. The result was a ranking of documents. TREC organizers used a pooling method that took the documents from the top of the ranking of all algorithms for a given search topic and merged them into one set (removing repetitions). The relevance of these pooled documents to the search topic was then evaluated by a single expert [60, 61].

To summarize, relevance judgments used to evaluate and improve Web information retrieval systems and algorithms at the TREC were made by human evaluators. This is a similar approach to the one used in research on Web content credibility today.

In order to further the comparison of epistemic difficulty involved in research of credibility and relevance on the Web, one may wonder whether relevance judgments are more or less uncertain or subjective than credibility judgments.

This question could only be answered with certainty by a comparison of datasets that contain multiple human evaluations of credibility or relevance per document. Unfortunately, such datasets are not available today. It is, however, possible to carry out a thought experiment that would attempt to apply one of the theories developed to understand Web content credibility judgments to relevance judgments. The reader is left to judge whether the theory proposed to understand credibility applies well to relevance judgments. If it does, then relevance judgments should not be any easier to understand and study than credibility judgments.

The theory proposed to apply to relevance judgments is called Prominence-Interpretation theory. It has been introduced by Fogg based on research by the Stanford team on Web content credibility [40] during 1999–2003. According to the Prominence-Interpretation theory, there are two stages in Web users' credibility evaluations. In the first stage, users investigate the Web content and notice some credibility cues. Some other (possibly important) cues may go unnoticed at this stage. Prominence is the likelihood that an information contained in a webpage will be noticed or perceived by the user. Fogg claims that at least five factors influence prominence: the motivation ("involvement") of the user, the ability ("experience") of the user, the task of the user, user's individual characteristics, and the topic of the webpage.

During the second stage, Interpretation, users make judgments about the cues they have noticed in the first stage. According to Fogg, many factors can influence interpretation: a user's level of competency (expertise) regarding the webpages topic, the context of the evaluation (consisting of the user's environment, expectations, and situational norms), as well as a user's assumptions consisting of heuristics, past experience, and culture.

In this thought experiment, the example search topic from the TREC, quoted above, is considered. A situation is given when Web users, or evaluating experts, need to judge the relevance of a retrieved webpage to the search topic. The judgment would not necessarily be binary, but could be done on some evaluation scale (such scales will be discussed in more detail in the next chapter). The search topic description asks the user to look for several kinds of information. The first question is whether the retrieved webpage is related to strikes. However, it should not be too difficult for a good retrieval algorithm to disregard pages that do not include strikes as the keyword (the only problem could be multiple meanings of a search term). Next, the user has to check whether the webpage contains information on the strike's location, ongoing negotiations, date and length of the strike, and current status of the strike or negotiations. The presence or absence of any of these kinds of information should affect the relevance judgment. However, it is clear that in a larger webpage, depending on user's attention, concentration, and time used for evaluation, some of these kinds of information may go unnoticed by the user (even if they are present in the page). These factors are influenced by the user's involvement, experience, and individual characteristics, as foreseen by the first stage, Prominence, of the Prominence-Interpretation theory.

Once the user has searched for the important content in the webpage, he or she still needs to make a relevance judgment. The search topic does not prioritize the kinds of information to look for (with the exception of information about a strike's location, which is explicitly mentioned as being a necessary condition for relevance). Therefore, the user is left to decide how relevant a webpage is that, for example, contains information about a strike's location and time, but no information about negotiation or current status. This stage requires an interpretation of the kinds of information in the search topic. Such decisions by the Web user clearly resemble the Interpretation stage of the Prominence-Interpretation theory. Clearly, the decision would also depend on a user's experience and understanding of the topic. For example, expert users who have experience in evaluating relevance may find it easier than ordinary users to interpret the information contained in the webpage. Still, even for an expert, determining the relevance ranking of two webpages about strikes may be difficult, if—for example—one webpage contains only information about the time of the strike, while the other only about the negotiation status.

The reader is left to judge for himself whether the proposed application of the Prominence-Interpretation theory is valid. There is, at the very least, a strong analogy between the decision process of evaluating the relevance and the credibility of a webpage. The conclusion is that relevance judgments are not any easier to make, nor less dependent on a user's attention, concentration, and experience than credibility judgments. Therefore, the creation of information systems and algorithms that support the evaluation of Web content credibility should in principle be not more difficult than the creation of such tools for supporting Web search. This is an optimistic conclusion for researchers working on Web content credibility evaluation support. However, an improved understanding of the concept of credibility by computer science is a prerequisite for advancing the state of the art of research on Web credibility. It is also one of the main goals of this book.

1.2 Why Does Credibility Evaluation Support Matter on the Web?

The current World Wide Web is characterized by two factors: a low price of producing Web content and very high incentives for producing Web content that can influence the beliefs of Web users. The incentives are, firstly, of commercial nature, which accounts for the rapid development of Web-based marketing and advertising, as well as the success of Google. However, Web content affects not just our purchasing decisions but also several other aspects of human behavior, ranging from lifestyle to political decisions.

Credibility evaluations of Web content are regularly made by ordinary users. The goal of research and development on Web content credibility evaluation should be to support and improve these evaluations, so that Web users can distinguish between truthful and untrue Web content (whenever this distinction is possible). The following section contains examples of Web content that is untrue, and can potentially have a high social impact. It also presents examples of existing services aiming to support Web content credibility evaluation.

1.2.1   Examples of Non-credible Medical Web Content

The Web contains information on almost all aspects of human behavior, and human knowledge. In order to focus our analysis on the credibility of current Web content, the discussion will be limited to a few areas of Web content. The first is Web content related to health and medicine. This is a large and important category of Web content, to the extent that Web users have coined the term "Dr Google." The medical domain is important because it is an instance of a larger category of Web content based on factual, specialized knowledge.

This section describes just three examples of non-credible medical Web content, which should be enough for the reader to realize the potential impact of this content, and therefore the significance of research on Web content credibility evaluation support in the medical domain. Still, it is important to remember that these examples are just a tip of the iceberg of non-credible medical content on the Web.

1.2.1.1   Vaccines and Autism

A Web search for the query "vaccines and autism" will have a plethora of results. Many of the found webpages will still support the view that a connection between vaccines and autism exists, although as of now a majority of webpages will refute the claim. The supposed connection between vaccines and autism dates back to the thiomersal controversy. The causal link between the mercury based vaccine preservative, thiomersal, and autism has been proposed in a scientific article published in 1998 by *The Lancet*, a highly reputed medical journal. The author of the study, Andrew Wakefield, has been found guilty of dishonesty by the British General Medical Council in 2010[9] and subsequently barred from practicing medicine in the UK. *The Lancet* has retracted Wakefield's article.[10] However, for 12 years, the controversy remained unresolved in the scientific community, and even today it lingers in the opinion of the public.

The anti-vaccination movement is a global community, largely present on the Web. One of the strongest supporters of the link between vaccines and autism was Jenny McCarthy, an American model and celebrity. Her son was diagnosed with autism at the age of 2.5, following a series of vaccinations. McCarthy had launched a foundation called "Generation Rescue" that promotes alternative therapies and alternative theories debating environmental causes of autism, including vaccination. The "Generation Rescue" website is an excellent example of the difficulty involved in evaluating Web content credibility. It is professionally designed, informative, and supported by a large community of users. Nevertheless, it is also rated as non-credible by existing credibility evaluation support tools, such as WOT.

---

[9]http://briandeer.com/solved/gmc-charge-sheet.pdf.

[10]http://www.thelancet.com/journals/lancet/article/PIIS0140-6736(97)11096-0/abstract.

The proposed example is one of many, and a good example of a specific type of medical Web content: content based on scientific facts (frequently, however, subject to simplification or incorrect interpretation). Only the scientific community could have refuted the claim underlying the belief that vaccines cause autism. The majority of this community has agreed that this belief is unsubstantiated. However, the process was time-consuming and obscure to the lay Web users and thus could not avert the general surmise that vaccines may indeed cause autism. This resulted in a decrease in the number of vaccinations in the USA and worldwide. The seriousness of the situation manifests in increasingly large measles outbreaks, such as the recent outbreak in 2015 in Germany. It involved over 570 reported measles cases and caused infant deaths.

1.2.1.2   Consuming Placenta

Examples of non-credible medical Web content can be much more humorous than the case of the anti-vaccination movement. An increasingly popular, and probably harmless, trend is for women to consume their own placenta post-partum. Ingesting one's own placenta is supposed to help avoid after-birth mood swings or depression (the so-called baby blues). The trend has supporters among celebrities, including Kim Kardashian.[11] This example is food for thought regarding the link between non-credible, controversial health and medical decisions, and the notoriety (and public exposure) of celebrities. Whatever the reason for her decision, Kardashian's impact on other women may be similar to her influencing women by declaring that she is using a new cosmetic.

Similarly to the previous example, a critical Web user should be able to find reputable Web content that refutes the claim that eating a placenta has health benefits.[12] However, the exposure of such content on the Web is much lower, proving that medical professionals are no match for celebrities online.

1.2.1.3   Colloidal Silver

The Web is a medium that is almost ideally suited for the proliferation of alternative medicine. One of the reasons is that many of the commodities required for alternative therapies can be readily purchased on the Web. One such example is colloidal silver. A search query for this term will result in many pages that recommend supposed benefits of using colloidal silver for the treatment of infections, ranging from ear infections to pneumonia, as well as on wounds or lesions.[13] This view is

---

[11] http://www.mirror.co.uk/3am/celebrity-news/kim-kardashian-eating-placenta-again-7013283.

[12] https://www.nichd.nih.gov/news/releases/Pages/062615-podcast-placenta-consumption.aspx.

[13] https://draxe.com/colloidal-silver-benefits/.

not supported by established medicine.[14] Rather than healing sinus trouble, colloidal silver (if ingested) can cause argyria, a permanent bluish-gray discoloration of the skin. Similarly to placenta ingestion, the use of colloidal silver is promoted by celebrities: this time, it is the well-known actress, Gwyneth Paltrow, who promoted the use of a spray with colloidal silver in the American health show, *Dr Oz*.[15] The price of colloidal silver health supplements ranges from 10 to 60 US dollars on Amazon (where it is one of the most popular health products).

The above three examples have one thing in common: Web content from reputable sources (such as the National Institutes of Health[16]) exists that contradicts non-credible claims present in other places on the Web. Critical Web users, who are willing to spend time and effort on verifying medical claims made on the Web, should be able to correctly evaluate the credibility of content from these three examples. This might not be the case for medical content that concerns new or emerging alternative medicine therapies or unconfirmed medical claims.

1.2.2   Fake News in Web-Based Social Media

"Fake news" is a term that has "gone viral" after the 2016 American presidential election. While the existence and potential political consequence of fake news is probably as old as civilization itself, the situation in 2016 has been significantly different: in the USA, over 60% of adult citizens get their news on social media [4]. Popular fake news can be more widely shared on Facebook than mainstream news. Last but not least, fake news stories circulated on social media during the 2016 election in the USA has favored one candidate at the expense of another. The ratio of the amount of fake news that were pro-Trump (or anti-Clinton) with respect to those that were pro-Clinton (or anti-Trump) was almost 3:1, while the ratio of Facebook shares of these fake news is over 4:1. This strong partisanship has most likely contributed to the results of the American presidential election in 2016 [4].

Here, let us give one striking example of political fake news from the American election in 2016. While many other examples have been identified, the case of the infamous "Pizzagate" is sufficient to describe the problem.

In early November 2016, Internet users received access to the e-mails of John Podesta, Hillary Clinton's campaign manager. The e-mails have been released on WikiLeaks after a successful phishing attack. At the same time, another anonymous source released the claim that the New York City Police Department (NYPD) was investigating a pedophile ring linked to members of the Democratic Party. The combination of these two news has led to claims that food-related words in Podesta's e-mails were code words for pedophilia, sex trafficking, and even satanist ritual

---

[14]https://nccih.nih.gov/health/silver.

[15]http://colloidalsilversecrets.blogspot.com/2013_08_01_archive.html.

[16]https://nccih.nih.gov.

practices. For example, the words "cheese pizza" were claimed to be a code word for "child pornography," since they have the same initials.

Altogether, claims related to "Pizzagate" formed a full-fledged conspiracy theory. Multiple fake news emerged from that theory, such as the alleged raid of the NYPD on Hillary Clinton's property, or a claim that the FBI had confirmed the existence of an underground sex network. The spread of these fake news on Twitter and several news websites was viral. It is estimated that over 1 million tweets related to "Pizzagate" have been published on Twitter by the end of the 2016 US election.

Apart from political consequences, the fake news' spread on social media resulted in real consequences that affected owners of restaurants claimed to be involved in sex-ring meetings. These businesses received large amounts of threatening phone calls, including death threats, and also experienced online harassment. The public reaction to fake news culminated in a shooting in one of the restaurants, Comet Ping Pong.[17] A self-proclaimed "investigator" fired three rifle shots in the restaurant, but let himself be arrested without resistance afterwards. Luckily, no one was hurt.

The "Pizzagate" conspiracy theory has been finally discredited on the Internet. A significant role in the process has been played by one of the credibility evaluation support systems described in the next section: Snopes.com. Mainstream news organizations, such as *The New York Times*, *The Washington Post*, and others, have also played a part in discrediting and denouncing "Pizzagate." Debunking of this conspiracy theory involved disproval of several fake news that used images of children from Instagram and falsely claimed that these were sex-ring victims, kept in a non-existent of the Comet Ping Pong restaurant. Despite early warnings that the news related to "Pizzagate" were fake, the "Pizzagate" theory continued to spread on social media and alternative Web-based news sites. It is important to note that an author of a fake news article about "Pizzagate" has been quoted to express her satisfaction by saying: "It's honestly really grown our audience."[18] This honest admission clearly shows the economic motivation of Web-based content producers in the production and dissemination of fake news, as well as other non-credible Web content.

1.2.3   Examples of Credibility Evaluation Support Systems

As it was already pointed out on the example of vaccines and autism, there are services aiming to support Web users in the evaluation of Web content credibility. In this book, such services will be referred to as credibility evaluation support (CS). While their current impact and popularity is still too low, they point out various

---

[17]https://en.wikipedia.org/wiki/Pizzagate_conspiracy_theory.

[18]https://www.thestar.com/news/canada/2016/12/07/belleville-woman-helped-cook-up-pizzagate.html.

possibilities for future research and development. A common feature of all the discussed services is that they are based on human evaluations, sometimes using a Crowdsourcing approach, and sometimes relying on experts.

1.2.3.1   Health on the Net

The first example comes from the medical domain and provides a follow-up for the discussion of non-credible medical Web content. Although activities of official health institutions (such as the National Institutes of Health) providing access to credible medical content are not a service supporting medical Web content credibility evaluation, such services exist. They are usually based on the principle of certification. One of the services providing certificates to credible medical websites is Health on the Net (HON).[19]

Established in 1996, Health on the Net is a foundation based in Switzerland. HON has been founded by experts on telematics and e-healthcare. HON collaborates with several medical institutions, as well as with the Economic and Social Council of the United Nations, the WHO, and the International Organization for Standardization's (ISO) technical committee for Health Informatics. To date, HON has certified over 8000 websites. While this number may seem small when compared to the number of websites that deliver medical content, it can be said that HON covers websites with highest source credibility.

Web content producers can apply for HON certification. They have to submit their websites for reviewing by a team of HON experts. The review is based on a publicly available set of criteria, summarized in the "HON code." According to the code, medical Web content needs to meet the following requirements:[20]

1. Authoritative. Any medical or health advice provided and hosted on this site will only be given by medically trained and qualified professionals unless a clear statement is made that a piece of advice offered is from a non-medically qualified individual or organisation.
2. Complementarity. The information provided on this site is designed to support, not replace, the relationship that exists between a patient/site visitor and his/her existing physician.
3. Privacy. Confidentiality of data relating to individual patients and visitors to a medical/health website, including their identity, is respected by this website. The website owners undertake to honour or exceed the legal requirements of medical/health information privacy that apply in the country and state where the website and mirror sites are located.
4. Attribution. Where appropriate, information contained on this site will be supported by clear references to source data and, where possible, have specific

---

[19] www.hon.ch.

[20] http://www.hon.ch/HONcode/Webmasters/Conduct.html.

HTML links to that data. The date when a clinical page was last modified will be clearly displayed (e.g. at the bottom of the page).
5. Justifiability. Any claims relating to the benefits/performance of a specific treatment, commercial product or service will be supported by appropriate, balanced evidence in the manner outlined above in Principle 4.
6. Transparency. The designers of this website will seek to provide information in the clearest possible manner and provide contact addresses for visitors that seek further information or support. The Webmaster will display his/her E-mail address clearly throughout the website.
7. Financial disclosure. Support for this website will be clearly identified, including the identities of commercial and non-commercial organisations that have contributed funding, services or material for the site.
8. Advertising policy. If advertising is a source of funding it will be clearly stated. A brief description of the advertising policy adopted by the website owners will be displayed on the site. Advertising and other promotional material will be presented to viewers in a manner and context that facilitates differentiation between it and the original material created by the institution operating the site.

HON certificates have expiration dates and must be periodically renewed. A Web content producer who obtains a HON certificate can display the certificate logo on his website. While the presence of such logo may be noticed by informed Web users, it is less likely to be known by lay Web users without a stronger interest in medical Web content credibility. Moreover, the absence of the logo cannot be interpreted as lack of source credibility, because only 8000 websites possess the HON certificate.

The certificate-based approach to selecting highly credible medical websites has been adopted by other organizations, such as the National Health Service (NHS) in England. This organization has introduced their own medical website certificate, the "Information Standard."[21]

HON provides other services, most notable of which is a prototype medical Web search engine, Khresmoi.[22] This search engine only indexes credible (official or certified) medical websites. Still, even Khresmoi cannot guarantee to always retrieve credible Web content, as demonstrated by a query for "eating placenta" that has returned a webpage with a detailed description of the procedure of cooking, powdering, and encapsulating the placenta, along with a recommendation to do so by mothers.[23]

---

[21] https://www.england.nhs.uk/tis/.

[22] http://everyone.khresmoi.eu/hon-search/.

[23] http://www.babycentre.co.uk/l1051310/how-to-eat-your-placenta-photos.

1.2.3.2   WOT

The expert-based approach used by Health on the Net may be suitable for a specialist-knowledge domain such as medicine and health, but cannot be expected to scale to the entire Web. The Crowdsourcing approach can be more suitable. That method is used by WOT,[24] the largest and most effective Web content credibility evaluation support system to date. WOT combines two tools: a community portal and a browser extension. The browser extension allows Web users to easily rate the credibility of browsed webpages. The extension also displays summaries for webpages that have already obtained sufficient ratings, in the form of small icons with colors indicating the credibility score—from red (not credible) to green (credible). The browser extension also modifies Google search results page by displaying an icon next to each result.

WOT has been successful because it attracts a large community of users. The portal claims to have 140 million downloads of the browser extension. Even considering that the extension may be downloaded multiple times by a single Web user, it is likely that WOT has tens of millions of users. This allows the system to cover a significant amount of websites, including the "Generation Rescue" website mentioned in Sect. 1.2.1.1 that is rated as not credible. WOT covers webpages on all topics and in various languages.

Apart from the browser extension, the WOT portal allows users not only to rate or check a webpage's credibility but also to discuss various kinds of webpages. The WOT system generally tends to focus on the less credible Web content, especially on content related to scams, frauds, and virus or malware threats. Users can also rate websites' suitability for children.

The WOT system uses a simple scale for rating website credibility, but also allows rating users to select tags to circumstantiate their rating. This approach will be discussed in more detail in the second chapter. WOT also provides an API for users who wish to obtain credibility scores of websites and use them in their own Web applications.

WOT's success has been threatened by ownership changes in 2014. After the changes, in November 2016, the WOT service has been accused by German journalists of selling user data to third parties. Data collection is enabled by the WOT browser extension. While WOT claimed to have sold anonymized data, the investigators were able to discover the personal data of several users. Moreover, WOT has not obtained user consent for selling the data in accordance to law. As a result, the WOT browser extension has been removed by major browsers. The example of WOT serves as an important reminder about the trustworthiness of credibility evaluation support services. The use of commercial credibility evaluation support services with unclear business models may be unsafe. However, this observation does not detract from the overall effectiveness of WOT's Crowdsourcing credibility evaluation mechanism.

---

[24]www.mywot.com.

WOT browser extension has been reinstated in major browsers in December 2016. The WOT service has since changed its privacy policy,[25] providing an extensive explanation of uses of personal and non-personal data, as well as an opt-out option for users who do not wish to share any data. The WOT service continues to be the largest credibility evaluation support service in use today.

1.2.3.3 Snopes

While both Health on the Net and WOT deal with the credibility of websites, the credibility of rumors or urban legends is also evaluated and investigated by Web users. One of the best-known websites serving this purpose is Snopes, established in 1995. The first goal of Snopes has been to evaluate the credibility of "urban legends," defined as widely circulating rumors. However, it is interesting to note that Snopes deals with submissions of various kinds of information, such as Internet rumors, e-mail chain mails, or political opinions. Snopes treats different kinds of information in different ways. Statements which make factual claims are subject to verification—this is the main function of Snopes. On the other hand, stated opinions are merely checked to verify the authenticity of the source. This kind of common-sense distinction shows that various kinds of information must be verified in different ways. Indeed, there is also a significant difference between the credibility of urban legends or rumors (even if they contain factual statements) that can be well evaluated by a crowd of diverse, independent users, and the credibility of specialist factual information, for example, in the medical domain.

Snopes is a very popular website, receiving hundreds of thousands of visits daily. It is also frequently referenced in the media and by researchers of modern folklore. Medical claims, such as discussed in the previous examples of non-credible medical content, are discussed in a separate topical category. Snopes also publishes collections of urban legends and rumors on a subject: a good example is the collection of rumors about the 1969 Apollo 11 moon landing.[26]

Apart from typical urban legends, Snopes seems to contain a lot of information on statements made by well-known figures, politicians, or celebrities. The large number of these statements exposes a very human motivation: the urge to catch these famous figures when they are lying. However, the amount of political statements quoted on Snopes has led to allegations that the service (or its founders) has certain political (liberal) leanings. This allegation has been strongly refuted by Snopes and its founders; nevertheless, this demonstrates another issue of services for credibility evaluation support: the service's own source credibility and fairness is being questioned by Web users.

---

[25]https://www.mywot.com/en/privacy/privacy_policy.

[26]http://www.snopes.com/info/lists/moonlanding.asp.

1.2.3.4 PolitiFact

Launched in 2007, PolitiFact[27] is a service focused exclusively on the credibility of statements made by politicians, journalists, and other authority figures. The motivation of Web users utilized by this service is similar to that of some users of Snopes, discussed above. However, PolitiFact is run by an American newspaper, the *Tampa Bay Times*. The newspaper is owned by the Poynter Institute, a non-profit school for journalism. The *Tampa Bay Times* partners with several other American newspapers to run PolitiFact. PolitiFact has also received support from numerous non-profit organizations, such as the Bill & Melinda Gates Foundation, the Ford Foundation, the Democracy Fund, and several others. With such funding management, PolitiFact is able to employ about ten permanent staff members who write for the service and rate the statements. This means that contrary to Snopes, PolitiFact does not follow the Crowdsourcing approach, but uses a team of experts.

The veracity (not credibility) of statements made by politicians is evaluated on a 6-point scale:

1. True—The statement is accurate and there's nothing significant missing.
2. Mostly True—The statement is accurate but needs clarification or additional information.
3. Half True—The statement is partially accurate but leaves out important details or takes things out of context.
4. Mostly False—The statement contains some element of truth but ignores critical facts that would give a different impression.
5. False—The statement is not accurate.
6. Pants on Fire—The statement is not accurate and makes a ridiculous claim.

According to PolitiFact, the claims are verified by checking original sources, for example, government reports, rather than news stories, as well as by interviewing impartial experts. Claim evaluations are always followed by a longer explanation that resembles a journal article. The quality of these articles is usually high: PolitiFact has been awarded the Pulitzer Prize for National Reporting for its fact-checking journalism in 2009.

The evaluations of claims made by politicians are aggregated on PolitiFact into a distribution of ratings that can be thought of as approximating the source credibility of the politician.

Fact-checking services similar to PolitiFact are run by other American news-papers or news agencies, notably by *The Washington Post*[28] (since 2011 as a permanent feature) and ABCNews.[29]

Similarly to Snopes, PolitiFact has been accused of liberal political bias. A study of about 500 statements rated on PolitiFact found that while claims made

---

[27]www.politifact.org.

[28]www.washingtonpost.com/news/fact-checker/.

[29]http://abcnews.go.com.

by Republicans and Democrats are equally represented, Republicans received three times more "Pants on Fire" ratings than Democrats. PolitiFact staff has replied that all claims are analyzed objectively and the result is a "batting average" of source credibility of political parties.

The above four examples of existing services supporting credibility evaluations of Web content can serve as inspiration, as well as source of data, for researchers of Web content credibility. Together with numerous examples of non-credible Web content (out of many, three from the medical domain were described), the large number of users of these services demonstrates the importance attached to Web content credibility by the public. Moreover, in two domains—healthcare and politics—services involve the work of experts, rather than relying on Crowdsourcing. While the question of what is the right approach towards designing a scalable, robust Web content credibility evaluation service is still open, existing services demonstrate a range of working approaches. The rest of this book will be devoted to formulating an improved understanding of how these approaches work and how they can be improved.

1.3 Book Organization

The book is organized as follows. Chapter 2 presents definitions of credibility and related concepts of truth and trust. Readers only interested in the most important definitions should refer to Sect. 2.3. This book proposes a new, specialized definition of credibility as a signal. This definition is useful in thinking about credibility when trying to measure it or gain an understanding of how to support credibility evaluations. Yet, the definition presented in Sect. 2.3 is not mathematically formalized. Readers who are more interested in theoretical (and mathematical) models of credibility can skip forward to Chap. 5.

Section 2.2 considers the question of design goals for services of Web content credibility evaluation support. This lays a groundwork for proposed designs of a credibility evaluation support system in Chap. 3.

Theories of Web content credibility evaluation are presented in Sect. 2.4. Section 2.5 presents methods of measuring credibility that are the basis of algorithms that support credibility evaluation. Mathematical concepts used throughout the book, like the Earth Mover's Distance and the Leik measure, are introduced in this section. Section 2.6 presents the most important experiments and publicly available datasets of credibility measurements used in this book.

Section 2.7 deals with the impact of evaluation subjectivity on credibility measurement. Section 2.8 shows a method for defining classes of webpage credibility based on distributions of credibility measurements. Section 2.9 discusses criteria used by human evaluators to evaluate credibility and their impact on credibility evaluations.

Chapter 3 presents methods, algorithms, and user interfaces of systems support-ing Web content credibility evaluation. The chapter starts with a reference design of a credibility evaluation support system (CS). The rest of the chapter discusses elements of this design: webpage credibility classifiers (Sect. 3.3) and algorithms that recommend Web content for evaluation (Sect. 3.4).

Adversaries of the CS are discussed in Sect. 3.2, and reputation systems for users of the CS in Sect. 3.5.1. The main part of the CS is the Fusion Algorithm, discussed in Sect. 3.6. Section 3.7 describes the CS module that deals with credibility of statements contained in webpages.

In Sect. 3.8, methods of predicting the controversy of Web content and Web search topics are discussed. Section 3.9 presents various designs of the CS user interface and how this interface can present summaries of Web content credibility evaluation, together with an evaluation of how this presentation can influence users.

Chapter 4 concerns the credibility of social media. The chapter considers credi-bility of user-generated content on Twitter (Sect. 4.1), on Q&A systems (Sect. 4.2), and on Wikipedia (Sect. 4.3). These diverse systems and platforms have several things in common from the point of view of credibility evaluation. The most important common features are the increased amount of meta-information about the author of evaluated content (as compared to regular websites) and the ability to aggregate information from several users that leads to an improved evaluation of a content credibility.

Chapter 5 presents mathematical and simulation models of credibility evaluation. Readers who have a more theoretical interest can read this chapter right after reading Sect. 2.3. Section 5.1 introduces a model of Web credibility that is defined as a signal. Basing on this concept, a game-theoretic model of Web content credibility evaluation—the Credibility Game—is introduced in Sect. 5.2. The rest of the chapter is devoted to various extensions of the Credibility Game that can be used to for modeling scenarios of Web content credibility evaluation. Such scenarios can be studied using simulation, leading to startling conclusions, for example, about the ability of a reputation system to influence strategies of dishonest content producers, or about the effects of learning in a knowledge community that evaluates content credibility.

Chapter 2
Understanding and Measuring Credibility

Hard models, soft thinking; soft models, hard thinking.
Harold Barney, 1978

Everything we hear is an opinion, not a fact.
Everything we see is a perspective, not the truth.
Marcus Aurelius

When considering the subject of credibility, computer scientists are usually hesitant and doubtful. This is because of their background and education in science, with emphasis on mathematics. Mathematics is an area requiring precise definitions and deductive reasoning. Faced with an inherently ambiguous and fuzzy social concept, such as credibility or trust, computer scientists are concerned about their inability to understand and model this concept with precision required to formulate algorithms or design information systems. Moreover, many computer scientists consider informatics to be a deductive science, similar to mathematics. This view is hard to support, especially when one considers a research area such as information retrieval, which is important and productive despite being clearly an empirical area of science. However, it accounts for many misunderstandings regarding the possibility of studying subjects such as computer-supported Web content credibility evaluation.

The study of scientific literature on credibility may only add to the doubts computer scientists have towards social concepts. Social sciences are empirical and had not yet formulated universally accepted and comprehensive theories on human social behavior. The same concerns understanding of social concepts. Available studies on credibility and trust in social sciences will point out several phenomena (often giving a convincing empirical verification) and formulate various hypotheses regarding human behavior. However, these phenomena and hypotheses are complex and varied, and seem hard to capture in a comprehensive model or theory. Furthermore, it is often difficult or impossible to make predictions about human behavior based on findings from social science. In addition, the language used in social sciences to express theories of behavior is often hard to comprehend for computer scientists.

The goal of this chapter (and, as a matter of fact, of the entire book) is to bridge this gap. Based on a review of existing literature from social sciences, economics, game theory, and computer science, it shall attempt to reformulate the definitions of social concepts and the validated theories of human behavior into models that will be useful for computer scientists. This is, in fact, one of the main research goals of social informatics, a branch of informatics that deals with understanding and use of social concepts and realizing social goals in the design of information systems. It will be possible to show that the complex social concept of credibility may be approximated by mathematical models. These models can be useful and are comprehensible for computer scientists.

The concerns mentioned above apply to the study of all social concepts by computer scientists (e.g., the same concerns apply to trust and to credibility). However, there is one specific problem concerning only the study of credibility. It is the confusion of two concepts: credibility and truth. Truth is a concept that seems to have a close semantic relationship with credibility. It is easy to mistakenly equate those two concepts and, for example, assume that the evaluations of credibility are equivalent to the evaluations of information's truthfulness. This is not the case, and this chapter will endeavor to dismiss this misunderstanding. It is sufficient to state that it is possible to differentiate between the independent concepts of truth and credibility. Information can be true and not credible, true and credible, not true and credible, or not true and not credible. However, the concept of truth becomes important from the point of view of this publication's goals when designing credibility support systems.

This chapter is devoted to the study of how users make judgments about Web content credibility. It also lays definitional and theoretical ground for the rest of the book. The chapter will begin with an introduction to the basic concepts used throughout the book. A top-down discussion method has been chosen to present these concepts. This means that the discussion shall begin with the concepts of credibility and truth, and move on towards other concepts that are necessary to understand credibility. A reader looking forwards to reach more basic and simple concepts must be patient: all in good time. The top-down discussion will end with basic concepts that are already well explained in the related literature (also in computer science).

After the top-down discussion of basic concepts, the chapter moves on to various theories of how users make credibility judgments. The chapter also presents empirical results of using various credibility measures, and studies of sensitivity of credibility measures to social and psychological user characteristics. Empirical studies of credibility measurements and their textual justifications also reveal the criteria of users who evaluate credibility. The reports on these studies conclude the chapter, giving the reader a solid understanding on the modeling and measuring of credibility.

2.1 Credibility and Truth

This section explores the relationship between the two concepts: credibility and truth. The goal of this discussion is to create a basis for understanding what it means to successfully support credibility evaluation in the next section. Definitions of credibility will be introduced later, together with a decomposition of this concept into more basic concepts. This top-down order is chosen so that the reader can first get an intuitive grasp of the major goal of the book: the concept of credibility evaluation support. In order for it to be comprehensible, the concept of credibility must be initially discussed without recourse to a precise definition. However, this strategy should also allow the reader to get a first feeling of this concept, before it is formally defined.

Truth is a concept directly related to credibility, but inherently more difficult to understand. Without giving a detailed definition of credibility, one can still describe credibility as an inherently subjective mental state of humans. On the other hand, truth is a concept often understood as universal and objective. Discussions on the nature of truth are the domain of epistemology and philosophy. The goal of this section is not to make a complete presentation of the complex concepts of truth, but to present the two concepts of credibility and truth side by side, and to understand their relationship.

In an attempt to directly compare the two concepts of credibility and truth, Table 2.1 summarizes examples used for the comparison.

Is credible information always true? If it were, there would be no fraud.

Is true information always credible? Consider the following examples: the theory of Copernicus in the Middle Ages, the theory of evolution in the seventeenth century, a doctor diagnosing a serious disease in a seemingly healthy patient, and a trusting person finding out their trust has been abused. Certainly, truth doesn't always sound credible.

The categories of "credible" and "non-credible" used in this example are associated with quantifiers: "credible for most," "non-credible for some." Still, the above examples may change depending on meta-information that is not described in the examples. Consider the following sentence: "Aliens attacked New York." This sentence may seem completely not credible, but under special circumstances

Table 2.1 A direct comparison of credibility and truth of information

	False	True
Non-credible	1. Aliens attacked New York 2. The Earth is flat	3. The theory of evolution 4. A doctor's diagnosis for a healthy patient that he has a serious disease 5. Information to a trusting person about the abuse of trust
Credible	6. All successful fraud	7. Personal hygiene, like brushing your teeth, is necessary for your health

can be made credible, as has been demonstrated by the radio show "The War of the Worlds."[1] In this case, the missing meta-information concerns mainly the presentation of the information, as well as the medium.

The examples above serve to demonstrate that the concept of credibility cannot be mistaken for truth of information. Of course, one may hope that credibility mostly stems from truth—but this is not always the case. What should be clear by now is that credibility and truth are two different concepts. For the sake of this book, it is necessary to understand both of them and their relationship.

The concept of truth becomes extremely important from the point of view of design goals for credibility evaluation support systems. For this reason, this section will focus on understanding the concept of truth. Falling short of an epistemological discussion, it shall focus on a review of the most relevant, theoretical contributions towards an understanding of truth that would be required by social informatics.

2.1.1 Post-structuralist Truth

In the view of post-structuralist or post-modernist philosophy and epistemology, truth is just a social construct, a concept that does not have any objective meaning. The two theories support epistemic relativism and conclude that truth is inherently subjective (due to culture, gender, race, age, social class, etc.).

Upon a more careful consideration of post-structuralist theories, a surprising discovery is made: the post-structuralist notion of truth is quite close to the notion of credibility. Consider the following passages from the Wikipedia definition of post-structuralism:

> The author's intended meaning is secondary to the meaning that the reader perceives. (...) every individual reader creates a new and individual purpose, meaning, and existence for a given text.

> A post-structuralist critic must be able to use a variety of perspectives to create a multifaceted interpretation of a text, even if these interpretations conflict with one another. It is particularly important to analyze how the meanings of a text shift in relation to certain variables, usually involving the identity of the reader (for example: class, racial, or sexual identity)[2]

The above quotations refer to the "general practices" or reasoning methods in post-structuralism. They fit in with the view of credibility being subjective. Moreover, if truth is indeed just the outcome of a social discourse (as postulated by post-structuralism), then prototypes for credibility evaluation support—which aim to gather receivers' credibility evaluations and to facilitate a discussion on credibility—support the creation of post-structuralist truth, while remaining aware of the impact context has on credibility evaluations.

---

[1] http://en.wikipedia.org/wiki/The_War_of_the_Worlds_(radio_drama).

[2] "Post-Structuralism," Wikipedia, http://en.wikipedia.org/wiki/Post-structuralist.

However, there are some important differences. Post-structuralist truth depends almost entirely on the receiver. The author's "intended meaning," as quoted above, is irrelevant, and so is the identity of the author (at least to the receiver). On the other hand, as will be explained in more detail later, the credibility of the source may be an important factor in credibility evaluations. If a source's (author's) credibility can be estimated, it can be used to reason about the credibility of new information coming from the same source. Still, credibility of the sources is not the only factor that impacts credibility evaluations.

Also, post-structuralists seem to have assumed that truth is completely subjective, in the sense that an agreement about truth is impossible or, even if reached, still falls short of real objectivity. Our research indicates that agreement is possible in some cases, and indeed, this is one of the basic premises of credibility evaluation support. If agreement about what's credible or not would not be possible, one would be *forced to build a personalized recommender system that would recommend to each user the content that would be credible just for her* (in other words, supporting credibility evaluation would mean doing it for each individual Web user independently). In short, another "credibility bubble" like the infamous "filter bubble" should be created. *Such an application would fall short of supporting user decisions meaningfully*, as these decisions should be based on objective, verifiable information.

This approach is even more unacceptable if the most pessimistic conclusion from post-structuralist theory of truth is considered: that *different (and often contradictory) versions of post-structuralist truth can be promoted by their supporters using power or social influence*. Following this point of view, people choose among the many versions of truth not independently, but under social influence of others; *it is possible to make a version of truth accepted by the majority, if only it is supported by sufficiently powerful people*. Even our common sense tells us that there is a lot of truth in this pessimistic conclusion. A conclusion for practical credibility evaluation support is that consensus is not always good (as it may be the result of social influence of an oppressive majority) and that it is important to present diversified views (also from minorities).

2.1.2 Scientific Truth

This brings the discussion to another sort of truth, which can be called "Scientific truth" for short. Finishing up the discussion on post-structuralist truth, one must not forget that this notion has received significant criticism, also from modern philosophers and thinkers. One such critic is Daniel Dennett, a philosopher and cognitive scientist, who in his essay "Postmodernism and Truth" provides a following summary of the notion of "Scientific truth":

> We are the species that discovered doubt. Is there enough food laid by for winter? Have I miscalculated? Is my mate cheating on me? Should we have moved south? Is it safe to enter this cave? Other creatures are often visibly agitated by their own uncertainties about

just such questions, but because they cannot actually ask themselves these questions, they cannot articulate their predicaments for themselves or take steps to improve their grip on the truth. They are stuck in a world of appearances, making the best they can of how things seem and seldom if ever worrying about whether how things seem is how they truly are.

We alone can be wracked with doubt, and we alone have been provoked by that epistemic itch to seek a remedy: better truth-seeking methods. Wanting to keep better track of our food supplies, our territories, our families, our enemies, we discovered the benefits of talking it over with others, asking questions, passing on lore. We invented culture. Then we invented measuring, and arithmetic, and maps, and writing. These communicative and recording innovations come with a built-in ideal: truth. The point of asking questions is to find true answers; the point of measuring is to measure accurately; the point of making maps is to find your way to your destination.[3]

The notion of "Scientific truth" is quite different from "Post-structuralist Truth," as it focuses on the existence of an empirical ground truth. Dennett also renders an evolutionary view of scientific truth, even making truth-seeking as a central element of the development of culture and science. Without going into details, it should be remarked that this notion of scientific truth is in agreement with Karl Popper's critical rationalism.[4] This epistemic theory claims that scientific truth is a process that attempts to critically verify all claims of truth, with empirical tests as the most important benchmark.

There are several problems with the notion of scientific truth. Most importantly, statements related to the human mental processes are quite hard to verify, and indeed this has been the main challenge for social sciences such as psychology or sociology. Yet, scientific progress is possible also in these areas, and empirical methods can be applied. Still, humans are capable of making statements (and claiming the truthfulness of these statements) that cannot be verified using empirical tests (such as all metaphysics). Also, science itself is never entirely in agreement about all claims, a fact that is noticed by Dennett as well:

> Yes, but science almost never looks as uncontroversial, as cut-and-dried, as arithmetic. Indeed rival scientific factions often engage in propaganda battles as ferocious as anything to be found in politics, or even in religious conflict. The fury with which the defenders of scientific orthodoxy often defend their doctrines against the heretics is probably unmatched in other arenas of human rhetorical combat. These competitions for allegiance–and, of course, funding–are designed to capture attention, and being well-designed, they typically succeed. This has the side effect that the warfare on the cutting edge of any science draws attention away from the huge uncontested background, the dull metal heft of the axe that gives the cutting edge its power. What goes without saying, during these heated disagreements, is an organized, encyclopedic collection of agreed-upon, humdrum scientific fact.

This observation has been the basis of post-structuralist and post-modernism critiques of science, which, for post-structuralist theorists, is merely another form of social discourse that creates claims which are no more true than the claims of any other social discourse. Nonetheless, it should be mentioned how Dennett stresses *the*

---

[3]D. Dennett, "Postmodernism and Truth," http://ase.tufts.edu/cogstud/papers/postmod.tru.htm.
[4]"Critical Rationalism," Wikipedia, http://en.wikipedia.org/wiki/Critical_rationalism.

existence of a large, uncontested collection of agreed-upon scientific facts. From the practical view of supporting credibility evaluations, this is a promising observation. Still, post-structuralists stipulate that the verification of such scientific facts is usually up to trusted experts with access to specialist equipment, and ordinary people must take up on the results of this verification.[5]

2.1.3   Semantic Truth Theory

Yet another theory of truth, also applicable to scientific truth, should be mentioned here: Alfred Tarski's Semantic Theory of Truth.[6] In brief, this theory states that truth is a logical property of sentences, but is relative to a model that expresses the semantics of these sentences. This view explains several apparent paradoxes of scientific truth, such as the disagreement between Newton's laws of motion and Einstein's theory of relativity. One can say that Newton's laws are valid if the model that expresses their semantics is limited to macroscopic objects in everyday conditions, but are not valid for a model that takes into account microscopic objects and objects moving at very high speeds.

Semantic Truth Theory also provides a different way of thinking about credibility evaluation. *There may be several models (or even sets of models) that are differently and independently used by people to evaluate truth: models for human beliefs, models for everyday facts, and models for specialist knowledge.* This simple initial classification will be of use in the next section, in proposing a general method of credibility evaluation support.

2.1.4   Incompleteness and Undecidability of Truth

In mathematics, logic, and computer science, the undecidability of truth is an important fact and constraint. Mathematicians like Gödel have proven that the truth of certain logical statements cannot be decided within an axiomatic system. This applies even to seemingly simple logical systems that can express basic arithmetic. From this perspective, objective (even mathematical) truth is shown to be sometimes unreachable via deductive reasoning (although, on the other hand, statements that cannot be proved from axioms using deductive reasoning may still be proved in

---

[5]For example, the following statement, "Neutrinos can move faster than light," has initially been supported by CERN in 2011. This statement was extremely hard and expensive to verify. However, it has eventually been verified as false, and the controversy had significant personal consequences for the involved scientists (the scientific coordinator of the involved group resigned). This shows that the verification processes of scientific truth are in good shape, after all. Source: Wikipedia, http://en.wikipedia.org/wiki/Faster-than-light_neutrino_anomaly.

[6]"Semantic theory of truth," Wikipedia, http://en.wikipedia.org/wiki/Semantic_theory_of_truth.

another way, or in another logical system). Undecidability of truth may concern empirical statements that may be (currently) impossible to evaluate in practice: consider, for example, the hypothesis that a nuclear reaction is occurring in the Earth's core.

Moreover, the fact of theoretical or practical undecidability of a statement's genuineness does not prevent humans from evaluating that statement's credibility. A striking example of this fact comes from computer science. Consider the famous and extremely important hypothesis concerning inequality of two well-known complexity classes: P and NP. Several practically used algorithms, such as the RSA public key encryption, are based on the implicit acceptance (or assumption) that P is not equal to NP. Indeed, according to a poll of over 150 computer scientists published in *ACM Communications* in 2012 [48], 83% of respondents find the statement $P \neq NP$ credible (a steep increase of over 20% since 2002). Only a stubborn 9% of skeptics does not (this number has not changed for 10 years). Over 10 years, the number of undecided expert respondents has dropped to below 1% for a controversy that may still never be resolved.

2.2 What Does It Mean to Support Credibility Evaluation?

In the previous section, the two concepts of credibility and truth have been compared. The concept of truth has been defined and introduced in detail, while the concept of credibility will receive a detailed definition in the next section. The following section provides another look at the two concepts from a different perspective. *Credibility is an input, while truth is an output of an information system that will be referred to as a credibility evaluation support (CS) system in this book.*

It should be noted that in the most general meaning, a CS is an information system that includes human users, as well as (potentially) artificial agents, programs, algorithms, or other information systems (such as search engines). Still, in this extended meaning, *a CS can be described as a social information system that aims to produce (a type of) truth from credibility evaluations; a socio-technical machine for producing truth.* Truth can also be viewed as a process; however, an information system (and a CS system as well) is a process, too. This means the result in question is not an output that is just a single piece of information; rather, it is the results of the credibility evaluation support process, and this result should be true. The reader can recall the examples of CS systems described in Sect. 1.2.3 and consider whether these existing CS systems indeed attempt to reach this goal.

The above observation clearly shows the importance and challenges of designing CS systems. The topic of this design is developed in Chap. 3. At this stage, the difficulty involved in the design of CS systems has been made clear: the subject matter at this point is ways of backing up decisions about the truth of information. The consequences of an error can clearly be critical.

The goal of this section is to pose (and partially answer) the following question: what does it mean to effectively support credibility evaluation? In the beginning, the identity of the intended user(s) of a CS system must be considered. Whose decisions should be supported by a CS system? There is a number of possible answers:

1. Individuals browsing the Web
2. Every Web user
3. A majority in a social group (the social group could be every Web user)
4. A topical knowledge community
5. Several social groups, differing in fundamental social characteristics, such as race, age, gender, social class or wealth, and nationality

Support for credibility evaluation tailored to just an individual Web user has already been criticized here. This approach would be liable to manipulation, as other individuals would use social influence to make others accept their versions of truth. Personalized credibility evaluation support tools could not counteract such a process; rather, they would tend to reinforce it, by reinforcing the beliefs of each individual user. *Every other approach to credibility evaluation support requires achieving the agreement of several Web users regarding the evaluation of Web content credibility.* It remains to be decided: who should be agreeing? Is agreement always possible?

The possibility of disagreement is obvious in controversial information. The existence of controversy in science or in other forms of social discourse is not, in itself, a bad thing from the point of view of supporting credibility evaluation. Researchers have found that tools warning Web users who search for information that the queried topic is controversial can encourage users to consider information credibility, prevent them from consuming suspicious information, and make them spend more time searching the Web [221].

An important function of credibility evaluation support is distinguishing between information that can have an agreed-upon credibility evaluation from controversial information. Information is controversial if users cannot agree about its credibility. This definition requires another explanation—that of agreement, but for the moment a common-sense interpretation of near consensus (almost everyone agrees) can be considered. If information can be diagnosed as controversial, it will still be possible to support debate on its credibility. Such debate may not bring a resolution, but is useful in itself, as it can lead to the creation of new knowledge (as in science) or to the creation of social agreement (as in politics).

An assumption can be also made that all information semantically related to human beliefs is controversial (humans will not be able to agree about it). This may be too strong an assumption (as, e.g., some social norms that can be classified as human beliefs are universally accepted). On the other hand, if it is possible to diagnose a piece of information as not controversial, best efforts should be taken to classify its credibility, based on its features and on available credibility evaluations. This once again elicits the question about what does it mean to support credibility evaluations in such a case. It may be useful to recall the discussion on Semantic Theory of Truth and to consider the existence of (at least) three sets of models used by people to evaluate truth (which should probably use different methods of credibility evaluation support): human beliefs, everyday facts, and specialist

Table 2.2 Credibility evaluation support methods for various kinds of information

Semantic truth model	Methods of credibility evaluation support	Receivers who benefit from credibility evaluation support
Human beliefs	Discussion, with the goal of presenting diverse views	Social groups that differ by fundamental social characteristics, such as race, age, gender, social class, wealth, culture, or nationality
Everyday facts	Wisdom of Crowds	Everyone
Specialist knowledge	Seeking evaluations by trusted, objective experts	Topical knowledge communities

knowledge. Information related to human beliefs includes all human opinions that cannot be verified objectively. Information related to everyday facts is the type of information that can be verified using one's ordinary senses and everyday knowledge. Specialist knowledge is a set of models for information that cannot be verified without specialists and expensive specialist equipment.

In Table 2.2, the three models are shown along with proposed methods of credibility evaluation support, and the receivers who could most benefit from these methods. The table may not be comprehensive, but it serves to show that various approaches to credibility evaluation support can be attempted for various truth models and various intended audiences.

Credibility evaluation of information related to human beliefs, even if this kind of information may be controversial, can be supported by a free discussion. The goal of the credibility evaluation support should be the presentation of diverse points of view, especially diversified with respect to fundamental social characteristics, such as race, age, gender, social class or wealth, and nationality. This could be achieved by a diversifying recommendation approach that would invite new discussion participants that could contribute a new point of view. In this aspect, credibility evaluation aims to support the discovery of post-structuralist truth.

The Wisdom of Crowds approach (gathering many evaluations from independent, diversified Web users) can be successful especially for information that can be verified using one's own senses, intelligence, and common knowledge (or common sense). For example, statements such as "George Bush said that he would not raise taxes, but did" belong to such category. This approach works under the assumption that a consensus emerges from available credibility evaluations.

We ourselves cannot support the discovery of specialist scientific truth through an empirical verification. A good method of credibility evaluation support for this kind of information is through the work of trustworthy experts. That means the support of learning; our users can, over time, achieve expert knowledge in an area of interest. One may even try to support the creation of entire, new topical knowledge communities.

Note that the two latter approaches have one thing in common: they attempt to support credibility evaluation by bringing it closer to scientific truth. On the other hand, if information is controversial, one may still (by supporting debate) bring credibility evaluations closer to post-structuralist truth. In other words, *successful credibility evaluation support causes individual credibility evaluations to agree with one of the two kinds of truth that is appropriate to the type of evaluated information*. This can be achieved, for example, by recommending a credibility evaluation selected by the credibility evaluation system for individual users.

Credibility evaluation support can be expressed by the following procedure:

1. Diagnose the type of truth model or the existence of controversy within the considered information.
2. For human beliefs or controversial information, support debate and try to present diversified credibility evaluations.
3. For non-controversial everyday facts, gather as much diversified, independent credibility evaluations as necessary to establish consensus.
4. For non-controversial specialist knowledge, gather credibility evaluations from trustworthy experts, and compare them to information of non-experts to evaluate non-expert user's reputation in the context of credibility evaluation. Then, combine (fuse) all available evaluations into one, using users' reputation scores as weights.
5. Recommend a credibility evaluation chosen based on point 3 or 4 or present diverse evaluations discovered in point 2.

The first step can be achieved through simple tagging of statements or webpages. It might be difficult to classify webpages as belonging to any category, as they may contain various kinds of information. Another approach for webpages could be to ask users to tag them as controversial, which would mean an attempt to apply step 2.

A prototype credibility evaluation system may actually attempt to follow steps 2, 3, and 4 at the same time, while trying to reach a conclusion about 1. When the conclusion is reached, the use of methods deemed inappropriate may be discontinued. For example, if the system realizes that a consensus has been reached about some information, it may close the discussion and move this information to a repository of uncontested facts. On the other hand, if the system realizes that some information is controversial, it may stop actively seeking expert opinions or applying Wisdom of Crowds—this will save user time and attention for information where consensus may still be reached. The system will still allow self-motivated users to continue debate, while classifying the information as controversial.

Steps 2, 3, and 4 of the proposed procedure are not mutually exclusive, but they differ in the allocation of scarce resources of user attention and time. In 2, users are allowed to continue a discussion and are self-motivated to do so. The information was already classified as controversial, but the discussion may still lead to learning about user behavior and to updating user reputation. In 3 and 4, the system actively tries to obtain expert opinions or a consensus. This means that the system chooses users and invites them to evaluate the information's credibility, and then motivates them by rewards (higher reputation gains, etc.). If such behavior is accepted for controversial information, it will merely result in wasting scarce resources.

Table 2.3 Comparison of goals of empirical credibility research and design of credibility evaluation support methods and systems

Empirical research of credibility	Design of credibility evaluation support methods
Study the impact of individual receiver's properties on credibility evaluations	Attempt to reduce the impact of individual receiver's judgment on credibility evaluations recommended to users
Propose models of credibility evaluations based on individual evaluations	Propose operational models of credibility evaluations based on aggregates of evaluations from many users
Do not influence receivers of information	Attempt to influence receivers of information to discourage dishonest or manipulative credibility evaluations

Finally, note a significant difference between two possible research goals of credibility evaluation support. The first such goal is the scientific study of credibility and credibility evaluation as phenomena or processes, using empirical methods. It shall be referred to as "empirical research of credibility." The second goal is the scientific and technical study of methods of credibility evaluation support. It shall be referred to as "design of credibility evaluation support methods." The difference between the two scientific goals is summarized in Table 2.3.

Table 2.3 summarizes the conclusions about credibility evaluation support methods discussed in this section. Since the objective of credibility evaluation is to propose evaluations that are closer to (one of two kinds of) truth, credibility evaluation support methods must focus on aggregates of credibility evaluations and study models created basing on these aggregates. This contrasts empirical research on credibility aiming to understand how individual credibility evaluations are made. Similarly, credibility evaluation support methods must be aware of attempts of manipulation and attempt to discourage them. That requires influencing the evaluations made by receivers. On the other hand, empirical studies of credibility evaluations should avoid influencing the participants.

2.3   Definitions of Credibility

In the previous two sections, the two concepts of truth and credibility have been compared. There is an important relationship between them: credibility is one of the inputs, while a type of truth (depending on the type of input information) is the output of a credibility evaluation support (CS) system. Various types of truth and their relationship to the type of information that is evaluated by a CS have been discussed in detail. In this section, the input of the CS system, credibility of information, is discussed.

The concept of credibility, similarly to the concept of trust, is grounded both in science and in common sense. Credibility has been subject to research by scientists, especially in the area of psychology and media science. Since the World Wide Web (WWW) has become commercialized and ubiquitous, credibility has found itself within the research scope of computer science and social informatics.

One of the earliest theoretical works on credibility dates back to the 1950s. The influential work of the psychologist Carl Hovland [67] introduced the distinction between *source, message, and media credibility*. Recent work [49] introduces the complementary concept of *system credibility*. Before introducing another definition of credibility, one should consider each of these four aspects of credibility separately. This is equivalent to making another step in the top-down discussion of the concept of credibility: from credibility to its components, focusing mainly on source and message credibility.

2.3.1 Source Credibility

Credibility concerns an act of communication, involving a source and a receiver of information (a message). Credibility is therefore a concept that is inherently relational. According to [193], source credibility is evaluated using two criteria: trustworthiness and expertise. Interestingly, this view of source credibility is close to the natural language (dictionary) definitions of the term "credibility." In the English language dictionary (*Oxford Advanced Learner's Dictionary*), credibility is defined as "the quality that somebody/something has that makes people believe or trust them." When this definition is applied to a person ("somebody"), it closely approximates source credibility. However, notice that the dictionary definition of credibility can also be applied to "something"—in this book, it will be the message itself. Also, the dictionary definition misses an important element: that of the receiver who makes a source credibility evaluation. Source credibility is, after all, always evaluated by a receiver.

At this stage, the top-down discussion of the concept of credibility has reached a point where it is possible to make another step. The goal of this step is to reduce the concept of source credibility to simpler and well-understood concepts of social informatics and the social sciences. Two concepts will need to be introduced before that is done: the concept of trust and the concept of reputation.

2.3.1.1 Credibility Trust and Reputation

To better the understanding of source credibility, some attention should be devoted to the concepts of trust and reputation. These concepts are frequently used to reason about credibility and can be a basis for defining source credibility. In this section, the concepts of trust and reputation will be introduced briefly, with a focus on understanding the aspects that are related to source credibility. For a more detailed and comprehensive explanation of trust and reputation, the reader is referred to [213].

Trust is a concept derived from the humanities and common experience. While the two definitions of trust will be discussed in more detail below, first a more general definition of trust (and distrust) in the most abstract manner as a *relation between a trust giver and a trust receiver in a context* must be given. The existence of this relation can be represented as a specific state of the trust giver. Both parties are agents (human or artificial). Unless it is stated otherwise, the analysis shall focus on human trust that is a mental state of humans. Human trust has been studied by psychology, sociology, anthropology, economics, and other sciences (such as neuroscience).

An important distinction can be made between *cognitive trust* and *emotive trust*. This distinction does not affect the definitions of trust given below; rather, it concerns the basis and factors that affect human trust. It is important to keep in mind that while humans are capable of rationally reasoning about trust (cognitive trust), they also can establish trust based on emotions or emotional relationships. This common-sense observation applies more to real, face-to-face relationships than to relationships mediated through technology or the Internet; on the other hand, it is important to keep in mind that our attempts to understand how trust works may be limited to cognitive trust.

The concept of trust is defined here as a relation. However, a related concept is *trustworthiness*, which is not relational, but is instead a property of an individual agent (or a group of agents). Following [213], trustworthiness can be defined as the *objective, context-dependent quality of deserving trust*. In other words, an agent is trustworthy in a context if many other agents can trust him in this context. The concept of trustworthiness can differ depending on how many agents should trust the trust giver: it can be required that all agents or a majority of agents do so. Frequently, trustworthiness is believed to be a function of an agent's attributes, like the agent's professional standing, external appearance, or other objective properties. However, this is a misconception. The attributes of an agent that are believed to be the causes of trustworthiness are the reason for trust propagation based on similarity. Trustworthiness is an intrinsic property of an agent that can be thought of as a function of the agent's norms or values (if the agent is human). Moreover, it is hard to use the concept of trustworthiness in practice, because it is very hard to measure. Almost all data that can be obtained by a trust management system is relational in nature; because of this fact, it is much easier to evaluate or estimate trust than it is to judge the trustworthiness of an agent.

Expectancy Trust

Expectancy trust is the first and most commonly used definition of trust. According to this definition [213], *human trust is a subjective, context-dependent expectation that the trust receiver will choose a specific action in the encounter*. An encounter is simply a situation when two or more agents can choose among certain actions, and the outcome of these actions is mutually dependent on all agents' choices. An encounter also has context that can be summarized as all encounter and agent properties that can affect the choice and outcome of actions. This definition of trust is close to these proposed by Gambetta or Mui [46, 124].

An example of expectancy trust is when a buyer on an Internet auction pays for a product in advance (this method is preferred by sellers). The buyer then expects that the seller will send him the purchased item.

Note that in order for this definition to apply, it is not necessary that a human should explicitly calculate and compare the probabilities of choosing an action by the trust receiver. It would suffice that the trust giver would be able to choose a particular action and expect that the trust receiver will also choose this action. Note also that if the giver is able to form such an expectation about all other agents in the encounter, then it will follow that he will be able to choose his own best action and to form an expectation about his own outcome in the encounter.

Apart from considerable support for this definition in the literature of social sciences, expectancy trust has also received some recent empirical support. The expectation is formed based on some information that is relevant to the future outcome of the encounter. In order to verify whether humans form an expectation about the outcome, it is necessary to observe their behavior when the provided information is varied. If the behavior varies, it can be concluded that an expectation is formed and is affecting behavior (under the ceteris paribus assumption that no other factors impact behavior). In [8], the finding that people form expectations based on information about trust receivers is verified. Barr used an economic investment experiment conducted in small communities in Zimbabwe and tried to verify whether people acted based on expectations about the trust receiver in the absence of any other mechanism that would facilitate cooperation (this included the absence of reputation: players were paired into anonymous pairs, and interactions were not repeated). In the experiment, both trust giver and trust receiver came from the same community. The experiment was designed in such a way that the trust giver's decision depended on the expected payoff received due to the decision of the trust receiver, and on the variation of this payoff. If the players expected a higher payoff, they invested more. If the players expected a high variation in payoffs, they usually invested less. Thus, the findings of Barr give empirical support to the theory that human trust is an expectation. The expectation in the experiment could only be formed based on the experiment setup and based on the knowledge of the participants about their communities.

Dependency Trust

After [213], **dependency trust** can be defined as **the subjective, context-dependent extent to which the trust giver is willing to depend on the trust receiver in a situation of uncertainty**. This definition is an adaptation of dependency trust definitions proposed by Josang et al. and Marsh [76] and [112]. A similar definition has been used in sociology [185, 186]: trust has been defined there as the attitude that allows the trust giver to accept a bet on the trust receiver's behavior. Accepting such a bet would mean a willingness to depend on the trust receiver.

The example of Internet auctions can also be used for dependency trust. When a buyer on an auction pays for an item in advance, he expects that this item will be sent to him; however, he also depends on the seller to send the item, and this dependency is high and can be adequately measured by the amount of money paid to the seller.

The two definitions of human trust are not contradictory: rather, they can be seen as complementary. The premise that a particular concept can be defined only in one way may make sense in the exact sciences or mathematics, but does not necessarily apply to humans, and it is human trust that is being defined here. It should be possible for humans to use both kinds of trust simultaneously, considering, perhaps, only expectancy trust if the risk is low, and requiring dependency trust when the risk is high. A well-designed trust management system should allow its users to express, and be able to process, both expectancy and dependency trust.

2.3.1.2 Reputation

Another concept that can be derived from one's common sense, and from economics, is the concept of *reputation*. The most abstract definition of reputation is [213] *information about the trust receiver that is available to the trust giver and is derived from the history of the trust receiver's behavior in some contexts*. Note that from this definition it can be seen that reputation can establish human trust.

Reputation, like trust, is subjective and context dependent. What follows the definition of reputation is that it can only be influenced by the history of the trust receiver's behavior. A detailed classification of reputation types, following [124], is shown in Fig. 2.1. Examples of reputation include the simple reputation used in

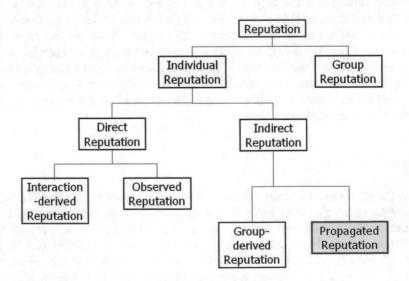

Fig. 2.1 A classification of types of reputation based on [124]

Internet auctions, where each buyer can read the feedback about a given seller and decide whether to trust that seller.

Note here that a distinction exists in the literature between *local* and *global* reputation. Local reputation is equivalent to reputation as defined here: it is subjective with respect to the trust giver. On the other hand, global reputation is not subjective to the trust giver, although it can be context dependent. Global reputation is related to trustworthiness, not to trust.

The most important distinction used in the presented classification is between direct and indirect reputation. Direct reputation is based on information about the history of an agent's behavior that is directly available to another agent. For example, reputation based on firsthand experience belongs to this category (referred to as interaction-derived reputation by Mui). Another type is observed reputation that can be obtained if an agent can observe interactions of other agents without participating in them. Indirect reputation is based on information obtained through third parties that cannot be directly verified. Reputation systems used by online auctions or other e-commerce enterprises belong to that category, referred to as propagated reputation. The distinction between direct and indirect reputation stresses the difference between using verifiable information and information that cannot be verified. The latter approach, most common in reputation systems used today in online auctions, is especially vulnerable to strategic manipulation [82, 123].

2.3.1.3   Normative Trust and Credibility Trust

In [32], Elgesem provides a definition of trust that is significant from the point of view of understanding the concept of source credibility:

> trust is a normative notion in the sense that an essential ingredient in all cases of trust and trustworthiness is the existence of a set of norms that provide the motivation to cooperate.

Elgesem's definition can be reconciled with the definition of expectancy trust. Trust can be an expectation about the behavior of a trust receiver based on a model of his reasoning. Elgesem's view on trust supports that more general definition of *normative trust*: an *expectation that the trust receiver follows certain norms of behavior*. Barber [7] states that these norms can be the "natural and moral social order," the norms that describe technical competence and professionalism, or the norms that govern legal obligations. Elgesem provides a more abstract view of "norms that provide the motivation to cooperate." In [212], trust is redefined as an expectation of or dependency on fair behavior.

Credibility trust is the most significant variant from the point of view of studying source credibility. Using the definition of normative trust, *credibility trust* can be defined as *the expectation that the trust receiver will follow the social norm of not lying*.

Using the concept of encounter context, it is possible to show that credibility trust is indeed a special kind of trust. Consider agents who meet solely for the purpose of exchanging information. In other words, during an encounter of these agents, the only action that can be taken is giving information (true, false, or partially true) to other agents. The context of this encounter is information sharing. After receiving new information, an agent will have some possibility to evaluate its correctness (perhaps not immediately, but during a period of time after the encounter). The trust in the agent that has provided this information to the trust giver in the context of information sharing is credibility trust. Based on that trust, the trust giver may or may not accept information from trust receivers in information sharing encounters. Note that the trust giver's outcome may vitally depend on the received information, and the information sharing encounter is associated with uncertainty about the information's correctness.

2.3.1.4 Source Credibility Defined as Trust

Drawing from this observation, one can conclude that *source credibility is closely related to credibility trust*. It is an expectation that the source will follow the social norm of not lying (not communicating a false message). Following the analogy to trust, source credibility can also be based on the trustworthiness of the source in the context of veracity—however, it is difficult to reliably observe, measure, or predict this property. Most observations or valuations concerning credibility are done in a relational context (context of a communication of information). A proxy for credibility trustworthiness may be reputation in the context of veracity.

This distinction is easy to accommodate using the definitions of trust and reputation that all included a context of evaluation. Therefore, it can be concluded that *source credibility is a combination (or multiple criteria evaluation) of two kinds of trust: credibility trust and the trust in the expertise of the source*.

At this stage in the top-down discussion of credibility, the discussion of source credibility is concluded and reduced to the concept of trust. It is now time to move on to the other three aspects of credibility: media, system, and, most importantly, message credibility.

2.3.2 Media and System Credibility

Media credibility has been the subject of research in media science and in computer science (since the introduction of the Web). On the Web, various media may be considered an important context for credibility evaluation: ordinary webpages, blogs, social media, and Q&A sites all have their own specific aspects that may influence credibility evaluation. Media credibility is a property of the medium that does not depend on the relation between the source and receiver. However, various media may modify the impact of source credibility and message credibility on overall credibility valuations.

System credibility, introduced by Ginsca et al. [49], is in some respects similar to media credibility. This aspect of credibility concerns information systems that actively support user judgments about information relevance, quality, credibility, or generally all recommendation systems and decision support systems on the Web. System credibility is especially significant for information retrieval systems (search engines) and recommender systems, but also for systems that support credibility evaluation.

2.3.3 Message Credibility

The majority of this book will be concerned with message credibility. This does not imply that the other aspects are less significant. However, source credibility is a combination of credibility trust and trust in expertise, and therefore can be considered a well-studied topic [213]. Media credibility is the subject of media science. System credibility, on the other hand, is an extremely broad aspect that exceeds the scope of this book, since it requires the consideration of information retrieval and recommender systems' quality and accuracy. For the above reasons, the medium and information system will be considered as fixed (given) and their credibility, unchangeable. Under this kind of ceteris paribus assumption, focus will be placed on understanding message credibility and source credibility.

It is important to note that message credibility, similarly to source credibility, is a context-dependent mental state of the receiver of the message. The seminal work of Tseng and Fogg [193] has introduced the following aspects of credibility that mostly concern message and source credibility:

- **Presumed credibility** is based on the general assumptions of the receiver regarding source credibility.
- **Surface credibility** is derived from a superficial examination of the message by the receiver. It is a first impression of message credibility. Evaluating surface credibility requires little time and effort on behalf of the receiver.
- **Earned credibility** refers to the evaluation of message credibility based on a more detailed investigation, personal experience, or expert knowledge. If possible, the evaluation of earned credibility should be the result of verification of the information.
- **Reputed credibility** refers to indirectly acquired evaluations of source credibility. Evaluation of reputed credibility requires reliance on third-party opinions. Reputed credibility can be considered equivalent to reputation in the context of veracity.

It is important to point out here that credibility is evaluated not just by the receiver but also by the sender of the message. And, in many cases, the sender knows the ground truth regarding the communicated information, while the receiver does not (this is not the same as evaluating the information's credibility; the relationship between credibility and truth of a message is discussed in the next section). A sender may be able to know the truth of a message in the case that the objective truth exists, and especially if the communicated information originates directly from the sender. In other cases (for propagated information), the sender may have better experience or expert knowledge than the receiver, and therefore can make a much better evaluation of earned credibility. In many cases (e.g., for specialist factual information), the receiver is only able to evaluate surface or reputed credibility, while the sender can evaluate earned credibility.

The situation when the sender knows the ground truth of his message or can evaluate the message's credibility better than the sender will be referred to as the *asymmetry of credibility evaluation*. The sender of information not only knows the truth or is able to make a better evaluation of the earned credibility of his own message, but also is able to recursively evaluate the credibility of the message as judged by the receiver. The ability to do so is considered by Tomasello to be a defining feature of human thought and reasoning (see Sect. 1.1.1) [192]. This ability increases the strategic advantage of the sender over the receiver in the case of asymmetry of credibility evaluation.

At this stage, a simple thought experiment can be conducted. In an experiment aiming to evaluate Web content credibility, a user is asked to look at a webpage and then to evaluate and rate the credibility of the webpage. Which of the four aspects of Web credibility would be evaluated by the user?

It is simple to rule out the aspect of presumed credibility. While the user may have a general assumption regarding the credibility of the webpage, he or she has been asked to evaluate one, specific webpage. The user's attention should therefore be focused on that page. It may be still possible that in their mind, the user would compare the credibility of this webpage against some benchmark. However, this is not equivalent to presumed credibility, but rather is a mental heuristic that could be used by the user to evaluate the credibility or quality of the webpage.

Similarly, it is simple to rule out the aspect of earned credibility, unless the user has expert knowledge about the webpage's content. This possibility should be controlled by the experiment designer. Under the additional assumption that the user does not have expert knowledge about the webpage's content, it is unlikely that he or she will be able to make a detailed investigation and verify the information contained in the webpage.

Reputed credibility may be taken into account by the user if, for example, he or she recognizes the domain in the webpage's URL. For example, if the webpage is a news article from a reputed newspaper (or from a tabloid), the name of the newspaper is likely to be contained in the DNS domain name of the URL, and the user could take this information into account. Again, this possibility can be controlled by experiment design: the user may be asked to evaluate a webpage without having access to the webpage's URL. In an experiment, it would even be possible to first show the webpage without the URL, obtain a first evaluation, and only then, upon showing the page's URL to ask the user for a second rating.

Finally, the last remaining aspect is surface credibility. This aspect is possible to evaluate by the user even if he or she has no expertise or firsthand knowledge about the webpage's content. Moreover, a user does not need information about the source (such as the domain in the webpage's URL) to evaluate surface credibility. Under the abovementioned assumptions about experiment control, surface credibility is the only aspect of credibility that can be evaluated by a user. Note that it does not take artificial conditions for this conclusion to hold: all users are often faced with webpages containing information from foreign sources and pertaining to issues outside of their expertise. In the case of asymmetry of credibility evaluation, the disadvantaged receiver of the information often can only evaluate surface credibility. For these reasons, it is important to understand how surface credibility is evaluated by Web users and how to model surface credibility.

2.3.4   Proposed Definition of Credibility

An attempt at formulating a new definition of message credibility will now be undertaken. The main theoretical contributions of previous work must be taken into consideration. The new definition will be based on the setting of Shannon's Information Theory, and will place the concept of credibility in the context of an act of communication requiring a source and at least one receiver. It must also be considered that the communicated information is associated with meta-information that can include several attributes, such as the topic of the communicated information, type of the medium used to communicate the information, properties of presentation of the information, and many more. In this model, communicated information is entirely contained in the message, while all other properties are considered part of the meta-information. The one exception is information about the identity of the source, which is treated separately in the receiver's investigation of source credibility; as explained in the previous section, this boils down to a consideration of trust in the context of credibility and expertise.

The proposed new definition of message credibility will be inspired by economic theory, in particular, the *concept of signal* [177]. The idea of signal has been introduced in economic models with asymmetric information, such as the job market, but lately also to model car sales on eBay [103]. Signal can be thought of as a summary of all information and meta-information received by a buyer that may convince him or her to buy a product (or hire an employee). In asymmetric information models, the buyer does not have access to crucial information about the product's quality, possessed by the seller. In order to convince the buyer, the seller may invest in the construction of a costly signal (e.g., repaint the car).

Credibility may now be defined as a **signal that may make a receiver believe that the information is true**. Note that while the definition contains a reference to the concept of truth, this concept may be actually understood differently by each receiver, and can depend on the type of communicated information. The crucial aspect is the relationship between the signal and the mental state of the receiver: the receiver's belief in the truth of communicated information. Significantly it shall be considered that *credibility is a function of attributes of communicated information and meta-information*.

In the case when the ground truth of the message can be defined, it is possible, using the proposed definition, to understand the relationship between credibility and truth. Ground truth (correctness or reliability of the information) is one of the factors that influence the signal of credibility. Even if ground truth is not (entirely?) available to the receiver, it may affect the signal that is credibility. On the other hand, the credibility signal can also be affected by many other factors, besides truth.

Since meta-information includes the type of the medium, this definition encompasses media credibility as well as message credibility. The distinction between surface and earned message credibility becomes possible upon considering that *signal may be multi-dimensional, the receiver may use various actions to evaluate the credibility of information, and these actions will use various dimensions of the signal.* Various receivers may also have various abilities (expert knowledge or personal experience) to evaluate credibility. All these and other factors will also have an impact on how receivers evaluate credibility of information. However, the input for all receivers is the same: it is the attributes of information and meta-information. The proposed definition could be extended to encompass source credibility if information about the source is considered to be a part of meta-information. However, the reduction of source credibility to trust in the context of credibility and expertise presented in the previous section shows that source credibility can (with advantage) be treated separately using established methods of trust and reputation management. This means that focus can shift to a better understanding of message and media credibility, as proposed in the new definition.

The proposed new definition brings the realization that credibility is subjective. The various attributes of information may be differently perceived and interpreted by various receivers (see Sect. 2.4.4). However, credibility also has objective aspects, insofar as human perception and interpretation of the properties of information and meta-information agree. This apparently high subjectivity of the proposed definition makes it necessary to explain the usage of categories such as "credible information" or "non-credible information." Unless a direct reference is made to the receiver of the information that is included in the proposed definition, the category of "credible information" will be using a universal quantifier and imply information that is found credible by all or the large majority of receivers. On the other hand, non-credible information (in the absence of a third category) is information that is not found credible by at least a significant minority of receivers.

It has been stressed before that not just the receiver but also the sender of the information can evaluate its credibility. The ability to do so is easily accommodated by our definition if we allow for the sender to make a thought experiment and put himself in the role of the receiver. (In this thought experiment, the sender sends the information to herself.) The sender also has access to all attributes of information and meta-information that he or she sends. The difficulty of the sender to predict the receiver's credibility evaluation is therefore due to the same reason as the subjectivity of credibility evaluations by various receivers. The sender and the receiver may use different actions (mental heuristics) to evaluate the credibility of information, which may result in different signals. However, according to Tomasello, the sender's ability to recursively evaluate the credibility and relevance of communicated information is a basic (and distinctive) feature of human reasoning. This ability puts a limit on the subjective differences of credibility evaluations by the sender and the receiver of the same communicated information.

In the case of credibility evaluations asymmetry, the sender knows the ground truth of his message or is able to make a more accurate credibility evaluation than the receiver. Using the aforementioned definition, it is better to think of the sender being able to perform two credibility evaluations. One of them is done in the role of the sender, using his own experience and ability, which results in a more accurate signal. The second credibility evaluation is performed by the sender in the role of the receiver. The sender assumes the receiver's limited experience and ability, resulting in a less accurate signal. The sender is therefore able to compare the two signals and to use the results of this comparison in his strategic behavior.

As it was mentioned in Sect. 2.2, credibility is an input for credibility evaluation support (CS) system. Using the worked out definition, it can be said that a CS system processes signals of credibility, along with other input (such as reputation of sources). On the other hand, the output of the CS system should be, as discussed in Sect. 2.2, an appropriate type of truth. This outcome can be seen as a design goal for CS systems. However, this definition of credibility can also aid in appointing another, less ambitious goal for CS systems: that the output of the CS system should be an *improved credibility signal*. What is meant by improved is a signal that is less noisy and more accurate in predicting the actual ground truth, if available for the considered type of information.

2.3.5 Conclusion of Top-Down Discussion of Credibility

In this section, the concept of credibility has been discussed in a top-down manner. The following main steps have been made in this discussion. First, the concepts of credibility and truth have been compared, and shown to be significantly different and partially independent. On the other hand, a relationship exists between these two concepts and another core concept: that of credibility evaluation support. Credibility evaluation support systems (CS systems) are information systems that take credibility as one of the inputs, while attempting to produce (a type of) truth as an output. A better understanding of various types of information, associated types of truth, and methods of credibility evaluation support have been discussed in Sect. 2.2.

Thereafter, the discussion focused on understanding the input of CS systems: credibility. First, the distinction between source credibility and message credibility has been made. Next, it was shown that source credibility is reducible to a concept that has already received significant attention in social informatics and social science, that is, the concept of trust. Source credibility can be thought of as equivalent to trust in the context of credibility and expertise. This realization has some practical consequences: there are numerous proposed methods of trust and reputation management that can directly be applied to handling source credibility [213].

The next important step was a new proposed definition of message credibility (that encompasses media credibility as well). This definition is based on signal, already an established concept from game theory and economics. Defining message credibility as signal allows to discuss it using established methods. In Chap. 5, this reasoning will be used to construct theoretical models of credibility evaluation and effectiveness of CS systems.

The remaining part of this chapter turns to theories that attempt to explain how humans make credibility evaluations. These theories shed more light on the process of credibility evaluation, as well as on how the signal of message credibility is constructed and interpreted by humans. Further in the chapter, methods of measuring the signal of message credibility are presented. Based on several experiments and datasets, empirical results about credibility evaluations allow to quantify and evaluate the potential subjectivity and bias of the message credibility signal. The results indicate clearly that the signal of message credibility can be successfully measured and used as an input for credibility evaluation support systems.

2.4   Theories of Web Content Credibility

As shown in Sect. 2.3, theoretical work on credibility of information dates back to the 1950s. However, since the commercialization of the Web has begun, research has focused increasingly on credibility of Web content. Several theories concerning the factors and processes underlying Web content credibility evaluations have been proposed. This section presents an overview of these theories.

2.4.1   Credibility Evaluation Checklists

One of the goals of research on how users make credibility evaluations on the Web was the improvement of Web content design methods. In other words, the goal was constructive: how should webpages, and Web content, be designed, structured, and displayed in order to make it more credible? This line of thinking has led to the development of guidelines or methods of credible Web content design. These guidelines were often formulated as checklists. One of the best-known examples is the checklist of the Stanford Web Credibility Project.[7] The checklist includes the following points:

1. Make it easy to verify the accuracy of the information on your site.
2. Show that there is a real organization behind your site.

---

[7]http://credibility.stanford.edu.

3. Highlight the expertise in your organization and in the content and services you provide.
4. Show that honest and trustworthy people stand behind your site.
5. Make it easy to contact you.
6. Design your site so it looks professional (or is appropriate for your purpose).
7. Make your site easy to use and useful.
8. Update your site's content often (at least show it has been reviewed recently).
9. Use restraint with any promotional content (e.g., ads, offers).
10. Avoid errors of all types, no matter how small they seem.

The Stanford guidelines are based on researching factors that affect Web content credibility evaluation [39, 40] and on models of Web content credibility evaluation, such as the Prominence-Interpretation theory [38, 40]. The Stanford Web Credibility group has conducted a series of research projects on Web content credibility in 1999–2003 and was one of the first groups to research this subject. Some of the models of Web content credibility evaluation are based on older theoretical information processing models grounded in psychology, such as the Heuristic-Systematic Model [17] and the Elaboration Likelihood Model [142]. For an overview of these models, see [49]. Here, stress will be placed on the adaptations of these models to the subject of Web content credibility evaluation.

2.4.2 Iterative Model [207]

Wathen and Burkell [207] presented an early synthesis of previous research on Web content credibility, as well as psychological research on the process of persuasion and attitude formation. According to their proposed model, credibility evaluations are iterative and follow at least two steps. In the first step, called "surface credibility evaluation" by the authors, a Web user only considers the appearance/presentation, usability/interface design, and the organization of information of a webpage. In the second step, called "message credibility evaluation," a user considers source credibility and message credibility. Source credibility is viewed as a function of a source's expertise and trustworthiness. Message credibility depends on a webpage's content, relevance, currency, and accuracy. In a final step, the user evaluates the content taking into account his or her own previous knowledge.

The iterative model does not fully agree with the distinction between surface credibility and earned credibility as proposed by Fogg. Firstly, both surface credibility and earned credibility are various aspects of message credibility. Source credibility, on the other hand, is completely distinct from message credibility, as it is usually evaluated in different ways. As was discussed in Sect. 2.3.1.1, source credibility is a special kind of trust, and its evaluations can be supported using trust management methods. On the other hand, message credibility evaluations differ from trust evaluations in several ways.

Contrary to the iterative model, this chapter will contain evidence (based on empirical studies and data mining) that surface credibility evaluations are influenced by source credibility, as well as by an examination of the Web content's accuracy and currency. In other words, the results of the conducted experiments do not support the distinctions of steps made by the iterative model. This does not imply that the concept of iterative credibility evaluations is incorrect. However, if the first step of the iteration is surface credibility evaluation, the next step is concerned with earned credibility evaluation and a possible updating of source credibility.

2.4.3   Predictive and Evaluative Model [65, 150]

The Predictive-Evaluative model of Web content credibility evaluation has been formulated by Rieh [150] and is based on earlier work of Hogarth [65]. The model bases on a classification of human judgments that divides all judgments into two types: "predictive judgment" and "evaluative judgment" [65]. Predictive judgment, according to Hogarth, refers to what people expect to happen, while evaluative judgment concerns human preferences among possible outcomes.

According to Rieh, credibility evaluation is made in two stages. First, a Web user makes a predictive judgment that leads her to the decision about an action. In the context of the Web, this predictive judgment could be a choice of a search result or the decision to follow a hyperlink. Therefore, the initial *predictive judgment is actually a judgment about the relevance of the information* to a user's information needs.

Next, a webpage is displayed to the user, and she makes an evaluative judgment about the webpage's credibility and quality. Rieh is mostly concerned with an evaluation of the "information quality" and "cognitive authority."

Rieh's model attempts to integrate credibility evaluation and relevance evaluation into a single model of interactive information-seeking behavior on the Web. While this may be a useful approach in the context of using a search engine, the model is less applicable to open browsing, and even less useful in Web 2.0 social media, where users often have to evaluate the credibility of information that they did not search for and that is pushed to them by other users. Still, Rieh's model is a good step towards the understanding of interactions between relevance judgments and credibility evaluations.

2.4.4   Fogg's Prominence-Interpretation Theory (2003)

Early research on Web content credibility originates from the Stanford Web Credibility Research Lab. One of the earliest large-scale (2500 users) empirical studies of Web content credibility evaluations was conducted by the Stanford team. While the study did not create an openly available dataset, it resulted in an influential theory of Web content credibility: the Prominence-Interpretation theory [40]. According to this theory, Web users use two stages in credibility evaluations. In the first stage, users investigate the Web content and notice some credibility cues. On the other hand, other (possibly important) cues may go unnoticed at this stage. Prominence is the likelihood that a webpage element will be noticed or perceived. Fogg claims that at least five factors influence prominence: the motivation ("involvement") of the user, the ability ("experience") of the user, the task of the user, a user's individual characteristics, and the topic of the webpage.

During the second stage, Interpretation, users make judgments about the cues they have noticed in the first stage. According to Fogg, many factors can influence interpretation: a user's level of competency (expertise) regarding the webpage topic, the context of the evaluation (consisting of the user's environment, expectations, and situational norms), as well as a user's assumptions that consist of heuristics, past experience, and culture.

According to Fogg, the Prominence-Interpretation process is iterative, as users may repeat the procedure at any time, resulting in new cues that are noticed and evaluated (interpreted).

Fogg's theory has been very influential in underlying the subjective aspects of credibility. Not only are both processes heavily dependent on user characteristics, but the first stage may also depend on a combination of webpage design (presentation) and user's attention and concentration. Basing on the Prominence-Interpretation theory leads to two important practical conclusions for designers of Web content credibility evaluation systems:

1. Webpage credibility needs to be evaluated by several users independently, to decrease the likelihood that important cues will not be noticed.
2. Systems for credibility evaluation support can benefit from standardized interfaces for collecting information about a webpage's credibility. By suggesting evaluation criteria, tags, or checklists, such tools reduce the subjectivity due to prominence of cues.

2.4.5   Dual-Processing Model [118]

Similarly to Fogg's Prominence-Interpretation theory, the Dual-Processing model of Metzger [118] focuses on the process of making credibility judgments. The model introduces two variables that have a crucial impact on credibility evaluations: the user's motivation and ability to evaluate credibility. According to the model, only if the user has sufficient motivation and ability will she or he be able to make a "systematic/central" evaluation. Even a user lacking motivation or ability can nevertheless make a credibility judgment; however, this judgment will be the result of a "heuristic/peripheral" credibility evaluation. The "systematic/central" credibility evaluation in the Dual-Processing model is therefore equivalent to earned credibility, while the "heuristic/peripheral" evaluation is equivalent to surface credibility. The Dual-Processing model resembles Prominence-Interpretation theory because it also introduces two phases of credibility evaluation: the exposure phase and the evaluation phase. However, Prominence-Interpretation theory did not distinguish between surface and earned credibility ratings. The Dual-Processing model is also in close agreement with Kahneman's theory of two mental systems [78]. According to Kahneman, two mental systems are involved in a human's decision making and reasoning: the automatic System 1 and the deliberative, lazy System 2. Using System 1 is almost effortless and very fast, but can result in systematic flaws in reasoning. This would be the equivalent of a "heuristic/peripheral" (surface credibility) evaluation if the user does not have sufficient motivation. On the other hand, a higher motivation allows to use System 2 and to make a "systematic/central" (earned credibility) evaluation.

2.4.6   MAIN Model [183]

Sundar [183] lists as many as 26 factors affecting credibility judgments that make up the MAIN model of credibility evaluations. According to this model, the four affordances (Modality, Agency, Interactivity, Navigability) generate cues that are utilized by Web users in heuristics that lead to quality and credibility evaluations. However, the MAIN model is mostly based on a synthesis of research into the quality and ergonomics of online media, and not on empirical user studies. Some of its factors do not even seem to be related to credibility (such as relevance, which is an orthogonal concept). The large number of cues (which have many synonyms that are used in other research papers) mentioned by the MAIN model emphasizes the difficulty of choosing the right criteria to evaluate credibility when designing interfaces or systems that support credibility evaluation. This difficulty can be best solved by considering only the criteria that are most important for users in real credibility evaluations.

2.4.7   Ginsca's Model [49]

In his comprehensive review of credibility research, Ginsca et al. [49] have also proposed a model of credibility in the context of information retrieval. In their work, the authors describe four aspects of credibility: quality, trustworthiness, expertise, and reliability. These four general terms are used to systematize the diverse terminology used in credibility research so far. The authors do not propose their own definition of credibility; rather, they rely on existing definitions from the literature.

   However, the work of Ginsca et al. makes an important contribution to the understanding of Web content credibility. Apart from the well-known aspects of media, source, and message credibility, Ginsca et al. add the fourth aspect of system credibility. This aspect can be understood as the credibility of current search engines, or rather their ability to support users in finding not just relevant but also credible results. However, the authors also mention the application of the concept of system credibility to the credibility evaluation support system itself. This seemingly recursive relationship covers several aspects, from the quality of the system and its ability to serve credible information, to the transparency and intentions underlying system design, as well as the system's robustness to manipulation. All of these aspects must be taken into account in designing a credibility evaluation support system.

2.5 Measures of Credibility

The reader may recall that by definition from Sect. 2.3.4, credibility of information is a signal that can induce a mental state of the receiver: make him or her believe that the information is true. What follows from this definition is that measuring credibility would require a measurement of signal. This problem is very similar to issues known in group decision making, economy and market research, or methods from mathematical psychology, where multiple persons are asked about their opinion or preference about some objects in order to rank them in some way. Various approaches to this problem differ by the tasks of respondents:

(a) *Monadic ratings*, where respondents are asked to rate objects on some scale (such as the Likert scale [71]).
(b) *Comparisons*, where respondents have to rate presented options in relation to other options, for example, saying that one option is better than another. The most well-known method is pairwise or paired comparison, where there is a choice between two objects.

The main advantage of monadic ratings is clearly their efficiency. Comparisons naturally require many more evaluations to compute a full rating of evaluated objects (smaller numbers of evaluations suffice to establish partial orders). Moreover, the study of information credibility requires not single but multiple evaluations of each object in order to investigate whether consensus is achievable. These considerations make the use of comparisons impractical for large experimental studies or large-scale systems. On the other hand, as demonstrated by Orme [137], pairwise comparisons give better results than monadic ratings with respect to discrimination among objects (ability of drawing statistically significant distinctions from a set of ratings of similar size) and prediction (ability to predict ratings in a validation set). Pairwise comparisons have one more advantage over monadic ratings: they can be more intuitive for respondents, although this may not apply for complex objects such as webpages.

2.5.1 Ordinal and Cardinal Scales of Credibility

The use of monadic ratings for credibility evaluations raises another methodological question. It concerns the use of ordinal versus cardinal scales.

One of the most popular rating scales in social science research is the Likert scale. Likert scales are commonly used to measure attitudes or preferences. For each question (there may be several), a Likert scale questionnaire provides five categories of response, typically from "strongly disagree" (1) to "strongly agree" (5). From a strict methodological point of view, the Likert scale is ordinal, not cardinal. This means that while responses on a Likert scale may be used to create rankings, they should not be used to calculate means, standard deviations, or for parametric statistical analyses such as ANOVA [71]. This is because the distances among the Likert scale evaluations (even though they are nominally equal to 1, if one considers just the response numbers) are unknown. For example, the intensity of feeling between "strongly disagree" and "disagree" may be different from the intensity of feeling between "neutral" and "agree."

If ratings on Likert-type scales are treated as ordinal data, one should employ ordinal statistics such as the median or mode as measures of central tendencies. Ordinal data may also be represented using distributions (frequencies of ratings for each value on the scale). Statistical inferences using these distributions should employ non-parametric tests, such as the Mann-Whitney U-test, chi-squared, or Spearman's rho. For modeling the data, methods such as ordinal or logistic regression may be used. Neither of these methods requires information about the length of intervals between consecutive scale values.

However, there exists a widely used variant of an ordinal scale that may be interpreted as a cardinal one. It is the popular "star rating" scale used in numerous Web services (e-commerce sites like eBay, Amazon, travel sites such as Booking.com, and many others). Two arguments may be given in favor of interpreting this scale as a cardinal one:

1. The "star rating" scale does not introduce a verbal interpretation of the scale values.
2. Web users with some experience are quite familiar with "star ratings" and use them to evaluate various objects. The diversity of evaluated objects (goods, services) leads users to interpret stars as simple numerical values that express their satisfaction.

An argument against the interpretation of "star ratings" as a cardinal scale is related to the underlying semantics of the criterion (question) for which the scale is used. For example, imagine there is a star rating system for restaurants. One restaurant receives 1 star, while a second one receives 2 stars. Is the second restaurant really twice better than the first one? What about the ratio between a "two-star" and "four-star" restaurant—is it really the same as between a "one-star" and "two-star"? One of the reasons why this is not the case is the prevalent positive bias (negative skewness) of star ratings or Likert ratings [79, 92]. This bias also concerns credibility ratings [79]. A response to this concern may be that the "star rating" system may still be interpreted as a cardinal scale, but the intervals between consecutive stars must be calculated in a way that discounts the bias. Alternatively (and this is the approach chosen by practical systems such as eBay), star ratings may be reinterpreted in terms of quality evaluations—this is equivalent to "raising the bar" for objects or services that must receive a mean rating of at least 4.5 (or even above a higher threshold) on the 5-point star rating scale in order to be considered high quality.

2.5.2   Example Credibility Rating Scale

An exemplary credibility rating scale could follow the approach outlined above. Using a star rating interface, the scale would be displayed following a prompt or question asking the user to evaluate the website's credibility. A user can select from 1 to 5 stars. When the cursor of a user moves over a star, the following hints may be displayed:

1. Completely not credible
2. Rather non-credible
3. Fairly credible, although has major flaws
4. Credible, with some flaws
5. Completely credible

The hints can be provided for less experienced users not familiar with the star rating. Also, it should be possible to switch hints off for certain experiments.

2.5.3   Consensus Measures

An important issue in measuring credibility is the decision whether or not users agree in their evaluations (regardless of whether the used scale is interpreted as ordinal or cardinal). Inter-rater agreement measures (e.g., Fleiss' kappa or intra-class correlation coefficient), or dispersion measures of results (e.g., standard deviation), are usually used to assess agreement. For a 5-point ordinal scale, the use of classic dispersion measures becomes difficult (since the use of standard deviation is unjustified [71]). This issue must be addressed with a proper measure tailored to ordinal scales. Historically, the first measure of this type was Leik's ordinal consensus, introduced in 1966 [100]. It was based on cumulative frequency distributions. This measure is used throughout this book; however, other ordinal consensus measures exist [189, 198]. Ordinal consensus measures are capable of identifying polarization or agreement in ordinal scaled values; they are typically normalized from 0 (representing polarization) to 1 (representing perfect agreement).

However, for a uniform distribution of variable levels, the frequencies of Leik's consensus value depend on the rating scale levels (0.4 in the case of a 5-point scale).

2.5.4 Distribution Similarity Tests

Statistical tests can be used to compare distributions of credibility ratings. The Kruskal-Wallis test is a non-parametric statistical method used to compare multiple samples in terms of their original distribution. This method is suitable for data measured on an ordinal scale, as it bases its calculations on ranks assigned to observations. The test does not assume a normal distribution of the analyzed data. However, it does make an independence assumption (similarly to the Mann-Whitney test): data in various samples is assumed to be independent. The sample sizes may be different.

The null hypothesis in the Kruskal-Wallis test states that mean ranks in analyzed groups are equal. In other words, data from compared samples come from the same distribution. Compared to the Mann-Whitney test, the Kruskal-Wallis test can simultaneously compare several samples (groups), instead of two at a time. For a detailed description of the test, the reader may refer to [52, 169].

2.5.5 The Earth Mover's Distance (EMD)

Distributions of credibility ratings may also be compared in another way—by computing a distance measure among two distributions. This requires the ability to interpret a credibility measurement as a cardinal scale (although for many measures, the intervals among subsequent points on the scale need not be equal to each other nor equal to 1).

Many measures designed to compare probability distributions are extensively described in the literature. These methods can be grouped into two categories: bin-by-bin and cross-bin dissimilarity measures. The former are based on comparisons between corresponding histogram bins of analyzed distributions, whereas the latter also include non-corresponding bin comparisons. Rubner et al. [154] list the Minkowski difference, histogram intersection, Kullback-Leibler divergence, and c2 statistics as illustrations of bin-by-bin dissimilarity measures. The cross-bin category includes quadratic form distance, Kolmogorov-Smirnov distance, and the Earth Mover's Distance.

The Earth Mover's Distance (EMD), also known as the Wasserstein metric, is a measure based on the solution to a transportation problem raised in linear programming. It reflects the minimal cost necessary to transform one distribution into another. When comparing two probability distributions, one can be treated as a supplier and the second as a consumer. All of a distribution's mass must be moved from the first distribution to the second. The costs of transportation of one unit of goods to every consumer by different suppliers are known: they can be set to the distance between elements of the first and of the second distribution. The goal is to find the cheapest flow of goods that will satisfy the consumers' needs. The solution to this problem is the minimal amount of work required to transform one distribution into another [154]. A formal definition of EMD for the distributions of 5 scale values is presented below.

$U = \{(u_1, p_{u_1}), \ldots, (u_n, p_{u_n})\}$ and $V = \{(v_1, p_{v_1}), \ldots, (v_n, p_{v_n})\}$ are two distributions with $n = 5$ discrete values, where p_{u_i}, p_{v_j} are probabilities of values. It is assumed that $\sum_{i=1}^{n} p_{u_i} = \sum_{j=1}^{n} p_{v_j} = 1$.

$D = [d_{ij}]$ is the ground distance matrix of distances between u_i and v_j (it is here that the assumption of having a cardinal scale comes in and can also be tailored by specifying various distances among various values).

To calculate EMD, it is necessary to find the optimal flow $F = [f_{ij}]$ between u_i and v_j that would minimize the general cost:

$$WORK(U, V, F) = \sum_{i=1}^{n} \sum_{j=1}^{n} d_{ij} f_{ij}$$

where the following constraints are imposed:

$$f_{ij} \geq 0 \text{ for all } i, j$$

$$\sum_{j=1}^{n} f_{ij} \leq p_{u_i} \text{ for all } i$$

$$\sum_{i=1}^{n} f_{ij} \leq p_{v_j} \text{ for all } j$$

$$\sum_{i=1}^{n} \sum_{j=1}^{n} f_{ij} = min(\sum_{i=1}^{n} p_{u_i}, \sum_{j=1}^{n} p_{v_j}) = 1$$

When the optimal flow is found (the transportation problem is solved), EMD is defined by the work normalized by the total flow. However, for distributions, the total flow is 1 so the normalization factor can be ignored.

$$EMD(U, v) = \sum_{i-1}^{n} \sum_{j=1}^{n} f_{ij} d_{ij}$$

Note that the optimal flow may "move" distribution mass among the same values (if the probabilities for the values are equal in both distributions). In this case, the distance $d_{ii} = 0$ and this part of the flow is ignored, leaving only the parts that need to move distribution mass from one value to another.

2.6   Credibility Measurement Experiments

2.6.1   Fogg's Study

The earliest large-scale study of Web content credibility has been carried out by
Fogg in 2003 [40]. Two thousand five hundred respondents evaluated 100 webpages,
both assessing their credibility and leaving a comment on what influenced their
credibility evaluation. The comments were used as a source of a page's most
prominent features. The participants of Fogg's study were the supporters of some
charity organization, plus their circles of friends. The motivation to participate in the
study was the researcher's pledge to donate to the charity organization. Moreover,
the participants were not obliged to leave demographic information.

Fogg's study did not result in a publicly available dataset of credibility evaluations that could be used for machine learning.

2.6.2   Microsoft Credibility Corpus

One of the earliest datasets of webpage credibility evaluations has been created
by Schwarz and Morris in 2011 [160]. The goal of their study was to select
the most promising features of webpages that could be used to augment search
results to support credibility evaluation. The dataset contained 883 webpages from
five topics: health, finance, politics, celebrities, and environment. Each webpage
was augmented by 37 features. Credibility evaluations were done manually by
researchers, with a single evaluation per webpage.

The drawback of the Microsoft credibility corpus is that it contains only a
single evaluation for each webpage. It can be therefore used as a dataset to test
machine learning algorithms for automatic classification of credibility, but not to
study consensus levels or methods of determining reliable credibility classes. Also,
while a single evaluation can be considered an expert evaluation for some of the
classes (such as politics or celebrities), it cannot be considered an expert evaluation
for health, finance, or environment topics.

2.6.3   Panel Experiment (IIBR)

In order to verify hypotheses related to the subjectivity of credibility evaluations,
evaluations from many users must be obtained preferably from a representative
or sufficiently varied sample. Subjectivity can be due to socio-economic or demographic status, but also psychological factors or the skills and experience in using
the WWW.

With such goals in mind, within the Reconcile project in September 2012, a dataset of credibility evaluation was constructed in cooperation with one of the largest Polish research institutes specializing in online social opinion polling [79]. Over 1500 (1503) users participated in the experiment. The respondent group was randomly selected from the population of Polish Internet users and was controlled for demographic and social characteristics, such as gender, age, and education, as well as for Internet usage skills measured by a modified version of the Web-Use Skill Index proposed by Hargittai and Hsieh [59].

The dataset contains 155 Polish language webpages on 17 topics, grouped into four categories: healthy lifestyle, cancer treatment, parenting, and personal finance. The dataset contains over 4300 webpage evaluations, an average of over 28 evaluations per webpage. Evaluations were done using seven criteria: credibility, presentation, author's expertise, author's intentions, clarity, completeness, and validity. Furthermore, evaluations were done in three experimental conditions: topic browse (the participant evaluated three randomly selected webpages), topic search (a participant evaluated three webpages on a similar topic and had to answer a question related to their content), and topic keywords (a participant had to evaluate three randomly selected websites and propose keywords to describe their content). Notably, the three conditions did not affect the median of the credibility evaluations (verified by a Kruskal-Wallis test).

2.6.4   The Content Credibility Corpus

The Content Credibility Corpus (C^3 for short) is a dataset that will be used throughout this book for various analyses or machine learning experiments. The C^3 dataset has been collected as a part of the Reconcile project, with the goal of creating semi-automatic tools for website credibility assessment, and is available for download[8] [80]. All experiments were conducted using the same credibility evaluation system (the Reconcile prototype). Websites for evaluation were archived (including static as well as dynamic elements, e.g., advertisements) and presented to users together with an accompanying questionnaire. The study was carried out between February and November 2013 on the Amazon Mechanical Turk platform. Participants were recruited from the US population. Their task was to evaluate the credibility of the presented websites. Each participant could evaluate any number of websites (but not more than 50) and was given a proportional monetary reward. Additional characteristics of users were controlled during the study.

Experiment participants were asked to evaluate four more dimensions on the 5-point star scale using the following five criteria:

1. Credibility of the webpage
2. Appearance (presentation) of the webpage

---

[8]https://rawgit.com/s8811/reconcile-tags/master/describe_data.nb.html.

3. Completeness of information on the webpage
4. Expertise of webpage's author(s)
5. Intention of webpage's author(s)

Evaluators needed to justify their evaluation with a short comment (min. 150 characters).

The corpus of webpages was gathered using three methods: manual selection, RSS feeds subscription, and customized Google queries. It spans various topical categories grouped in five main topics:

- Politics and economy
- Medicine
- Healthy lifestyle
- Personal finance
- Entertainment

The selection aimed to achieve a thematically diverse and balanced corpus of a priori credible and non-credible pages, thus covering most of the possible threats on the Web. As of May 2013, the dataset consisted of 15,750 evaluations of 5543 pages from 2041 participants. Users performed the evaluation tasks over the Internet on our research platform via Amazon Mechanical Turk. The respondents evaluated the archived versions of the gathered pages independently, not knowing each other's ratings.

Participants also responded to a psychological questionnaire. Literature studies dedicated to positive bias have led to the selection of the following psychological dimensions in the study: trust (expectancy that others can be relied upon), need for cognition (deriving pleasure from cognitive activities), risk-taking (tendency to involve in risky behaviors), conformity (understood as a sub-dimension of cooperativeness), and intellect (estimations of one's own intellectual abilities). The study checked the hypothesis that users showing high level of trust, risk-taking, and low level of need for cognition, conformity, and intellect will more often overestimate the credibility of the evaluated website [147]. Psychological traits were measured using selected scales from the International Personality Item Pool: NEO:A1 to measure trust, JPI:Cpr to measure conformity, JPI:Rkt to measure risk-taking, AB5C:V+/V+ versus V−/V− to measure intellect, and CHS to measure need for cognition. The results were analyzed using a graded response model from Item Response Theory (IRT). Internet experience was measured with the same modified Web-Use Skill Index scale as in the panel experiment described in the previous section.

During the study, the following characteristics referring to users were gathered:

- Age (groups: 10–20, 20–30, 30–40, 40–50, 50–60, 60–70, 70+)
- Education level (groups: no schooling completed, to grade 12 but no diploma or lower, high school graduate, some college credit but no degree, associate's degree, bachelor's degree, master's degree or higher)
- Internet experience (groups: high, average, low)
- Political views (groups: 10-step slider, from "left wing" to "right wing")

- Gender (groups: male, female)
- Income (less than 10,000, 10,000 to 25,000, 25,000 to 50,000, 50,000 to 75,000, 75,000 to 100,000, more than 100,000)
- Psychological traits (trust, risk-taking, conformity, intellect, need for cognition; analyzed groups: low or high in every analyzed trait)

Several quality-assurance heuristics were implemented during the study. The evaluation time of a single webpage could not be shorter than 2 min; the links provided by the users should not be broken and were required to link to an English language webpage. Additionally, the textual justifications had to be at least 150 characters long and written in English. As a quality-assurance element, the comments were also manually monitored for spam.

2.6.4.1 C^3 Dataset Augmentation with Tags

As mentioned in the previous subsection, the C^3 dataset of credibility assessments initially contained numerical credibility assessment values accompanied by its textual justification. These accompanying textual comments referred to the issues underlying particular credibility assessments. Using a custom-prepared code book, these texts were manually tagged to perform quantitative analysis of the related issues frequency.

The tagging was performed via Crowdsourcing rather than delegating this task to a few annotators. As the number of possible distinct tags exceeds 20, tags were grouped in several categories. Workers had to make a multiple choice (min. 1, max 4) of best suitable tags. The meaning of particular tags, accompanied by several example phrases which correspond to that tag, was provided to simplify the tagging task.

2.6.5 Fake News Datasets

Because of the rising importance of the fake news detection problem, datasets of fake news have been developed by the research community. These datasets are actually credibility evaluation datasets used as ground truth for fake news detection research. Three example datasets listed in this section have been developed using various methods of credibility evaluation: expert-based and Crowdsourcing-based.

1. The LIAR dataset originates from PolitiFact (see Sect. 1.2.3.4). The LIAR dataset has been collected using the PolitiFact API and includes 12,836 statements obtained from news releases, speeches, or interviews with politicians [205]. Because of the use of PolitiFact, the statements of LIAR dataset are labeled by PolitiFact experts (typically journalists who specialize in fact-checking), using PolitiFact labels: true, mostly true, half true, barely true, false, and "pants on

fire." PolitiFact is also used to create fact-checking datasets by other sources
[200].

2. The CREDBANK dataset contains about 60 million tweets related to fake news.
   The dataset has been labeled using Crowdsourcing on Amazon Mechanical Turk.
   The tweets contained in the CREDBANK dataset are related to over 1000 news
   events. The credibility of each event has been evaluated by 30 workers on mTurk
   [121]. The tweets in CREDBANK have been published on Twitter in October
   2015.
3. FakeNewsNet is an ongoing effort to create a dataset of fake news from
   PolitiFact and BuzzFeedNews. BuzzFeedNews is sample of news published by
   nine news agencies during September 2016 (prior to the US election). Similarly
   to PolitiFact, BuzzFeedNews is fact-checked by journalists. Additionally, the
   dataset is enriched by linked articles, including their Web content (media,
   metadata). By December 2017, the FakeNewsNet contained about 420 news
   items, balanced between fake news and true news. The dataset contained over
   60,000 engagements with these news from about 40,000 users on Facebook and
   Twitter [167, 168].
4. SemEval-2017 task[9] [25] had two parts: one of stance detection and the other of
   rumor veracity. The dataset consists of about 300 fake news threads from Twitter,
   totaling about 5500 tweets.

Apart from these datasets, some research on fake news detection uses the
DBpedia as a data source [21]. DBpedia, and, more generally, the Wikipedia, can
be viewed as a source of encyclopedic facts (see Sect. 4.3 for a discussion of the
credibility of Wikipedia content). The drawback of this approach is the lack of non-
credible examples. This weakness can be partially compensated by projects such as
the Uncyclopedia[10] (a humorous and sarcastic "encyclopedia" of misinformation) or
UnNews[11] (a sister project of Uncyclopedia that focuses on bogus news). However,
the weakness of using these projects for fake news detection is that by definition,
sarcasm does not count as fake news that are defined intentionally and verifiably
false news articles [167].

2.7   Subjectivity of Credibility Measurements

According to the definition of credibility (Sect. 2.3.4) and theories of credibility
evaluation (Sect. 2.4.4), credibility is subjective. Fogg's Prominence-Interpretation
theory predicts that even though credibility is a function of attributes of information
and meta-information, this function may vary for different users and indeed also for

---

[9]SemEval-2017 Task 8: RumourEval: Determining rumour veracity and support for rumours.
[10]http://uncyclopedia.wikia.com.
[11]http://uncyclopedia.wikia.com.

situational contexts. By definition, the credibility signal is also specific to a person, as various receivers can have different capability to evaluate credibility.

Taking all these considerations into account, the question remains: how strong is the subjectivity of credibility? In other words, does the signal generated by a webpage and received by various users differ significantly from user to user? Answer to this question can be obtained if based on several empirical results.

The question of subjectivity of credibility also has practical value. If credibility is highly subjective, then creating models to predict credibility evaluations just based on webpage features, and not on receiver features, would be impossible. On the other hand, if the subjectivity is low, it would be feasible to focus on the signal generated by various webpages. It would also become feasible to compare these webpages with each other with regard to their credibility.

The first systematic study of webpage credibility evaluation subjectivity to demographic, social, and psychological factor, as well as Internet usage skill, was based on the Panel dataset described in Sect. 2.6.3. The study compared distributions of credibility evaluations according to gender, education, Internet efficacy, and psychological factors. The results are shown in Figs. 2.2, 2.3, and 2.4. The impact of gender (which was almost balanced in the sample) on credibility ratings is very low, with females being slightly more likely to give the highest rating than males. The impact of education is a little stronger; respondents with higher education (almost half of the sample) are slightly more critical in their credibility ratings. The impact of Internet skills, ranked in three grades (light, medium, and heavy Internet users), was also small—Internet novices (about 30% of the sample) are a little more likely to give highest credibility ratings.

Fig. 2.2 Credibility ratings subjectivity to gender. Source: [79]

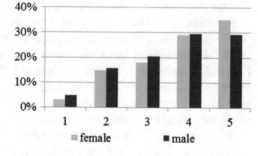

Fig. 2.3 Credibility ratings subjectivity to education. Source: [79]

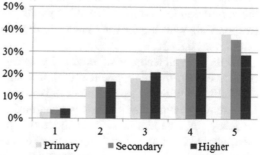

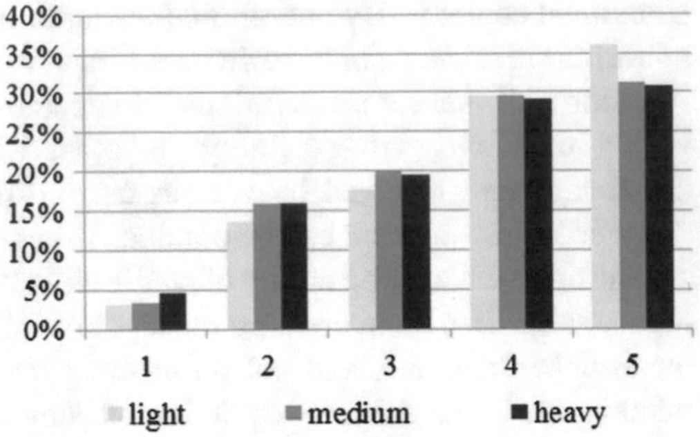

Fig. 2.4 Credibility ratings subjectivity to Internet usage skill. Source: [79]

Fig. 2.5 Credibility ratings of ordinary users and experts. Source: [79]

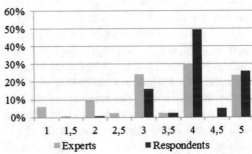

While statistical tests show that the differences between the distributions are significant, it is evident from the examination of the distributions that for practical purposes, the difference is negligible. The impact of other respondent characteristics, such as age, was even smaller—the Kruskal-Wallis test indicates that age does not have any significant impact on credibility rating distributions.

A similar situation occurred when psychological factors were examined. Two psychological factors were investigated in the study: "need for cognition" and "trust." Psychological traits were measured using scales from the International Personality Item Pool. "Need for cognition" is a personality trait that can be understood as a higher cognitive ability. "Trust," on the other hand, describes a general tendency to trust others. While statistical tests indicated significant impact of psychological variables on credibility ratings, this impact was weak. For example, "need for cognition" is negatively correlated with the tendency to overrate webpages (defined as giving a rating that exceeds the median rating by at least 1 score), but the correlation is -0.0875. "Trust" is positively correlated with credibility ratings (respondents with higher trust gave slightly higher ratings), but the correlation is even lower: 0.0421.

While the subjectivity of credibility ratings in the panel experiment turned out to be low, the experiment revealed a strong tendency to overrate webpage credibility by ordinary users. The negative skewness (shift towards positive values) of credibility rating distributions is apparent. The question remained whether this tendency constituted a bias. To evaluate this possibility, the medical webpages in the study (119 out of 154 webpages) were evaluated by medical experts. Figure 2.5 demonstrates that experts give much more critical credibility ratings than ordinary users (regardless of their Internet experience or education level). Since this result concerns the sensitive area of health-related Web content, it demonstrates a real need for supporting credibility evaluation on the Web.

2.7.1 Robustness of Credibility Rating Distributions to Sample Composition

Another, practical view of the subjectivity of Web content credibility ratings concerns the question of whether it is practically possible to get a robust estimate of a webpage's credibility from a small sample of credibility ratings. In an ideal situation, one could ask a representative sample of Internet users to evaluate each website and, based on the collected data, draw reliable conclusions. However, such a scenario is not realistic in practical applications. Considering the unlimited resources of the Internet, assuming a high response rate for every website or movie included in the rating system is unrealistic. Rather, one should expect small samples of evaluations for a subset of all objects. In practice, it would be quite good if the researcher could receive more than 10 ratings for more popular webpages. Due to the power-law structure of popularity distributions, most webpages would receive zero or at most 1 rating, while a small part would be able to receive a relatively high number of ratings. The question of how to deal with unpopular webpages is left for the next chapter.

If, for example, credibility ratings would be highly subjective with regard to gender, and the credibility evaluation support system would base its operation on webpages that receive at least 10 ratings, then what would be the impact on the system if a webpage would be rated by a sample composed only of males, and no females? A similar question concerns other demographic, social, or psychological characteristics.

This question can be answered by a systematic comparison of distributions from small samples size of 10, drawn at random from the dataset, from the overall distribution of all ratings, and similarly by a comparison of distributions from samples of the same size, but only from respondents with a fixed characteristic (e.g., only from male respondents). Distributions will be compared using the EMD (see Sect. 2.5.5). First, to set a benchmark, distributions from small samples shall be repeatedly drawn (1000 times) and the EMD of these distributions to the reference distribution from all evaluation will be calculated. This will serve to establish a benchmark: the effect of sample size on the EMD.

Table 2.4 shows statistics of EMDs obtained from 1000 random draws of subsamples from the credibility evaluations in the panel experiment dataset (see Sect. 2.6.3) and the C^3 dataset (see Sect. 2.6.4). For comparison, the experiment was repeated with another dataset: the MovieLens dataset of movie ratings. MovieLens is a project conducted by the Social Computing Research group at the University of Minnesota, which aims to produce reliable recommender systems

Table 2.4 Summary statistics of EMDs between reference distribution of credibility ratings and distributions from small random subsamples for various datasets

Dataset	Min	Second quintile	Median	Mean	Third quintile	Max
Panel N = 10	0.11	0.32	0.36	0.40	0.41	1.92
Panel N = 50	0.04	0.14	0.16	0.17	0.18	0.35
Panel N = 100	0.04	0.11	0.12	0.13	0.14	0.32
C^3 N = 10	0.10	0.30	0.34	0.35	0.36	0.77
C^3 N = 50	0.02	0.12	0.13	0.15	0.15	0.47
C^3 N = 100	0.01	0.1	0.1	0.12	0.13	0.23
Movies N = 10	0.13	0.31	0.36	0.39	0.38	1.82
Movies N = 50	0.05	0.14	0.15	0.17	0.17	0.43
Movies N = 100	0.03	0.11	0.11	0.12	0.13	0.29

designed specifically for recommending movies. The dataset contains over a million anonymized ratings of approximately 4000 movies by more than 6000 users who joined the MovieLens platform in 2000. Basic demographic information (gender, age, occupation) was added to the dataset. Every user rated at least 20 movies. On average, every user rated 166 (with a median of 96). The most active user rated 2314. Over 70% of evaluators were males (a 72:28 ratio); 73% of the evaluators were within the 18–44 age range. The two most frequent occupations were managers and students.

Not surprisingly, the results show that the larger subsets differ to a lesser degree from the respective reference distribution. However, in real-life situations, smaller samples of evaluations for every object are to be expected. Therefore, summary statistics calculated for subsamples of size 10 will be treated as a benchmark for further comparisons.

In order to explore how extreme cases affect evaluations uploaded to a quality evaluation system, for every value of an independent variable included in the analyzed datasets, random samples of size 10 are drawn. For example, for the gender variable, samples are drawn of size 10 of evaluations submitted only by men and samples submitted only by women. The distributions obtained from these samples are compared using EMD with respective reference distributions. The experiment is repeated 1000 times. The median EMD is then calculated for each value of an independent variable. The maximum EMD median for all values of a variable is used to evaluate the impact of that variable on sample composition. The value is compared to the benchmark EMD obtained from perfectly random samples of size 10.

The analyzed datasets contain several demographic characteristics of users. The datasets related to Web content credibility evaluation (C^3, Panel) contain richer information about users; the remaining datasets (Article Feedback Tool (AFT), MovieLens) contain only basic demographic data. Additional information about the relation between demographic factors and credibility evaluation can be found in Rafalak et al. [147]. In subsequent analysis, a certain feature can be sometimes omitted if it is not present in a dataset. Common variables contained in different datasets are unified in terms of measurement scales. Maximum medians of EMD

Table 2.5 Maximum medians of EMD for samples of size 10 selected using demographic variables or content topic, compared against respective benchmarks

	Age	Gender	Education	Internet (experience)	Politics	Income	Occupation	Topic	Second quintile (benchmark)	Median (benchmark)	Third quintile (benchmark)
C^3	0.35	0.33	0.34	0.34	0.34	0.34	NA	1.68*	0.30	0.34	0.36
Panel	0.39	0.39	0.38	0.39	NA	NA	NA	0.41*	0.32	0.36	0.41
Movies	0.38	0.38	NA	NA	NA	NA	0.42*	0.42*	0.31	0.36	0.38

Fig. 2.6 Credibility ratings subjectivity to webpage topic. Source: [79]

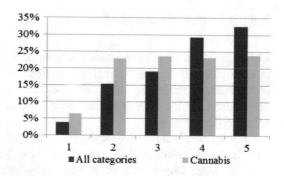

distributions for subsamples selected using demographic variables are summarized in Table 2.5.

The obtained results show that maximum medians for the analyzed homogeneous samples representing demographic variables fit almost perfectly into the range between the second and third quintile of respective benchmark distribution (values that do not fit into this range are indicated with stars in Table 2.5). Those limits slightly exceeded (by 0.04) only for the "occupation" variable in the MovieLens dataset. The range between the second and third quintile contains the middle 20% of analyzed distributions. Therefore, even in the most extreme cases, where all users represent the same level of a demographic factor (i.e., all are men), the observed EMD from respective reference distribution is very similar to the benchmark. This means that credibility distributions derived from small samples of size 10 are robust against demographic user characteristics.

The situation is quite different if ratings are selected by content (website or movie) topic. In all three datasets, the maximum median of EMD distributions sampled using topics is greater than the third quintile of the respective benchmark. In the Movies and Panel datasets, this difference is rather small, but in C^3 it is quite high. It is worth mentioning that C^3 is more diversified than the Movies and Panel datasets in terms of website topical category. This is probably why the obtained results show the strongest impact for the website topic in the C^3 dataset.

The effect of the webpage's topic is visualized in Fig. 2.6. It shows the distribution of all credibility ratings from the Panel dataset, compared against the distribution of credibility ratings only for webpages on the topic of "Cannabis." The effect is quite strong, which is confirmed by statistical tests.

Kruskal-Wallis comparisons of credibility evaluation distributions calculated for websites grouped by topical category confirm the significance of content topic. In all analyzed datasets, these comparisons reached the level of statistical significance. This result suggests that credibility ratings given by users are dependent on the subject category of the evaluated website. A practical conclusion would be that a credibility evaluation support system should use the topic of content as a context for presenting ratings and recommendations.

2.8   Classes of Credibility

In the previous section, the robustness of distributions of credibility ratings to sample composition has been demonstrated. With respect to several social and psychological user features, distributions of credibility ratings are not strongly affected even if the sample is extremely biased (all users in the sample have one identical characteristic).

On the other hand, distributions of credibility ratings are definitely affected by attributes of the evaluated webpages. One example, shown in the previous section, is the webpage's topic. The above analysis supports the view that credibility, defined as a signal that is a function of attributes of communicated information and meta-information, can be measured by the proposed "star rating" method. Distributions of credibility ratings from at least 10 respondents seem to be a good method of such measurement.

It was mentioned in Sect. 2.2 that supporting credibility evaluation for a large class of Web content—the non-specialist, factual Web content—should be based on consensus. Such consensus can be established based on distributions of credibility ratings by assigning such distributions to classes of credibility. For example, a distribution of credibility ratings that focuses on the most positive rating scores can be assigned to a "Highly Credible" class. Similarly, a distribution that focuses on negative ratings can be assigned to a "Highly Not Credible" class. Assignment of a distribution to a class is based on the fact that consensus has been reached about the webpage's credibility.

Before deciding on a procedure to assign distributions to credibility classes, one must address the issue of class design. Usually, this issue is solved by selecting thresholds for averages or other statistics (median values, modes, etc.) obtained from a sample of evaluations and using these thresholds as boundaries for classes. The thresholds will typically be based on examination of the data, but the data scientist often needs to make an ad hoc decision in order to set threshold values. Clustering or other unsupervised approaches based on averages or medians will not work well in cases where raters often disagree, leading to dispersed distributions of ratings. A threshold is also required for a dispersion measure such as the Leik coefficient in order to determine whether consensus can be reached.

Instead of directly selecting such thresholds to define classes of credibility, the EMD can be used to cluster distributions of credibility ratings. This section first shows the result of this approach for the two datasets of credibility ratings: the Panel and C^3 datasets (as well as additional datasets for comparison). A method is proposed based on an observation of discovered clusters, aiming to define credibility classes directly using distributions and the EMD measure. This method has the advantage of naturally dealing with distributions with high dispersions and other issues of distribution shape such as bias (or skewness).

The proposed approach to defining classes yields good results on several datasets. Furthermore, clusters should be the basis for creating operational definitions of quality classes that can be used to classify new Web content. The proposed method to define simple and intuitive classes using entire distributions of ratings fits discovered clusters better than classes defined using distribution means. The fit is good not just for individual datasets: proposed classes are fitted to clusters from four datasets using just two parameters. The proposed method for defining classes for highly dispersed distributions is also compared with a method that uses known dispersion measures.

2.8.1 Clustering Credibility Rating Distributions Using Earth Mover's Distance

In this section, four datasets are analyzed with the aim of discovering clusters of distributions. Clustering, one of the unsupervised machine learning techniques, helps in finding hidden structure in unlabeled data. From the perspective of this research, clustering can be helpful in better understanding gathered data, finding typical distributions, and showing any similarities between different datasets.

2.8.1.1 The AFT Dataset of Wikipedia Quality Ratings

The four datasets used in the clustering study are the Panel dataset, the C^3 dataset, the MovieLens dataset introduced in the previous section, and the AFT dataset.

The Article Feedback Tool (AFT) is a Wikimedia survey for article feedback, aimed at engaging readers in the assessment of article quality. AFT was used on Wikipedia in five different versions. Currently discontinued, it was in use for over a year, enabling the compilation of a large dataset of Wikipedia article evaluations made by volunteer Wikipedia users.

The dataset used here is based on AFTv4 that used a simple GUI with a "star rating" in four categories: trustworthiness, objectivity, completeness, and quality of writing. These criteria closely resemble criteria used for webpage evaluation in the Panel and C^3 datasets. The original AFTv4 dataset contains over 11M ratings of articles based on 5.6M different revisions of over 1.5M distinct articles, collected between July 2011 and July 2012.

2.8.1.2 Clustering Algorithm

EMD is used to measure distances between distributions, and the k-medoids algorithm is used to find cluster centers. This algorithm has an advantage—every center of a cluster must be an actual observation. This allows for an intuitive interpretation of the results. However, one of the drawbacks of this method is that it is computationally expensive and requires constructing an N–N distance matrix between observations. For an AFT dataset this is virtually impossible, as it would require the construction of a matrix with over 1010 entries. Therefore, a sample consisting of 1000 observations randomly chosen from the dataset has been used for clustering.

2.8.1.3 Determining the Number of Clusters

Because of the positive bias that is present in all datasets, using just two classes of Web content quality results in great diversity within one of the two classes. For example, warning users about highly non-credible Web content would be impossible with a binary classification that matched the clusters discovered in the C^3 dataset, as the cluster of non-positive evaluations contains distributions focused on the middle of the Likert scale together with distributions focused on the negative ratings. A binary classification may also be insufficient for applications that require a zero false positive (or false negative) rate, for example, the recommendation of highly credible medical Web content. For this reason, K = 3 or K = 4 classes are considered for various datasets. The use of K = 3 is hoped to discover a cluster of positive quality evaluations of Web content called Pos, a cluster of negative quality evaluations called Neg, and a cluster of neutral quality evaluations called Neu.

Adding a fourth class should result in the discovery of a cluster of conflicting evaluations of Web content, which are referred to as controversial, called Con. To decide whether it is possible to identify such clusters in the data, the shape of medoids for K = 4 is examined.

2.8.1.4 Notation for Extreme Distributions

In order to better evaluate the discovered medoids, their EMDs from extreme distributions focused on the positive or negative evaluations on the star rating scale can be calculated. The following notation is introduced: $P = \{p_1, p_2 p_3, p_4 p_5\}$—distribution of ratings on a 1–5 scale. For all considered datasets, ratings were submitted on the star rating scale where 1 is the most negative and 5 is the most positive value. $p_1 + p_2 + p_3 + p_4 + p_5 = 1$.

Table 2.6 Definitions of extreme distributions of values on the star rating or Likert scale

$P_{Neg} = \{p_1 = 1\}$	Extremely negative rating distribution
$P_{Pos} = \{p_5 = 1\}$	Extremely negative rating distribution
$P_{Con} = \{p_1 = 0.5, p_5 = 0.5\}$	Extremely controversial rating distribution

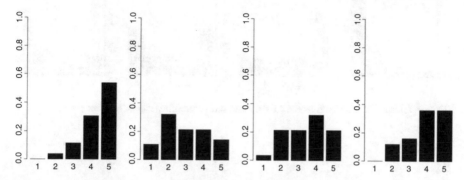

Fig. 2.7 Clusters of distributions for Panel dataset with credibility labels. Source: [148]

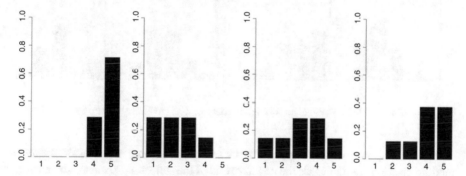

Fig. 2.8 Clusters of distributions for C^3 dataset with credibility labels. Source: [148]

In this notation, p_i denotes the probability that an evaluation has a value of i on the star rating scale, while a notation of $\{p_1 = x_1, p_2 = x_2, \ldots, p_5 = x_5\}$ denotes the shape of a distribution. For the sake of conciseness, $p_i = 0$ can be skipped.

$EMD(P_1, P_2)$: the Earth Mover's Distance between two distributions.

Table 2.6 contains the definitions of extreme distributions. The first two distributions focus all mass on one end of the star rating scale, while the last distribution focuses all mass on both ends and represents extreme disagreement of ratings.

The shape of medoids for the four clusters differs visibly in every dataset (see Figs. 2.7, 2.8, 2.9, and 2.10). Nevertheless, for every dataset, a medoid which can be referred to as representative of a positive class can be identified. This is the first medoid shown in the figures. These medoids are, to various extents, focused on the right end of the star rating scale. The closest is the medoid from the C^3 dataset, whose EMD from P_{Pos} is equal to 0.29. The furthest is the medoid from the MovieLens dataset; its EMD from P_{Pos} is 1.10.

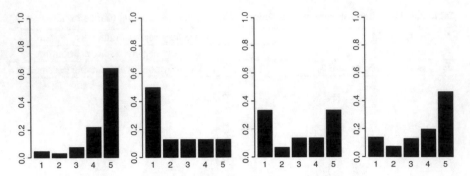

Fig. 2.9 Clusters of distributions for AFT dataset with credibility labels. Source: [148]

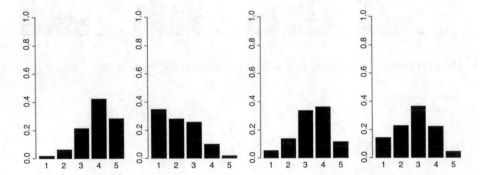

Fig. 2.10 Clusters of distributions for MovieLens dataset with credibility labels. Source: [148]

A similar approach can be applied in the search for the negative cluster. Again, a medoid that is shifted towards the negative end of the star rating scale exists in every dataset, as illustrated by the second medoid in Figs. 2.7, 2.8, 2.9, and 2.10. However, due to the positive bias of ratings in all datasets, this medoid is less distinctively focused on the extreme negative evaluations. The tendency of ratings to be J-shaped makes most distributions left-skewed. This results in greater EMDs of discovered negative medoids from the ideal P_{Neg} distribution (Panel, 1.96; C^3, 1.29; AFT, 1.25; MovieLens, 1.16).

Since a positive and negative cluster has been identified for each dataset, all of the remaining observations could be grouped into a neutral cluster, resulting in K = 3. However, potential disagreement of ratings for a significant set of Web content still needs to be taken into consideration. Knowledge of the domains suggests that this is a real possibility; for example, Wikipedia (which is the source of content evaluated in the AFT dataset) includes procedures for identifying controversial articles and dealing with controversy.

It is not possible to identify medoids that belong to the controversial class for every dataset. It seems that for most of the datasets, controversy is not a part of their natural structure. Only in the AFT dataset (from Wikipedia) are controversial observations frequent enough to constitute a separate cluster (third medoid in

Fig. 2.9). This medoid is characterized by a clearly U-shaped distribution quite close to the extremely conflicting P_{Con} distribution (an EMD of less than 0.3). The fourth cluster's medoid for AFT is characterized by a J-shaped distribution that cannot be interpreted as representing clear disagreement.

Medoids which have not been selected as representatives of positive or negative clusters can be thought of as belonging to the neutral cluster. If no cluster matches the controversial class, the two leftover neutral clusters can be merged into one. The shape of the neutral cluster may vary, as it is simply the cluster that contains all remaining observations.

For every dataset, two distinct clusters exist that can be treated as the positive and negative class, respectively. For the AFT dataset, the controversial class can also be introduced, whereas for other datasets this class does not occur. This results in our choice of K = 3 for the MovieLens, C^3, and Panel datasets and K = 4 for the AFT dataset.

Following this qualitative analysis, the fitness of the proposed classes to discovered clusters will now be subject to a quantitative evaluation.

2.8.2   Classes of Credibility Based on Distributions

This section introduces definitions of rating distribution classes that can be used to interpret clusters discovered in the data. These definitions are dedicated to ratings on a 1–5 star rating scale but can be easily generalized to other scoring options. The definitions do not require rating aggregation, since they use entire distributions, so the question of whether the scale is ordinal or cardinal is irrelevant. Moreover, the class definitions can be made independent of the data, so they can be applied to training machine classification algorithms without the danger of information leaks.

Classes of distributions are defined using the extreme distributions P_{Pos}, P_{Neg}, and P_{Con} introduced in the previous section. The classes use the two parameters R and α:

- Class of positive rating distributions:

$$Pos_{\alpha_1}^{R_1} = \{P : EMD(P_{Pos}, P) < R_1; \ p_1 + p_2 + p_3 < \alpha_1\}$$

- Class of negative rating distributions:

$$Neg_{\alpha_2}^{R_2} = \{P : EMD(P_{Neg}, P) < R_2; \ p_4 + p_5 < \alpha_2\}$$

- Class of controversial rating distributions:

$$Con^{R_3} = \{P : EMD(P_{Con}, P) < R_3\}$$

- Class of remaining rating distributions. $\mathscr{P}$ is the family of all rating distributions for values $1, \ldots 5$:

$$Neu = \mathscr{P} \setminus Pos_{\alpha_1}^{R_1} \setminus Neg_{\alpha_2}^{R_2} \setminus Con^{R_3}$$

The same values for $\alpha_1 = \alpha_2 = \alpha$ shall be used. The parameter α is used to avoid moving too much of the distribution mass to the other end of the star rating scale. This may happen especially with distributions that are close to the threshold of R for the EMD. Note that for $\alpha = 1$, the class definitions only use the radius parameters.

2.8.2.1   Fitting of Proposed Classes to Distribution Clusters

Having clustered the data, what remains is to determine distance thresholds from the reference distributions. This will allow to assign any distribution for new Web content to a class. By fitting classes to all considered datasets using identical parameters, the generality of the proposed classes will be validated. If this approach would result in low accuracy, even assuming the fit could be improved for individual datasets using fitted parameter values, the approach would be insufficiently generic.

By iterating over a matrix of possible values for Pos, Neg, and Con radii (considering radii from 0 to 4 with a step of 0.01) and changing the value of α (considering the same values for both Pos and Neg classes, $\alpha \in \{0.1, 0.2, 0.3, 1\}$), an optimal point maximizing the geometric mean of the percentage of correctly assigned labels for all datasets is found. The geometric mean takes a value of zero if the percentage of correctly assigned labels drops to zero for any of the analyzed categories. Moreover, it is influenced to a greater extent by smaller values than the arithmetic mean.

The optimal point is found for the following parameters R of the Pos, Neg, and Con classes. The Con class is considered only for the AFT dataset, since this is the only dataset with four clusters.

$$Pos_{0.3}^1 = \{P : EMD(P_{Pos}, P) < 1; p_1 + p_2 + p_3 < 0.3\}$$

$$Neg_{0.3}^2 = \{P : EMD(P_{Neg}, P) < 2; p_4 + p_5 < 0.3\}$$

$$Con^{0.7} = \{P : EMD(P_{Con}, P) < 0.7\}$$

The optimal radius R for these three classes has the following values: $R_{Pos} = 1$, $R_{Neg} = 2$, and $R_{Con} = 0.7$. The optimal value of $\alpha = 0.3$. In order to evaluate the effect of the alpha parameter on accuracy, this parameter has been varied together with the radius and the optimal value for proposed classes for all datasets has been found. This enables to compare obtained fit accuracies for various values of alpha. The results are shown in Table 2.7.

Table 2.7 Accuracy of optimal class fit to data clusters for various values of α

α	0.1	0.2	0.3	1
AFT (%)	64.1	78.0	85.3	85.8
C^3 (%)	78.4	85.3	81.8	75.2
Panel (%)	65.2	75.6	84.5	92.3
MovieLens (%)	60	67.9	62.7	48.6
Geom. mean accuracy (%)	66.6	76.5	78.0	73.3

The results show that increasing α from 0.1 to 1 results in an increase of the accuracy for some datasets, while for other datasets the optimal value of α is 0.2 or 0.3. Overall, the optimal value of $\alpha = 0.3$. Notably, there is a severe deterioration in the accuracy for the MovieLens dataset for $\alpha = 1$.

The overall agreement of the fitted classes with discovered clusters is high (the geometric mean of accuracy for all datasets is 78%). The highest agreement rate is observed for the Pos, Con, and Neg classes. Class Neu, containing all unclassified ratings, shows the highest misclassification rate. Most importantly, misclassification rates between the extreme classes—Pos and Neg—are extremely low. This is the advantage of introducing a third buffer class (Neu). For many applications, this kind of class design will have an advantage.

2.8.2.2 Fitting the Controversy Class to Discovered Clusters

The above analysis uses only two parameters (the radius R and α) to fit the proposed classes to clusters discovered in the empirical data. The obtained result shows quite a good fit. The only exception is the Con class, which is too small in the analyzed datasets. In order to improve the fit of the Con class, an attempt of a more sophisticated definition of this class should be undertaken. This enhanced definition uses classic dispersion measures that have also been frequently used to measure inter-rater agreement.

The definition of the extremely conflicting distribution (Con) can be extended by a parameter β that enables a shift of the mass from one end to the other: $P_{Con} = \{p_1 = 0.5 - \beta, p_5 = 0.5 + \beta\}$. The value of β must be limited so that P_{Con}^{β} does not change into P_{Neg} or P_{Pos}, respectively, for $\beta = -0.5$ and $\beta = 0.5$. The controversy defined using the P_{Con}^{0} distribution serves as a perfect illustration of opinion polarization, which can be identified using classic dispersion measures. In this section, one of the earliest proposed ordinal dispersion measures, Leik's ordinal consensus (see Sect. 2.5.3), is used. The performance of Leik's ordinal consensus against EMD in the detection of controversy can be tested by using the following variants of definitions for the Con class:

$$ConL^T = \{P : Leik(P) < T\}$$

$$ConD_{\beta}^{R,T} = \{P : EMD(P_{Con}^{\beta}, P) < R \vee Leik(P) < T\}$$

$$ConC_\beta^{R,T} = \{P : EMD(P_{Con}^\beta, P) < R \wedge Leik(P) < T\}$$

What is measured is the goodness of fit of these definitions by comparing the classes Con_0^R, Con^T, $ConD_\beta^{R,T}$, and $Con_\beta^{R,T}$ with the clusters from the AFT and C^3 datasets containing clusters with distributions that could be considered evidence of controversy. A binary classification case is assumed: the controversial cluster versus all other distributions in the dataset.

The space of parameters α, β, R, and T has been searched for the most promising parameter values yielding the best precision and recall for both datasets. Although no promising outcome is produced for a search executed on the C^3 dataset, the results for AFT show that the best performance is achieved for the last $ConC_\beta^{R,T}$ class (using a conjunction of Leik and EMD). The optimal parameter values of $T = 0.35$, $\beta = 0.1$, and $R = 0.8$ show the following performance: precision=78%, recall=82%, and f1=80%. In comparison, predicting the Con cluster in the AFT dataset using only the EMD radius and the simpler definition of the Con class results in precision of 75% and recall of 82%.

Note that the EMD of the uniform distribution for the 5-point star rating scale from the P_{Con}^0 distribution is 0.8. This value is the same as the optimal EMD radius for the Con class found using the fitting approach for the AFT dataset.

The poor results obtained for the C^3 dataset can be explained by the insufficient number of controversial examples in the dataset, which do not enable acquisition of a meaningful cluster.

2.8.3   Advantage of Defining Classes Using Distributions Over Arithmetic Mean

This section compares the use of the proposed classes with that of classes that use a simple arithmetic mean.

The first advantage of using the classes defined in this section is evident when dealing with conflicting ratings. If a significant amount of Web content generates disagreement regarding its quality evaluation, as in the AFT dataset, using means to define classes will introduce classification errors. The presented approach deals with this issue. However, it might be argued that the mean can be used together with a dispersion measure instead.

The use of the mean and the described approach can be compared by considering the extreme case of $\alpha = 1$. In this case, in the proposed class definitions, the condition of α is not used. Only the radius parameter determines the class. It can be shown that, in this case, the proposed classes are equivalent to using the mean. This is because $EMD(P_{Neg}, P) = \overline{P} - 1$ and $EMD(P_{Pos}, P) = 5 - \overline{P}$, where $\overline{P}$ is the mean of distribution P. This implies that classes constructed using the mean with threshold values $R_{Neg} + 1$ and $5 - R_{Pos}$ for the Neg and Pos classes, respectively, would be identical to classes with $\alpha = 1$. A comparison of the accuracy obtained using such classes with other values of α has already been shown in Table 2.7. The optimal fit is obtained for $\alpha = 0.3$ with a geometric average accuracy of 78%, while the accuracy for classes constructed using the mean would be 73.3%. However, for the MovieLens dataset, the loss of accuracy from using means is quite severe (48.6% vs. 62.7% obtained for $\alpha = 0.3$). This comparison shows the clear advantage of using a definition of classes that utilizes the α parameter, which is only possible if the entire distribution is used to define the Pos and Neg classes.

The classes proposed in this section are merely simple examples of how entire distributions can be used to define Web content classifications. The advantage of the proposed approach lies in its simplicity and generality. However, it is possible to use entire distributions to define classes that are much better fitted for specific applications. For example, these class definitions can be tailored so that the classes take into account possible bias of ratings (similarly as in the previous section for the Con class).

The exclusive use of arithmetic means for clustering or interpretation of the obtained clusters is likely to disregard important patterns in the data. This especially concerns the Con class, as its distribution concentrates mainly on the extreme points of the scale and therefore cannot be adequately reflected by the arithmetic mean.

2.9 Credibility Evaluation Criteria

In Sect. 2.5, the idea of using a star-based rating for an overall assessment of credibility has been proposed. Furthermore, Sect. 2.3.3 argued that such a method measures surface credibility (unless users are experts, or are additionally exposed to information about the Web content's source and know the reputation of this source). Such a holistic measurement of surface credibility has the advantage of simplicity and, as demonstrated in Sect. 2.8, can be used to create distributions of credibility evaluations that can robustly indicate a credibility class for the evaluated Web content.

The process of evaluating surface credibility on a star-based rating scale can be described and explained by psychological theory. In his seminal book, Kahneman [78] introduces the concept of two cognitive systems that are used by humans in all decision making. System 1 is responsible for "fast thinking" and usually uses mental heuristics that can be inaccurate, but require little mental effort. System 2 is the slower, deliberative cognitive system that requires more effort and time, but can be more accurate.

In the described experiments, surface credibility evaluations were usually completed quickly, in a matter of minutes. Three minutes were enough for most surface credibility evaluations. This implies that surface credibility evaluations of Web content are another instance of Kahneman's System 1 thinking. Therefore, it should not be surprising that several mental heuristics can be applied by Web users to evaluate credibility. On the other hand, earned credibility is better described by deliberative System 2 thinking; earned credibility evaluations also require more data, time, and effort on behalf of the users.

Moreover, Kahneman's theory suggests a method for improving the accuracy of System 1 evaluations [78, chapter 21, pp. 222–232]. The method relies on findings of psychological research, indicating that holistic System 1 evaluations (even when done by experts) tend to be less accurate than evaluations based on a predefined set of relevant criteria and a statistical algorithm. Kahneman proposes a procedure to improve the predictive accuracy of System 1 evaluations:

1. Determine a set of criteria that are relevant to the decision and can be evaluated as objectively as possible. It would be best if the criteria would be independent of each other.
2. Obtain human evaluations of these criteria (e.g., on a Likert scale) in a specific, predetermined order.
3. Use an algorithm (can be a simple sum) to aggregate evaluations of these criteria.

Kahneman also observes that if followed, the proposed procedure greatly increases the accuracy of a single, holistic System 1 evaluations, if the evaluation is done at the end of the procedure (after all criteria have been evaluated).

Kahneman propounds that evaluation criteria can be defined by a domain expert. However, an expert may not be necessary if a sufficiently large dataset of evaluations with appropriate justifications is available, such as in the case of the C^3 dataset. This dataset contains thousands of evaluations with textual comments. Moreover, these comments have been augmented by labels from a predefined set (see Sect. 2.6.4). This section introduces a comprehensive set of independent criteria for credibility evaluation, following Kahneman's procedure. It also describes a statistical algorithm for using criteria values to predict surface credibility. This algorithm can be used to aggregate criteria evaluations.

2.9.1 Identifying Credibility Evaluation Criteria from Textual Justifications

The results presented in this section are based on an extensive analysis of textual justifications contained in the C^3 dataset [80]. In order to identify credibility evaluation criteria used by over 600 evaluators who prepared the C^3 dataset, the 7071 textual justifications (comments) contained in the dataset were processed using unsupervised machine learning methods. The comments were analyzed using a TF-IDF term frequency matrix, and Latent Semantic Analysis and Singular Value Decomposition were used to reduce the dimensionality of the matrix. Next, the matrix was used to perform clustering of similar terms, as well as topic discovery algorithms. In order to decrease the impact of the topical categories of evaluated webpages on the clusters, a special list of topic-related stop-words was used. The resulting clusters of textual justifications can be interpreted as the criteria used for credibility evaluation.

The resulting 22 criteria can be grouped into seven categories. These categories can be thought of as types of cognitive heuristics used to evaluate surface credibility of Web content. Moreover, the categories are useful for organizing the criteria to increase the efficiency of using them in content evaluation. The following list summarizes the seven categories of credibility evaluation criteria:

1. What kind of webpage is it?
2. Is the content of commercial character?
3. Who is the author or publisher?
4. How is the webpage designed?
5. Is the information on the webpage verifiable?
6. Is the textual content of high quality?

The third category is clearly related to source credibility or reputed credibility. All other categories are directly related to message credibility. The individual credibility evaluation criteria are shown in Table 2.9. Usage frequencies for each criterion are given in the third column of Table 2.8, based on the C^3 dataset. Usage frequencies do not sum up to 100%, because some ratings used several criteria simultaneously. The usage frequency indicates how often a criterion may be used, but should not be confused with the criterion's importance. For example, "Design aesthetics" is a frequently used criterion, but its impact on credibility ratings (shown in the fourth column) is moderate. On the other hand, "Official page" is a criterion of moderate usage frequency, but with the highest (positive) impact on credibility ratings. Impact is defined as a difference between the mean of all ratings and the mean of all ratings that used a particular criterion. Note that as ratings are biased towards higher values, the means range from 3 to 5 (the overall mean is 4.06). Therefore, an impact of absolute value above 0.2 can be considered quite strong. Criteria with a positive impact are used in ratings that have an overall higher mean than the mean of all ratings, while criteria with a negative impact are used in ratings that have a lower mean. Some criteria, such as "Objectivity," have a negative impact because they are used in a negative context (in this case, when objectivity is being questioned or is clearly lacking) and not in a positive context (in other words, web-pages are rarely praised for their objectivity, but can be criticized for the lack of it).

From the table it is possible to notice the overall negative impact of the criteria category: "Is the content of commercial character?" On the other hand, the category "Who is the author or publisher?," which is strongly related to source credibility, has an overall positive impact. Some criteria clearly dominate others, both in terms of usage frequency and absolute impact. For example, "Source organization type" is a criterion that dominates several others (among them being "Easy to Google," which shows that Google is not enough to support credibility evaluations) and is by itself not dominated (Pareto-optimal) with respect to usage frequency and absolute impact.

The fifth column in Table 2.8 contains expert opinion on the ability to auto-matically compute an indicator for a credibility evaluation criterion. This analysis relates to author's experience with the automatic processing of Web content. For example, criterion 1 (Web media type) could be computed by an automatic detection

Table 2.8 Criteria discovered from C^3 dataset using unsupervised machine learning

Criteria category	Criterion	Usage freq.	Impact	Autom. comp.
What kind of webpage is it?	Web media type	16%	−0.08	Yes
	Celebrity gossip	N/A	N/A	No
	News source	N/A	N/A	Yes
	Scientific study	N/A	N/A	No
Is the Web content of commercial character?	Advertising	6%	−0.27	No
	Sales offer	5%	−0.48	No
	Unknown or bad intentions	8%	−0.68	No
Who is the author or publisher?	Author is known	9%	−0.01	No
	Author's authority	18%	0.13	No
	Official page	8%	0.38	No
	Source organization type	18%	0.33	Yes
How is the webpage designed?	Broken links	2%	−0.63	Yes
	A lot of links	7%	0.15	Yes
	Contact information	3%	0.12	Yes/No
	Content organization	11%	0.01	Yes/No
	Design aesthetics	22%	−0.10	No
Is the textual content of high quality?	Easy to read	9%	0.2	No
	Language quality	5%	−0.18	Yes/No
	Informativity, completeness	38%	0.08	No
Is the information on the webpage verifiable?	Easy to Google	12%	0.21	Yes
	Objectivity (personal opinion, review)	23%	−0.18	No
	References (citing credible references)	19%	0.03	Yes
	Freshness (publication date)	5%	−0.14	Yes
	Evaluator's experience	9%	−0.03	Yes/No
	Big community	3%	0.0	No

Source: [80]

Table 2.9 Overview of correlation between criteria used by evaluators, top four pairs, all significant

Criterion 1	Criterion 2	Corr. coef.
Design aesthetics	References	−0.19
Source organization type	Design aesthetics	−0.19
Author's authority	Design aesthetics	−0.16
Author's authority	Content organization	−0.15
...	...	...

Source: [80]

of templates typically used for media types. Criterion 3 (News source) could be computed using a database of recognized news sources. Criterion 10 (Source organization type) can be based on the DNS domain name (.gov, .edu, .com, etc.). Seven criteria have been marked as Yes/No as they could be partially automated. For example, criterion 14 (content organization) can be approximated by the analysis of the CSS of the webpage. Criterion 17 (Language quality) can be approximated using NLP techniques. Both of these criteria have been used in previous research and have been found significant for automatic classification of Web content credibility [136, 209]. Criterion 23 (Evaluator's experience) could be approximated by a reputation system or by an aggregation algorithm for credibility ratings similar to Expectation-Maximization.

To summarize, 9 out of 25 factors could be automatically computed according to the current knowledge; 7 additional factors could be partially automated, while 9 factors are hard to be automated at present.

2.9.2   Independence of Credibility Evaluation Criteria

The discovered credibility evaluation criteria are mostly independent. The absolute correlation of criteria co-occurrence does not exceed 0.19 (see Table 2.9). The highest correlations are negative (-0.19) and occur between the "Design aesthetics" (which has a slightly negative impact on mean credibility ratings) and two other criteria: "Source organization type" (which has a strong positive impact on mean credibility ratings) and "References" (which has almost zero impact). Interestingly, these two pairs of criteria belong to different criteria categories. One interpretation of this finding is that respected organizations usually have well-designed webpages. Another is that poor design can decrease the likelihood that users will notice references to credible webpages.

The overall low value of criteria correlation can be interpreted as independence (orthogonality) of discovered criteria. This notion is intensified by the results of an attempt to perform principal components analysis (PCA). A PCA on the occurrence data of criteria usage to evaluate webpages in the C^3 dataset confirms that the usage of criteria is independent, and the patterns of co-occurring criteria cannot be replaced with their linear combinations. The PCA results show that to retain 95% variance in the data, one would need to use 27 out of possible 30 principal components (criteria, thematic category of webpage, and mean credibility score). The most informative principal component would explain 7% of the data variance. This indicates that the set of criteria has been prepared well and that the proposed criteria are independent and clearly interpretable.

2.9.3   Modeling Credibility Evaluations Using Credibility Criteria

The definition of credibility employed in this book uses the concept of a signal understood as follows: it is a function of attributes of communicated information and meta-information which may make a receiver believe that the information is true (see Sect. 2.3.4). However, the details of this function have not been discussed so far. The credibility evaluation criteria discussed in this section are a first step towards a decomposition of the credibility signal. While understanding the exact functional dependence may be too complex, it is possible to introduce and validate models of credibility evaluations that use the introduced criteria. These models can also be the first step towards semi-automated credibility evaluation support, which will be discussed in more detail in the next chapter.

In order to model credibility evaluations, it is necessary to make an additional assumption about the ratings. This issue has already been discussed in Sect. 2.5.1; the star rating scale used for evaluating credibility (also in the C^3 dataset) may be interpreted as an ordinal or cardinal scale. In this section, it is assumed that the scale is cardinal, in order to apply linear regression models to predict credibility evaluations using frequencies of usage of credibility evaluation criteria.

The dependent variable in this model is, therefore, the average credibility evaluation. The independent variables are the frequencies of label usages for a webpage. Other independent variables are thematic categories (binary variables), as well as the number of textual justifications and the maximum frequency of label usage for all labels.

The proposed model was trained on the C^3 dataset which was split into training (75%) and validating (25%) datasets. The linear regression model achieved a Root Mean Square Error (RMSE) of 0.709 on the validating dataset, against a benchmark RMSE of 0.493, 0.852, and 1.702 for a random forest model, uniform random model, and constant value model, respectively. The better result of the random forest model shows the high potential of using the proposed independent variables to predict mean credibility evaluations. However, random forest models are hard to interpret, and the main goal of training the linear regression model is to gain insight into the functional dependence of credibility evaluations on the credibility evaluation criteria.

The impact of the most significant credibility evaluation criteria on mean credibility evaluations is shown in Table 2.10. By interpreting the sign and magnitude of the model coefficients, it is possible to interpret the impact of independent model variables. The interpretation is intuitive and convergent to previously reported findings from the other sections. The frequencies of usage of the credibility evaluation criteria that had the highest impact and frequency in Table 2.8 turn out to be significant and have the same signs in the linear regression model. The only surprising variables are frequencies of criteria: "Contact information," "Easy to read," "Language quality," and "Freshness." Overall, using linear regression allows to select the 11 most important credibility evaluation criteria from the total set of 22 criteria identified from the textual justification of credibility ratings in the C^3 dataset.

Some topical categories, such as *Healthy lifestyle*, tend to lower the mean credibility evaluation. This is probably due to the controversial nature of subject matter of webpages, for example, unconventional diets like *Paleo diet* or ear candling in case of *medicine* category.

Table 2.10 Impact of most significant independent variables in the linear regression model of mean credibility evaluations

Independent variable	Model coefficient
Sales offer	−0.09
Unknown or bad intentions	−0.25
Official page	0.08
Source organization type	0.15
Broken links	−0.17
Contact information	−0.05
Easy to read	0.08
Language quality	−0.10
Easy to Google out	0.08
Objectivity	−0.16
Freshness (publication date)	−0.07
Topical category "Healthy lifestyle"	−0.06
Maximum labels frequency	−0.08
Number of evaluations	0.09

Source: [80]

Chapter 3
Supporting Online Credibility Evaluation

Whenever we can replace human judgment with a formula, we should at least consider it.
Daniel Kahneman

This chapter focuses on methods, algorithms, and design of information systems for supporting Web content credibility evaluation. It presents an architecture of such a system created as part of the Reconcile project. The chapter introduces adversary models (strategies of adversary behavior) for such a system. Thereafter, the chapter discusses each element of the system in detail, including the design of the user interface and interaction, machine classifiers of credibility, algorithms that recommend content for evaluation, reputation algorithms, and aggregation algorithms. The chapter concludes with an empirical evaluation of the system's impact on user judgments of Web credibility.

3.1 Design of a Credibility Evaluation Support System

The design of a Web-based information system premised on the principle of open collaboration (or Crowdsourcing, or Web 2.0) should consider two aspects. First, the technical aspect. The task of designing the technical part of the system is similar to the design of application servers or information systems that are based on Web services. Using the divide-and-conquer principle, several modules and functions of the system can be identified. Next, these modules and functions need to be coordinated using a data- or workflow model.

The second aspect of the design of a Web 2.0 is the social one. Several questions need to be answered at this stage: Who will be the users of the system? What motivates the users to provide information required by the system? How should the system's user interface be designed to provide the most satisfying user experience?

The two aspects of the design of the credibility evaluation support system are described in this section.

© Springer International Publishing AG, part of Springer Nature 2018
A. Wierzbicki, *Web Content Credibility*,
https://doi.org/10.1007/978-3-319-77794-8_3

3.1.1 Architecture

The general architecture of a credibility evaluation support (CS) system is shown
in Fig. 3.1. It will serve as a blueprint of a CS system in this chapter, in order to
organize the description of algorithms that can be of use for the system. The design
of the CS system presented in this section is the result of a generalization of several
existing systems, especially the WOT system and the prototype CS system designed
in the Reconcile project. While actual designs of other CS systems may differ from
the one discussed here (e.g., focus only on the evaluation of statements, and not
webpages, or the other way around), most CS systems will include at least a part of
the proposed design. The proposed design can also be thought of as a comprehensive
reference model for designing a simpler CS system to be used in practice. However,
certain parts of the presented design are considered crucial for the CS system's
increased resistance to adversaries, as well as for its increased accuracy in credibility
evaluations. These design parts will be emphasized below.

The proposed reference design of a CS system is composed of several modules:

1. User Interface
2. Reputation Algorithm
3. Recommendation Algorithm
4. Webpage Analyzer
5. Statement Analyzer
6. Fusion Algorithm

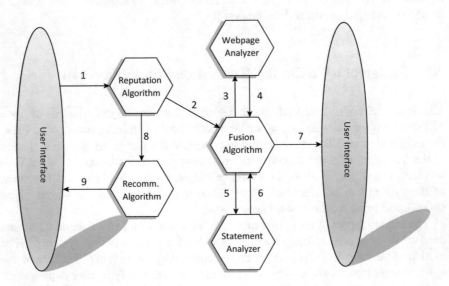

Fig. 3.1 Architecture of a credibility evaluation support system

The user interface can be implemented in several ways, for example, as a Web portal. Another alternative is a browser extension. The user interface could also be a Twitter bot or a Wiki extension. The first two alternatives will be discussed in Sects. 3.1.1.2 and 3.1.1.1, respectively. User interfaces for supporting credibility evaluation on Twitter will be discussed in Chap. 4.

In Fig. 3.1, the data flow within the credibility evaluation support system starts with a user's evaluation of the credibility of a webpage or statement (1). This evaluation is first processed by the reputation algorithm, since a comparison of the user's evaluation with other users' evaluations (or with an aggregated system evaluation) may affect the evaluating user's reputation. A CS system can be made resistant to adversaries through the incorporation of a specialized reputation system. This makes the Reputation Algorithm module an essential part of CS system design. The requirements and design of a reputation algorithm for a CS system are discussed in Sect. 3.5.1.

Alternatively, a user may request information about the aggregated credibility of a webpage or statement; in this case, the data flow still starts with the Reputation Algorithm, but will be forwarded directly to the Fusion Algorithm (2).

The main part of the CS system is the Fusion Algorithm. The role of this algorithm is to produce the final credibility evaluation for a webpage, statement, or domain. The fusion algorithm also creates its own internal evaluations of the credibility of CS system users. The requirements and design of a fusion algorithm for a CS system are discussed in Sect. 3.6. The user's rating (2) is an input to the Fusion Algorithm and contributes to the final credibility of the rated content. The Fusion Algorithm of the CS system also relies on input from three modules: the Reputation Algorithm that proffers the reputation of users who submitted evaluations, the webpage Analyzer that provides features of the evaluated webpage (3, 4), and the Statement Analyzer that processes information about statement credibility (5, 6). The requirements and design of the webpage Analyzer and Statement Analyzer are discussed in Sects. 3.3 and 3.7, respectively. The resulting aggregated credibility evaluation of the webpage, statement, or domain is the output of the Fusion Algorithm to be displayed by the User Interface (7).

Resistance to adversaries and manipulation can also be increased by the use of a recommendation system that recommends webpages to be evaluated by the CS system's users. The design of such a recommendation system and its role in increasing the CS system's resilience to adversaries are discussed in Sect. 3.4. The Recommendation Algorithm may choose several webpages to be evaluated by a user; this choice may include suggestions from the reputation system of webpages with known evaluations, in order to test a user and update his reputation. These suggestions are provided by the reputation algorithm to the Recommendation Algorithm in step (8). This function makes the Recommendation Algorithm an essential module of the proposed CS system design. The Recommendation Algorithm also chooses webpages that have an insufficient number of ratings, but seem of interest to users, and outputs a list of webpages suggested for a user's evaluation to be displayed by the user interface in step (9).

Steps (1) and (7) could be alternatively carried out as Web Service calls. The user interface could therefore be a separate application or system that uses the Web credibility evaluation support system as a Web Service.

3.1.1.1 Browser Extension User Interface

An effective way to implement a user interface for a CS system is through a Web browser extension. This method allows the interface to directly support the user's Web browsing. Most Web browsers today support extensions or plug-ins. The drawback of this method is that a separate extension needs to be implemented for each browser (or, at least, a single extension needs to be customized). Moreover, extensions may stop working if the browser version changes, and it would therefore need to be constantly updated.

Furthermore, it is best if the Web extension does not interfere too much with the browser and is as simple as possible. More complex functionality, such as support of online discussion or gamification, may be implemented through a dedicated Web portal (discussed in the next section). For this reason, a good software architecture would involve the use of a Web Service that provides most functionality of a CS system, while the user interfaces (browser extension, portal, or other) access the CS system through the Web Service.

The WOT service[1] is a good example of how a browser extension can be used as a user interface to a CS system. The browser extension provides three user interface functionalities: rating a webpage, warning about a webpage's credibility (or displaying a summary of ratings), and extending Web search results with aggregated credibility ratings.

This browser extension of a CS system can be designed similarly to the WOT system. WOT has developed a successful and effective Crowdsourcing mechanism for Web content credibility evaluation support, which can be thought of as a reference design for such services in the future.[2]

Figure 3.2 shows an example of webpage credibility evaluation using the WOT extension. As shown in the figure, WOT uses the popular "star rating" scale, which was discussed in Sect. 2.5.1. Moreover, WOT interprets the scale as a cardinal one, which is reflected by the usage of the rating mean to aggregate credibility ratings. Users rate webpages through the WOT extension using two main categories: "trustworthiness" and "child safety." Ratings are aggregated by WOT for entire domains, not individual webpages that belong to the same domain. Therefore, WOT's "trustworthiness" rating is equivalent to a source credibility evaluation of

---

[1]http://mywot.com.

[2]WOT is a commercial site that has been accused of violating user's privacy and tracking data. Since the accusation, the WOT service has changed and extended its privacy policy, providing an opt-out option for users who do not wish to share data. See Sect. 1.2.3.2 for further details.

Fig. 3.2 Example of a webpage credibility evaluation in the WOT browser extension. Source: WOT webpage

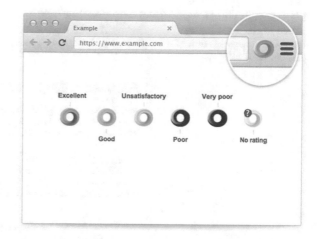

Table 3.1 Labels made available by the WOT credibility rating interface (Source: WOT Wiki, https://www.mywot.com/wiki/API#Reputations)

Category group	Category identifier	Description
Negative	101	Malware or viruses
	102	Poor customer experience
	103	Phishing
	104	Scam
	105	Potentially illegal
Questionable	201	Misleading claims or unethical
	202	Privacy risks
	203	Suspicious
	204	Hate, discrimination
	205	Spam
	206	Potentially unwanted programs
	207	Ads/pop-ups
Neutral	301	Online tracking
	302	Alternative or controversial medicine
	303	Opinions, religion, politics
	304	Other
Positive	501	Good site

the webpage's domain by the user. This is in agreement with the provided definition of source credibility's first dimension, credibility trust (see Sect. 2.3).

Despite the apparent simplicity of WOT credibility ratings, WOT allows users to provide more information using the browser extension. When a user selects a rating, a separate window displays labels that can be used to express the reasons for the evaluation (displayed labels depend on the value of the chosen credibility evaluation), summarized in Table 3.1. Users can also submit a textual comment that justifies or explains their rating.

An analysis of these WOT labels shows that they are primarily used to indicate reasons for negative credibility evaluations; labels in the neutral and positive categories represent a minority. Another set of such labels has been proposed in Sect. 2.9.

The power of the simple Web browser extension is fully displayed by the augmented Web search results (see Fig. 3.3). By displaying small icons next to the search results, users may be alerted about highly non-credible webpages before they even visit them, even if those pages have a high ranking in the search results. This method allows for a fully independent evaluation of a webpage's relevance to a user's query and the webpage's credibility. Critical users could, for example, only care about webpages that are highly credible (a small minority of typical search results).

This kind of service is important because current search engines are not enough to deal with credibility evaluation. The usefulness of Google as an indicator of medical websites' credibility has been evaluated by Frické et al. [42] who evaluated the PageRank score as one indicator of quality. Their results show that it is not inherently useful for discrimination or helping users to avoid inaccurate or poor information. Griffiths et al. [54] evaluated PageRank scores with evidence-based quality scores for depression websites (expert ratings). Again, PageRank scores correlated weakly with the evidence-based scores. This shows that, if considered alone, PageRank indicator is clearly insufficient to account for the quality of medical websites.

If a user browses a website that is rated as not credible or unsuitable for children, the WOT browser extension will display a warning window (see Fig. 3.4). This window presents the aggregated rating along with the labels used as justification. The user can choose whether to proceed to the webpage or to leave it.

An aggregated credibility rating of a webpage is also displayed by the WOT extension in the browser's toolbar, next to the URL. This aggregated rating display uses the same colored icons as used for the rating. If the user clicks on the aggregated

Fig. 3.4 Example of a warning window by the WOT browser extension. Source: WOT webpage

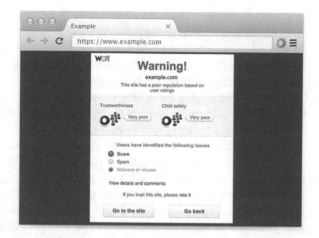

credibility rating's icon, WOT displays a summary of ratings in the two main categories (trustworthiness and child safety). If this summary is not enough, the user may click on a small link labeled "show details and comments" that leads the user to the WOT portal.

3.1.1.2   Credibility Evaluation Portal

While the WOT browser extension maintains a simplicity of interaction and presented information, the WOT portal allows for more complex interaction among users, as well as providing more arguments and justifications of the credibility evaluations. WOT also automatically retrieves additional information about the domain from trusted third-party sources, such as CERT, WHOIS, Google Safe Browsing, Symantec, listing of phishing sites such as PhishTank, and other sources. WOT presents the comments submitted by users that rated the webpages from the evaluated domain. Other users can downvote or upvote the comments.

Website owners can register on WOT and participate in the discussion by answering the comments of evaluating users. They can also request additional evaluations at the WOT forum, which is another functionality of the WOT portal. WOT portal users can be considered experts in credibility evaluation, who dedicate significant time and effort to evaluate earned credibility of a website identified by a domain name. This evaluation is different from the aggregation of surface credibility ratings from the WOT browser extension.

The criteria for rating credibility may vary for various kinds of webpages; for example, charity sites require the domain's owners to be listed on WHOIS and to be registered as a charity organization. Website owners can present arguments to get a higher credibility rating. The discussion for some charity sites can become heated, for example, for a Muslim charity website, whose owners accused users of rating the domain as not credible because of alleged racism. E-commerce websites

are another example. Here, the criteria for earned credibility evaluation are related
to the registered ownership of the e-commerce company, checking cash flows, and
investigating claims of fraudulent behavior or simply poor service by the evaluating
WOT users. Other criteria involve the usage of encryption (SSL/TLS), existence of
user data privacy policies, and their enforcement.

In some cases, WOT credibility evaluations, despite efforts, fail to be objective.
One particular example is the low rating of a blog "mywotlies.wordpress.com." The
blog has been started by a website owner dissatisfied with the WOT credibility rating
of his site. The blog lists all possible opportunities for manipulation of the WOT
rating and makes several accusations against the WOT site. It has been subsequently
evaluated as not credible by the WOT users, after a long discussion on the portal.
This evaluation cannot be seen as completely objective, especially since the blog
site does not contain any content inappropriate for children (and this category was
also rated low in the WOT users' assessment of the blog) or fraud attempts, unless
one considers some misleading arguments as fraud.

A CS portal can also contain functionality that aims to motivate users to rate
webpages. WOT assigns a simple activity score to its users; however, no rankings
of users by this score are provided by the portal.

Aggregating ratings into domains by WOT makes it easier to acquire a sufficiently large sample of ratings; on the other hand, it reduces the granularity of
credibility evaluation. Designers of a CS system should also keep in mind that
typically, users evaluate surface credibility of individual webpages, rather than of
entire websites or domains. For this reason, it is possible to aggregate ratings
for individual webpages, which does not preclude the possibility of aggregating
ratings for websites or domains, as well. Such an approach has been used by the
experimental CS developed as part of the Reconcile project.[3] This CS system also
uses a Web browser extension, like WOT. However, ratings are aggregated and
displayed in the plug-in for individual webpages. On the CS portal, it is also possible
to see ratings listed by domain names (websites).

Similarly to PolitiFact or Snopes, the Reconcile CS allows users to evaluate
statements made on webpages, as well. This possibility is supported by the browser
extension (see Fig. 3.5), which displays a context menu when the user highlights
a statement on a webpage in the browser. This additional information can also
be used by fusion algorithms that evaluate a webpage's credibility. Statement
credibility evaluations can also be propagated using Semantic Textual Similarity.
These functionalities will be discussed further in Sect. 3.7.

Section 2.2 discussed the five steps that make up a design of supporting
credibility evaluation. The Reconcile prototype CS has been designed in accordance
with this conceptual guideline. A central part of this credibility evaluation support
procedure is an evaluation the Web content's controversy. For controversial Web
content, supporting credibility evaluation means basically supporting discussion
and presentation of diverse points of view, which is also enabled by the Reconcile

---

[3] www.reconcile.pl.

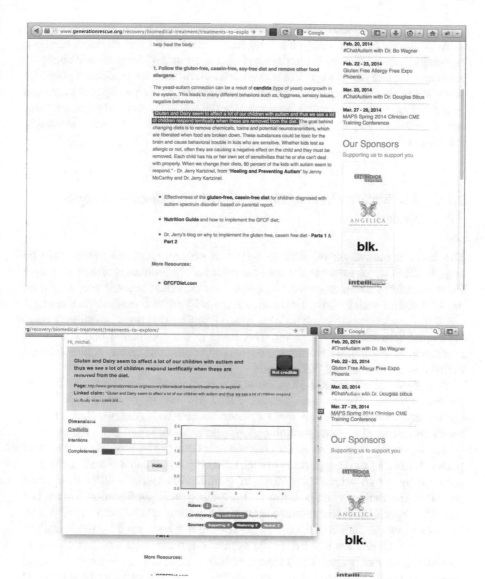

Fig. 3.5 Rating statements in the Reconcile CS portal

CS system and the WOT portal. Only for non-controversial Web content can the CS present aggregated credibility evaluations to the user. For these reasons, the Reconcile prototype supports tagging of Web content as controversial by users. If a webpage or statement receives a sufficient number of such tags from various users, it will be considered as controversial by the CS system.

The Reconcile CS also uses more advanced gamification features, as compared to WOT. These features aim to motivate Reconcile portal users to rate webpages, especially those chosen by the system and displayed in the "Suggested Webpages" panel on the main portal page. Reconcile portal users can earn reputation points by rating webpages. More reputation points are assigned for rating webpages suggested by the system. Reputation points are earned for rating each individual page, but users can also choose two gamification functions: quests and bets. These are discussed in the next section.

3.1.2   Motivating Users of the Credibility Evaluation Support System

The intrinsic motivation of users to rate Web content credibility may often be negative. This is, for example, the case for PolitiFact or Snopes, where users search for non-credible statements made by politicians, or urban legends propagated on the Web and in social media. However, the majority of Web content receives high credibility evaluations that can even be biased (credibility ratings by ordinary users are higher than ratings by experts). This leads to the conclusion that if negative motivation is the dominant intrinsic user motivation, then users require external motivation to rate credible Web content.

Scarcity of user time and attention is one of the main bottlenecks of Crowdsourcing systems. The problem lies not just in the scarcity of ratings but also in the inadequate time and effort spent by users to rate Web content. Both of these problems can be addressed by gamification approaches or reputation systems.

The basis of gamification approaches are user rankings by reputation or activity points. Achieving a higher position in such a ranking is the main external motivation provided by gamification. The designs of gamification systems differ in how the points for the rankings can be earned. One such typical gamification feature is a "quest": a special task that requires more activity (or a special activity) of a user, but also allows to earn more points. This feature has been used by the Reconcile CS system.[4] Quests are defined by the system's administrator and can consist of topically similar webpages (e.g., medical webpages) that need to be rated by special users (e.g., medical experts). A quest typically consists of a small number (three or more) of webpages to be evaluated by the user.

The Reconcile CS system also explored two other gamification features: "bets" and "quizzes." The bets gamification feature allows a user to bet with another user on his or her evaluation of website credibility. Every participant with a positive reputation score was allowed to place a bet. Users decided how many reputation points they would like to put as a stake. A user who won a bet gained two times his or her stake. Additionally, users ranked in the top 20% of reputation ranking

---

[4]http://reconcile.pl.

were allowed to settle bets placed by other users. A bet settlement consisted of another evaluation of the same webpage made by the settling user. The user whose evaluation matched exactly with the settling user's evaluation won the bet. The settling user gained more points for settling the bet.

Quizzes have been used in Crowdsourcing system as a gamification method [69]. In the Reconcile CS, quizzes are a feature for evaluating statements. Statement evaluations can be posed in the form of a question: "Is ... credible?" The question could be binary choice (a simple "yes/no" answer) or multiple choice, with an answer set that is equal to the statement credibility evaluations used in the system.

The effectiveness of using these features has been evaluated in an experimental study [77]. In the study, users (students) have been asked to evaluate credibility of webpages and statements related to Java programming (students participated in courses of Java programming). The webpages were specially prepared by an expert who modified the pages to include specific numbers of errors. The expert's credibility ratings of the webpages depended only on the number of errors in the page. Experiment participants were not aware that the pages have been modified, but could discover the errors on their own; therefore, the accuracy of the users' credibility ratings depended mainly on the prominence of the errors and the effort and attention of the users. Users were divided into three groups: a control group that did not have access to gamification features, but could earn reputation points through standard webpage evaluations (14 participants), a group that had access only to the bets feature (12 participants), and a group that had access to all gamification features (quests, bets, and quizzes—52 participants).

The results of the experiment indicate that the group that had access to all gamification features was much (almost three times) more active than the control group or the bets group. Moreover, users who had access to all gamification features took much more time on average to evaluate a webpage or statement: 1 min and 12 s, in comparison to about 40 s in the control group. However, when users chose to participate in quests or bets, their accuracy decreased in comparison to standard ratings. One explanation of this phenomenon is that the users in the gamification group were more aware of the changes in the reputation ranking than users in the control group (which explains their higher activity), but still achieved a higher accuracy when they used standard evaluations in comparison to evaluations made using bets or quests. In fact, bets or quests were much less popular than the usage of standard evaluations in the group of users who had access to all gamification features.

Bets were not a popular feature, but the usage of bets had an interesting impact. The overall distribution of user credibility evaluations in the study was found to be biased—user ratings were much more positive than expert ratings (see Sect. 2.7). This bias was reduced for ratings obtained through bet settlements. A similar effect was observed in the group of users with a higher reputation score (who were the users who could settle a bet). The conclusion is that users with higher reputation start behaving more similarly to experts and reduce their credibility evaluation bias. This fact makes the correct evaluation of user's reputation particularly important for the CS system, especially as reputation systems can be targeted adversaries. The reputation system is discussed further in Sect. 3.5.1.

A final possibility of externally motivating users to participate in credibility evaluation is by using external Crowdsourcing platforms, like Amazon Mechanical Turk (mTurk), and paying for the evaluation. This approach has been used successfully for many commercial and research projects. Crowdsourcing workers can be invited to use the CS to rate webpages suggested by the system for them (making use of the recommendation algorithm, and possibly of the quest feature, if it is implemented by the CS system).

The cost of a single credibility evaluation can be quite small; a budget of 500 USD should suffice (at the time of writing) for a 1000 webpage credibility evaluations on Amazon Mechanical Turk. However, this approach has several issues. The first is quality control. Since users are being paid for work, incentives exist for fraudulent behavior. Several approaches could be used here, for example, demanding that users write comments justifying their evaluation along with providing a minimum number of URLs used to check the credibility of a webpage. Several automatic approaches, such as checking the comment's language, visiting the URL's pages, and running topical classification on them, can be used to validate the work. Another approach can be used if the CS system is already operational. Crowdsourcing workers can be required to register in the CS system and become ordinary users. The reputation algorithm will calculate their reputation by comparing their ratings to ratings of other users, including experts. Crowdsourcing workers can then be paid for their work, under the condition that their reputation is above a minimum threshold.

3.2 Adversaries of Credibility Evaluation

Algorithms of the credibility evaluation support (CS) system have to be designed with the goal of providing correct and reliable credibility ratings. An important (perhaps the most important) design goal of CS system algorithms is resistance to adversaries. All of the algorithms used in a CS system (the reputation algorithm, the recommendation algorithm, the fusion algorithm) should be designed to be robust against adversaries who aim to manipulate them.

While there can be many adversaries of the CS system and many kinds of attacks on this system (e.g., a Denial-of-Service attack), the most obvious *adversary is a Web content producer who wishes to increase his Web content's credibility rating by the CS system in order to mislead or manipulate potential users*. The CS system's input are credibility evaluations, while the desired output of a CS system is the truth (see Sect. 2.2). The adversary's goal is to make the CS system produce an indication that the adversary's Web content is true, even when it is not (assuming that ground truth can be defined). This type of adversary will be referred to as the *basic CS system adversary*. The basic adversary can, of course, employ other adversaries and use coalition attacks or even Crowdsourcing systems, but all of these proxies will have a single, strategic goal dictated by the basic adversary.

There are many examples of adversaries who try to artificially increase the perceived popularity or reputation of their own goods or services in e-commerce reputation systems, directories, or quality evaluation systems such as Amazon, Booking.com, opinions, and many others. All of these adversaries have goals that resemble the goals of the basic adversary of the CS system. Because of the ubiquity of the basic adversary, all algorithms of the CS system should have a degree of robustness against this type of adversary. However, it is insufficient to make the CS system robust only against the basic adversary.

The analogy between the CS system and a reputation system reveals the need for taking into account other kinds of adversaries. In a reputation system, adversaries that wish to manipulate other's reputation may be combated by weighing their ratings with their own reputation. However, this recursive reputation algorithm can be targeted by a slightly more sophisticated adversary that will first behave fairly in order to justly get a high reputation, and then use this high reputation to manipulate the reputation of others.

This type of adversary is difficult to protect against especially if the final goal of the system is object evaluation or recommendation (as is the case for the CS system). This is because most algorithms for evaluating reputation do it by comparing a user's input (evaluations) to system evaluations. However, if the adversary has access to system evaluations in the first place, it is simple for him to copy them and provide them as his own input. This kind of adversary is called the *imitating adversary* [107]. There can be many types of imitating attackers, but the simplest kind will reduce his effort for object evaluation and at the same time maximize his reputation reward by directly copying system evaluations. If no system evaluation is available (for new objects), the attacker may just ignore them. If system evaluations are hidden until the user provides his input, the adversary may use a proxy to receive the system's evaluation and use it in a second interaction with the system.

In the following parts of this chapter, the robustness of algorithms of the CS system to the basic adversary and the imitating adversary will be considered.

3.3   Classifiers of Webpage Credibility

The credibility evaluation support (CS) system relies in its operation on user evaluations. However, this does not mean that the system only uses these evaluations as an input. The webpage Analyzer is a system module that provides additional, automatically computed inputs to the system. These inputs are webpage features that can be used in automatic classifiers of webpage credibility.

The webpage Analyzer is integrated with the fusion algorithm, the central module of the CS system. A fusion algorithm can incorporate a machine learning algorithm and use the webpage features directly, or it can use the output of a machine classifier of credibility—in the latter case, the automatic credibility classifier would be a part of the webpage Analyzer module.

There are two reasons behind this design. The first reason is due to the cold-start problem. A majority of Web content does not have a sufficiently high popularity to quickly attract a sufficient amount of evaluations by CS system users. This is especially true if Web content credibility classification uses rating distributions, as suggested in Sect. 2.8. In this case, a minimum number (e.g., 10) of ratings is needed before Web content can be assigned to a credibility class.

Before this happens, Web content with no evaluations or an insufficient number of them can either be ignored by the CS system or given a preliminary evaluation that is based on machine classification of credibility. The latter approach needs to be specially designed in order to reduce the likelihood of serious classification errors.

A second reason for using automatically calculated features is that this approach increases the robustness of the CS system against manipulation or wrong evaluations. The fusion algorithm takes features of automatically computed credibility classes as input and uses them in a manner similar to user evaluations. This means that in a situation when Web content would be the target of strategic manipulation, the automatically computed Web content features—independent of manipulation attempts—would increase the CS system's resilience to attacks.

3.3.1 Webpage Features

Following [136, 209], as many as 37 webpage features could be used in automatic classification of webpage credibility. This list might still be expanded as it depends on the inventiveness of future researchers. For example, if linguistic features from the General Inquirer (GI) are used, as many as 183 variables can be obtained, while it is reported that Google uses over 200 webpage properties to rank search results.[5] However, some of these features are only weakly correlated with webpage credibility evaluations. Therefore initially, a list of 22 features identified by Olteanu et al. [136] can be considered as having significant correlation with webpage credibility. These features can be grouped into two categories: content-based (using only the content of the considered webpage) and Internet-based (using additional information from the Internet).

Some features are expressed as numbers (usually ranged from zero to infinity), others are binary, and some are discrete (a selection from possible categories). Feature calculation relies heavily on external libraries, scripts, and APIs. Webpage category is detected using the Alchemy API,[6] all ad-related properties are measured using AdBlock scripts,[7] and text-related features are calculated using

---

[5]http://www.searchenginejournal.com/infographic-googles-200-ranking-factors/64316/.

[6]www.alchemyapi.com.

[7]www.adblockplus.org.

the NLTK library[8] or simple regular expressions (e.g., for calculating the number of exclamations). Some features like PageRank, Facebook share, or Alexa rating can be calculated only by invoking an appropriate API delivered by data owners (i.e., Google, Facebook, or Amazon). Note that previous work suggests that while PageRank is correlated with credibility, the correlation is weak, and the PageRank indicator by itself is unlikely to be sufficient to evaluate information credibility [42, 54].

Webpage features selected in [136] cover a broad range of aspects from presentation through popularity to content. On the other hand, the list of features is not exhaustive. As is shown in [160], position in search results correlates, although weakly, with webpage credibility judgments. Much stronger positive correlation is observed for popularity [136, 209].

Although context and popularity features correlate with credibility evaluation, it is not a simple cause and effect relationship. These kinds of features are used for approximating webpage credibility. However, credibility in the sense of factual correctness and completeness derives exclusively from text and pictures on the page.

Extensive use of external APIs for feature calculation, as in the case of [136, 209], has many advantages but also some drawbacks. First of all, it limits time and costs of implementation and makes research easier to replicate for other scientists. Instead of training new classifiers for webpage categorization, the API provided by Alchemy can be used (and indeed has been used in this research). To calculate other, global webpage properties, there exist no reasonable alternatives except for external APIs: calculation of PageRank requires crawling the whole Internet (although there exist heuristics that allow to estimate PageRank without taking into account the entire hyperlink graph), and popularity on Facebook or Twitter can be measured only by data owners. APIs provided by these companies are subject to many limitations, such as the number of requests per day and non-commercial applications. Additionally, vendors may change algorithms that calculate particular features without notification, and such changes may have consequences for credibility of classification algorithms. Therefore, features based purely on external APIs are difficult to use beyond scientific application and are prone to manipulation. On the other hand, features based exclusively on webpage text have been also tested [209]. These features can be calculated directly without the use of third-party vendors and used, with some success, for machine classification of webpage credibility.

3.3.1.1   General Inquirer Features

In addition to the Natural Language Processing (NLP) features proposed in [136] (see Table 3.2), features calculated with the aid of the General Inquirer tool have

---

[8]www.nltk.org.

Table 3.2 Webpage features significant for credibility evaluations (Source: [136])

Feature category	Feature name	Description
Content-based	#exclamations	Number of exclamation marks "!" in the text
	#questions	Number of question marks "?" in the text
	?polarity	0 if the overall sentiment of webpage text is negative, 1 otherwise
	#negative	Number of sentences with negative sentiment in webpage text
	#subjective	Number of subjective sentences in webpage text
	informativeness	Text informativeness measure of webpage text in corpus of all webpages
	smog	NLP text readability measure of webpage text
	#css_definitions	Number of webpage CSS style definitions
	#adverbs	Number of adverbs in webpage text
	domain_type	Type of webpage's DNS domain, for example, .org, .com, .gov
Internet-based	#fb_share	Number of Facebook shares for a webpage URL
	#fb_like	Number of Facebook likes for a webpage URL
	#fb_comment	Number of Facebook comments for a webpage URL
	#fb_click	Number of Facebook clicks for a webpage URL
	#fb_total	Total number of Facebook shares, likes, comments, and clicks for a webpage URL
	#tweets	Number of Twitter tweets mentioning a webpage URL
	#bitly_clicks	Number of Bitly short URL clicks for a webpage
	#bitly_referrer	Number of websites having Bitly short URL for a webpage
	#delicious_bookmarks	Number of Delicious bookmarks for a webpage URL
	aleksa_rank	Alexa rank
	#aleksa_links_in	Number of incoming links to webpage estimated by Alexa
	page_rank	Google PageRank

been proposed in [209]. The General Inquirer (GI) [178][9] is one of the most well-known content analysis tools. It consists of an application and an associated dictionary.

The dictionary contains 11,767 word senses mapped to 183 categories. The notion of category is central to content analysis. A category is a group of content—in this case word senses—that shares a commonality (possesses a shared feature or attribute). GI categories are linked with multiple psycholinguistic and psychosocial categories. The list of GI categories includes, for example, topic-based ones (politics, economy, religion) and several emotion-related categories such as pleasure, pain, feelings, or arousal. Two of the categories, positive and negative, represent evaluative dimension (sentiment). Category membership is binary: words either belong to a category or not.

For text processing, the GI application uses a dictionary-backed lemmatizer and word sense disambiguation rules by Kelly and Stone [86]. For a webpage that needs to be evaluated by the CS system, the GI application can produce a vector of 183 numbers, which represent counts of each category in every analyzed text. This entire vector can be used as features to train machine learning algorithms in order to predict webpage credibility. This approach has been used in [209] for binary classification of webpage credibility based on the Microsoft credibility corpus. The results had an average F-measure (for both classes) of 0.75.

Obviously, there are other linguistic resources and approaches available that might be used to compute word categories. For example, one might apply a word clustering algorithm or word grouping based on WordNet. However, the General Inquirer is a resource especially relevant to credibility evaluation due to its psychosocial characteristics, especially multiple psychological traits of language.

3.3.1.2   Difficulties in Feature Computation

The automatic feature computation presents several difficulties. Most of them concern Internet-based features. The first difficulty is time. Internet-based features of a webpage typically need seconds or even minutes to compute. This can be due to varying Internet throughput, as well as server load or limitations on APIs. For this reason, using Internet-based features for real-time webpage credibility evaluation may turn out infeasible.

Another difficulty involves the availability of some Internet-based features for webpages from different geographical locations. For example, Delicious and Bitly are services popular in the USA, but much less used in other parts of the world. For non-English language webpages, these features may not be available. The same concern might apply even to Facebook or Twitter, for example, in China.

Content-based features that rely on Natural Language Processing may also be difficult to calculate for languages other than English.

---

[9]http://www.wjh.harvard.edu/~inquirer/.

3.3.2   Performance of Classifiers of Webpage Credibility

Automatic Web content credibility classifiers can be designed in several ways, and their design determines their performance. The most straightforward way is to try and classify Web content credibility using the same star rating scale that is used to submit credibility evaluations by humans. Using methods such as logistic regression, it is possible to create models that will use the features described in the previous sections to achieve this goal.

Experiments with logistic regression have been reported in [209] on the Microsoft credibility dataset (Sect. 2.6.2). The logistic regression model has been trained with all features, but also with a subset of the features that had the highest F score. The best performing regression models used only top 20% of the features. The quality of regression models was tested on the Microsoft dataset using tenfold cross-validation. The best results have been obtained by a combination of features described in the previous section (including additional NLP features from the General Inquirer). The best model achieved a Mean Absolute Error (MAE) of about 0.75. In practice, this means that on a discrete scale, the model would make an average mistake of 1 on the 1–5 star rating scale.

This result is not too encouraging, especially for the medium credibility ratings. If Web content has an extremely high credibility rating (equal to 5), the model's average mistake would give this content a rating of 4; on the other hand, webpages with extremely low credibility ratings (1) would be given a rating of 2 by mistake (on average). However, webpages with credibility ratings of 3 can be given a rating of 2 or 4 by mistake. This shows that it should be possible, using automatic classification, to distinguish between webpages with extreme credibility evaluations with high certainty. However, it becomes much more difficult to distinguish between webpages of medium credibility ratings.

Another approach is to divide Web content into smaller sets of classes. For example, following the approach described in [209], it is possible to choose three classes: "low credibility" (credibility ratings 1–2), "medium credibility" (credibility rating 3), and "high credibility" (credibility ratings 4–5). These classes are usually unbalanced due to the bias in ratings. Alternatively, it is possible to divide all webpages into just two classes: "not credible" (credibility ratings 1–3) and "credible" (credibility ratings 4–5). The choice of the boundary between the two classes is once again justified by the rating bias.

The case of two classes will be considered first. For binary classification, traditional performance measures of precision, recall, and the F-measure can be applied. Wawer et al. [209] reported F-measures of approximately 0.75 for the binary classification case when using all features initially and using logistic regression as the machine classification method. However, precision for the "credible" class is usually much higher (approximately 0.82) than for the "not credible" class (0.66). This is good, because it means that the error of incorrectly assigning a webpage to the "not credible" class is larger than the error of incorrectly assigning an object to the "credible" class. The importance of these two kinds of errors depends on the application; however, if the CS system is applied for Web content where non-credible information can cause high damage to users (such as medical Web content), it is better to avoid incorrectly assigning webpages to the "credible" class. Still, this kind of error occurs almost 20% of the time. For the example of medical Web content, this may be unacceptable.

Where three classes are used, it is possible to avoid making the mistake of assigning webpages from the "low credibility" class to the "high credibility" class. Wawer et al. [209] report an F-measure of approximately 0.65 for predicting Web content credibility using three classes and using the most significant 20% of all features (including the General Inquirer features). While this is less than the F-measure for the binary credibility class case, the reference level also changes (since for three classes, the random reference level is 33% instead of 50% for the binary case). Moreover, it is possible to reduce the likelihood of error between the extreme classes almost to zero.

3.4   Recommending Content for Evaluation

The role of the recommendation algorithm in the credibility evaluation support (CS) system is based on the simple observation that ratings of content selected by users are more vulnerable to manipulation. If users rate content that is recommended to them by a recommendation algorithm, they are less likely to be interested in strategically submitting false ratings. Credibility ratings of content selected by users cannot be totally ignored or disallowed by a CS system. However, if ratings of content suggested by the recommendation algorithm are given a higher weight, the overall robustness of the CS system to adversaries that wish to manipulate credibility evaluations will be increased.

Another function of the recommendation algorithm is based on the fact that ratings are sparse and tend to be unevenly distributed. A small set of webpages is highly popular and likely to receive a lot of ratings, if content to be rated is selected by users. On the other hand, a large set of less popular (but still interesting to many users) webpages is unlikely to receive sufficient ratings. Recall from Sect. 2.7 that a minimum number of at least 10 ratings is required in order to reliably assign Web content to a credibility class, based on an empirical rating distribution. The recommendation algorithm acts as a load balancer that assigns resources (user ratings) to webpages that have an insufficient number of ratings, while skipping webpages that have already achieved a required number of ratings.

Last but not least, an algorithm that recommends content for evaluation cannot ignore user interests. Users are already deprived of their intrinsic (genuine or strategic) motivation to rate Web content that is selected by themselves. It is therefore very important that users should be suggested Web content to rate based on their own interests, expressed through past history of rating (self-selected) webpages. These webpages should be displayed prominently by the CS user interface, for example, on the starting page, like in the Reconcile CS prototype (Fig. 3.6).

Fig. 3.6 Starting page of Reconcile CS portal with "Suggested Webpages" panel containing webpages recommended to be rated by user

This double role of the recommendation algorithm makes its design quite challenging. The primary goal of the recommendation algorithm, that of guiding users to algorithmically selected content, is, however, achieved regardless of the recommendation algorithm design. This observation only leaves the other two goals to be obtained: guiding users to webpages that have insufficient ratings and selecting Web content that will be of interest to users. These two goals can be achieved by a small modification of standard recommendation algorithms [107, 130]. First, the algorithm uses a matrix of self-selected user ratings (with users in rows and webpages in columns) as input. This matrix can be factorized (e.g., using stochastic gradient descent) to obtain probabilities of interactions between a user and a webpage (or statement). This probability can be used to rank Web content in a descending order. From this ranking, webpages or statements that have a sufficiently high number of ratings can be removed. (As a matter of fact, webpages that do not have enough ratings can also be ignored. If a webpage has zero ratings, it would not appear in the CS system. A webpage that has 1 rating can be considered insignificant for the users. Only if a webpage receives at least 2 ratings from various users can it be considered as generating significant user interest.)

The drawback of the standard matrix factorization approach is that the matrix of user-content ratings may be too sparse. In such a case, information about webpage topics may be used. This is because based on just matrix factorization, it is often difficult to precisely predict the Web content topics that a user may be interested in. For instance, rating-based recommendation infers that a user is interested in sports news. However, this user actually only read and rated articles about basketball, and in particular, about NBA, so recommending other irrelevant sports news (based on similar users' ratings) like Formula One may not attract the user to rate. For recommender systems working on objects that are not easy to map into topics, matrix factorization may be the only possible approach. On the other hand, the CS Web content recommendation algorithm works on textual Web content (and not products or other objects). Textual topic modeling is able to infer latent topic variables from a corpus of documents [11], and such topics can be naturally applied to describe the interest of a user based on the textual contents he or she has interacted with. The proposition is therefore to integrate texts into MF to improve the accuracy of interest matching.

The combination of object- and topic-based recommendation may be achieved by redefining the objective function that calculates the sum of prediction errors to be minimized by stochastic gradient descent (for details, see [130]). The output are also probabilities that a user will rate a webpage or statement. By integrating topics that are extracted from textual contents into the algorithm, the probability that a user will rate a certain Web content can be predicted, even if the Web content has no or insufficient ratings. The list of candidate webpages or statements can be sorted inversely according to the predicted probabilities, in order to recommend the top-K ones to the user.

Importantly, in practice it is still necessary to filter the list of Web content selected for a user in order to remove unsuitable Web content. Even in the case when the content has insufficient ratings to determine its credibility class, spam or phishing webpages may be exposed by searching for their URLs or domain names in third-party services. Also, machine classifiers that work based on webpage features can be applied to obtain a first estimate of credibility. Together, these methods serve as an initial estimate of Web content credibility that can be taken into account by the recommendation algorithm. Web content with a low initial credibility should not be recommended to users for evaluation.

3.4.1 Robustness of CS Recommendation Algorithm to Imitating Adversary

Besides recommending interesting Web content to users to increase the system's coverage, another functionality offered by this recommendation component is to defend against the imitating attack, which is particularly harmful to a CS, that is, existing reputation system is ineffective in detecting such attacks. In this section, a defense mechanism by analyzing users' responses to recommendations is proposed.

As explained in [107], to quickly build high reputation, imitating attackers typically densely copy and resubmit system's ratings within a short period of time. The focus is therefore on the highly active users to detect imitating attack.

Based on their activities over the past period of time, for example, 24 h, a set of active users are selected. For each user, a list of webpages is recommended based on his or her interest. Figure 3.7 demonstrates how the imitating attackers and normal users are expected to react to recommendations. It is assumed that the

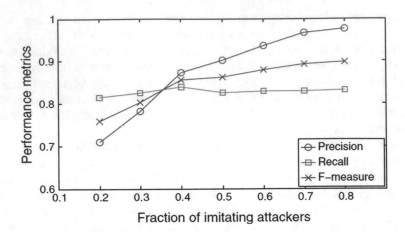

Fig. 3.7 Robustness of a CS system to imitating adversaries. Source: [130]

recommended webpages already have reliable credibility information, but instead of showing the exact ratings to users, the system provides fake ratings and asks for new ratings to make the current fake ratings more confident. For instance, a recommended Web content has a credibility rating of 4-point (assuming 5-point Likert scale), but the system displays 2-point to the selected users. The basic idea of manipulating ratings is to entice imitating attackers to copy the fake ratings, which can be used as evidence for attack detection. For a normal user, if he or she decides to rate the recommended Web content, the ratings are expected to be closer to the real credibility rating than to the displayed fake rating. On the other hand, imitating attackers may simply copy the fake ratings without actually assessing the recommended Web content so their ratings are close to the displayed fake ratings with high probability. It is worth mentioning that controversial topics, as well as users' bias/subjectivity, make the ratings comparison non-trivial. However, this issue is not the focus of this section, and it is assumed that the system has certain mechanisms to detect and handle controversial contents [18]. Another option is to recommend only the Web content whose credibility can be objectively measured.

Comparing the displayed fake ratings and users' ratings enables the estimation of a user's imitation behavior. This is done by modeling the user's behavior by a probabilistic model: a series of independent Bernoulli trials. In each trial, the user may behave consistently with the behavior of an imitating attacker or not. Each trial is initiated by the event of displaying a fake rating to an active user. If the user's rating is equal (or within a threshold, e.g., an absolute difference of 1 on the 1–5 star rating scale) to the fake rating, then his behavior is consistent with an imitating adversary; otherwise it is not. In each trial, the success probability is modeled by Beta distribution with parameters α and β (starting with $\alpha = \beta = 1$). After observing s successes (consistent behaviors) in n trials, the posterior density of the probability is $Beta(\alpha + s, \beta + ns)$. Accordingly, the density function of the probability p_u of performing imitation behavior (by user u) is given by

$$f(p_u|\alpha_u, \beta_u) = \frac{\Gamma(\alpha_u + \beta_u + 2)}{\Gamma(\alpha_u + 1)\Gamma(\beta_u + 1)} p_u^{\alpha_u}(1 - p_u)^{\beta_u}$$

where $\alpha_u \geq 0$ and $\beta_u \geq 0$ represent the numbers of u's ratings that are consistent with the fake ratings or not, respectively. $\Gamma()$ is the gamma function. The expectation probability is then obtained by

$$p_u = \frac{\alpha_u + 1}{\alpha_u + \beta_u + 2}$$

If a user's imitation behavior probability is higher than a predefined threshold, this user is considered an imitating attacker. In contrast to existing methods for detecting adversaries that rely on complex machine learning methods, the core of this defense mechanism is to derive a simple posterior imitation probability.

The effectiveness of such a defense mechanism depends on the performance of the recommendation model. If users actively rate the recommended Web content, their behaviors can be comprehensively analyzed, and malicious users can be reliably detected. Otherwise, if users refuse to rate, it is not possible to distinguish imitating attackers from normal users. In order to further motivate users to actively rate the recommended Web content, besides personalized recommendation, an adaptive reputation system is prepared. The next section elaborates upon this system.

3.5 Evaluating Users' Reputation

The results of user's work in the credibility evaluation support (CS) system are evaluations of Web content credibility along with their justifications. This information can be considered a kind of user-generated Web content. One way of looking at this information could also be as a special kind of answer to the question: how credible is the evaluated content? In this case, one could see the work of users in the CS system as answering questions in a specialized Q&A system.

The problem lies in finding an appropriate and reliable reference point for validating users' credibility evaluations. Existing online platforms use opinions about content generated by members of the community instead of automatic algorithms. Commonly used algorithms automatically modify the reputation of the content's author after receiving a single opinion about this content (positive or negative) from members of the relevant online community. In order to prevent manifestations of mindless and unjustified criticism, which can discourage authors from uploading new content, portals use a variety of techniques, such as:

1. Meta-moderation, that is, evaluations of evaluators (e.g., as introduced by the portal Slashdot)

2. A form of "reputation fee" or "reputation payment," paid by a user from his or her reputation points, for expressing a negative opinion (a "downvote")
3. A daily limit on the number of negative opinions expressed by an individual user (this solution, like solution (2), is used on Q&A portals, e.g., on sites from the family of Stack Exchange portals)

Potentially, meta-moderation is the most effective of the techniques used to control negative phenomena associated with the direct use of community members' opinions to calculate reputations. Unfortunately, this technique can also be the most expensive from the point of view of the platform's owner (assuming that the platform employs second-order evaluators). Additionally, it is also susceptible to manipulation; for example, where second-order evaluators are elected from ordinary members of the community, among whom might be a dishonest person (for instance, an evaluator who promotes the content of certain users and criticizes content published by others). The phenomenon of publishing biased opinions is known even on portals which enable users to publish reviews of products. The idea of peer prediction [120, 217] is a response to these situations. This concept assumes that by using a specific payoff structure (and if certain assumptions are met), the reputation algorithm is capable of motivating users to post honest opinions, even if the platform does not have a reliable point of reference which, for each user's opinion, would provide a basis for the validation process. However, the effectiveness of alternative models proposed to date, based on the peer-prediction model, has been confirmed mainly by theoretical analysis.

Among the models proposed so far, only one investigates the effect of negative payments, according to the current state of knowledge. Witkowski [217] created a model, based on game theory and using the peer-prediction approach, demonstrating that the introduction of penalties can discourage users with less knowledge from participating in the game, while those with more extensive knowledge are motivated to stay in the game and to invest effort into completing tasks. However, this model has not been verified under real conditions.

The reputation algorithm of the CS system proposed in this chapter makes use of the observation that users with a higher reputation in the prototype system start evaluating content similarly to experts. Also, for some types of Web content such as specialist Web content, experts are available and can be invited as users with an initial high reputation. This situation concerns, for example, medical Web content— a user with a medical degree can be thought of as a domain expert and receive an initial high reputation. For this reason, the principle of the proposed algorithm will be a comparison of chosen user evaluations to evaluations of the same Web content made by other users with a sufficiently high reputation. If the comparison shows that the user's and expert's evaluations are similar, the reputation of the user can be increased. Otherwise, it can be reduced. This principle is somewhat similar to meta-moderation. It is however automatic and does not require a special action from the expert (also leaving the expert with no possibility of strategic action).

Another unique principle of the proposed reputation algorithm is its integration with the recommendation algorithm. Because the recommendation algorithm will display fake ratings to specially chosen (high activity) users and, after a series of such trials, will calculate the probability that a user submits a fake (copied) rating, the reputation system can be aware of the user's imitating behavior and reduce the user's reputation accordingly.

3.5.1 Reputation Systems and Algorithms for Web Content Quality Evaluation

A user rates Web content in two ways: (1) He or she rates webpages that he or she selects. The CS system is not involved in the selection process. (2) She or he rates webpages that are recommended by the system (see Sect. 3.4). To make users more active in assessing Web content, reputation points can be awarded for users who submit Web content evaluations. Based on this principle, three scenarios can be identified, with different values of reputation points awarded in each scenario. If a user rates self-selected Web content, (1) if the CS system does not have sufficient evaluations of this content, the system will give reputation points R_0; (2) otherwise, if the system already has sufficient evaluations of this Web content, reputation points of R_1 are assigned to the user; (3) if the user rates recommended Web content, the system will give reputation points of R_3. Obviously, the ratings are particularly valuable if a Web content has little credibility information, so $R_0 \geq R_1$. Furthermore, since Web content recommendation serves the purposes of both increasing the system's coverage and detecting malicious users, R_3 is set to value larger than R_0. An example of reputation point distribution could be $R_0 = 10$, $R_1 = 0.1$, and $R_3 = 20$.

Reputation points can be not only awarded but also deducted. When the system detects that a user submitted a fake rating, the corresponding reputation points (previously awarded by the system) are deducted from her or his reputation. The awarded reputation will be deducted only if the fake rating concerns Web content that has a high-confidence credibility evaluation and the user's rating significantly deviates from the system rating. Since more reputation points give users more privileges such as becoming community leaders, reducing advertisements, etc., users are motivated to rate Web content with little credibility information, or those that are recommended by the system, thus increasing the system's coverage, as well as benefiting the recommendation-based defense mechanism. It is noted that imitating adversaries can still gain reputation if they refuse to rate the recommended Web content (avoid being detected) but keep copying system's ratings (e.g., slowly aggregating R_1). This effect can be reduced by setting a maximum limit on the number of submitted Web content evaluations by a user, for example, 100 per day.

In order to test the reputation system's effectiveness, a simulation experiment has been conducted. In the experiment, artificial agents submitted webpage credibility evaluations (on a star rating scale such as used in the proposed CS system). Agents could be honest (submitting non-strategic evaluations, modeled as random evaluations from a biased distribution), as well as one of three kinds of imitating adversaries. Naive imitating adversaries (50% of all imitating adversaries) would copy the system's rating with 0.8 probability. Medium imitating adversaries (30% of all imitating adversaries) would copy the system's rating with 0.5 probability, and smart imitating adversaries (20% of all imitating adversaries) would copy the system's rating with 0.2 probability. The behavior of smart imitating adversaries is not much different from the behavior of normal users; nevertheless, they were included in the evaluation. The goal of the evaluation is to determine how precisely the recommendation and reputation algorithm, when combined, can detect imitating adversaries. The goal of the algorithms is therefore to assign any agent to a class— be it an honest agent or an adversary. This is done based on the imitating behavior probability threshold calculated by the recommendation algorithm.

The results of the evaluation are shown in Fig. 3.7. The figure shows three performance measures: precision, recall, and the F-measure, as a function of the increasing fraction of imitating adversaries. The imitating behavior probability threshold has been set to 0.25 for this evaluation. It can be observed that recall is not affected by changing the fraction of imitating adversaries. However, as this fraction increases, the imitating adversaries become dominant in the system, so the fraction of predictions that are able to successfully detect adversaries (precision) also increases. As a consequence, the F-measure increases, as well.

The optimum threshold for the estimated imitating behavior probability can be determined by investigating the sensitivity of performance measures to this parameter. The results are shown in Fig. 3.8. From the figure, it can be observed that extremely low or extremely high threshold incurs extremely low precision or recall, which is not acceptable. When the threshold is 0.4, F-measure is maximized in this set of experiments.

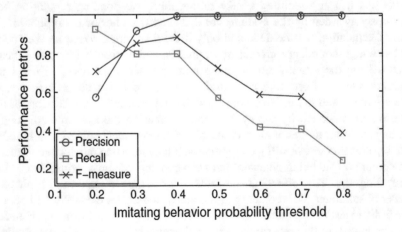

Fig. 3.8 Impact of imitating behavior probability detection threshold. Source: [130]

3.5.2 Role of Webpage Recommendations in Combating Adversaries

The interaction of the recommendation algorithm and the reputation algorithm can be investigated further by comparing the values of reputation calculated for honest agents and adversaries by the reputation algorithm with and without the recommendation algorithm's support. In other words, in this set of experiments, the recommendation algorithm could be switched on or off. Without the recommendation algorithm, all agents rate only self-selected webpages.

If a user rates a self-selected website that already has sufficient ratings (i.e., the number of ratings is larger than the median of the number of ratings for all websites in the system), 0.1 point is awarded; if the self-selected website does not have sufficient ratings yet, 10 points are given. On the other hand, if the user rates a recommended website, 20 points are assigned. This is to motivate users to more actively interact with the recommendation component. (Other variants of reputation payoffs yielded similar results.) In order to study the influence of the recommendation, two experimental settings were set up: a reputation system with recommendation functionality and one without recommendation. The simulator periodically checks the correctness of ratings. If a user's rating differs from the mean of all corresponding ratings (treated as ground truth), the rating is determined to be incorrect, and the points are deducted from the rating user's reputation.

Figure 3.9 demonstrates the cumulative distribution function (CDF) of reputation points of honest users and different types of attackers in the case when the recommendation system is used. Users' reputation points are divided into seven ranges: [0,1000), [1000,1100), [1100,1200), [1200,1300), [1300,1400), [1400,1500), and [1500,1600). Such ranges can help to distinguish different reputation levels, which are more meaningful and interpretable than directly displaying numeric values.

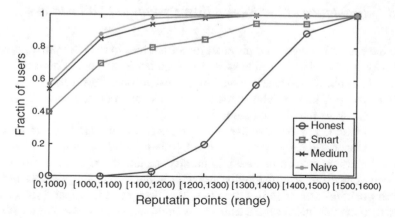

Fig. 3.9 Cumulative distribution function of reputation of honest users and adversaries with recommendation algorithm. Source: [130]

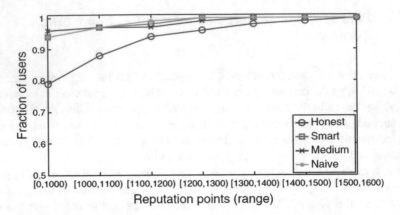

Fig. 3.10 Cumulative distribution function of reputation of honest users and adversaries without recommendation algorithm. Source: [130]

Figure 3.10 shows the same CDFs in the case when the recommendation system is not used.

By comparing the results in the two settings, it was observed that when recommendation functionality is provided, honest users' reputations are significantly higher than that of imitating attackers. On the other hand, when recommendation functionality is absent, although honest users' reputation points are generally higher than that of imitating attackers, the difference is not significant. The conclusion is that the integrated recommendation system not only helps to directly detect imitating attackers but also boosts reputation system, which provides an alternative way to study users' imitating behavior.

3.5.3 Resistance of the Reputation System to Sybil Attacks

Since the reputation algorithm plays an important role in the CS system, it would inevitably be the object of attacks and manipulation attempt. This section has discussed a sophisticated attack of the imitating adversary. However, a simpler form would be the well-known Sybil attack [30]: the use of a botnet or similar approach to insert fake users into the reputation system.

Many possible approaches have been proposed to mitigate Sybil attacks [75, 101]. Moreover, the simplest way to use Sybils to attack a reputation system is by ballot stuffing: a coalition attack to modify the target's reputation. However, it has been shown that peer-prediction reputation algorithms are provably resistant to such coalition attacks [43]. Of course, this does not mean that Sybils cannot be used to combat more sophisticated reputation algorithms. Reputation systems are constantly under attack in the Internet today, and reputation algorithms are in a constant arms race with adversaries. It is beyond the scope of this book to demonstrate the possibilities of reducing vulnerabilities of reputation systems.

However, there exists a practical, although costly, method of resisting Sybil attacks: improved authentication. Sybil attacks rely on the weakness of authentication systems used in the Internet today. Increasing the requirements of user registration and authentication may be the way to create a secure, practical credibility evaluation support system.

3.5.4 Tackling the Cold-Start Problem of the Reputation System

Another typical problem of reputation systems is the cold-start problem: the lack of a minimal number of users with known histories to evaluate their reputation. Here, we are going to suggest one possible solution of this problem.

Notice that contemporary CS systems used in practice, such as WOT or Snopes.com, do not suffer from a low number of users. There also exist practical ways of motivating users to join and start contributing into online communities that are just starting to develop—for an overview, see the seminal book of Kraut and Resnick [95].

A method that can be used to deal with the cold-start problem in the reputation system is a hierarchical reputation system design. This approach relies on introducing (at least) two roles of users in the reputation system: an ordinary user and an expert. The role of the expert can only be taken by trustworthy, active users who will play the role of evaluating contributions of ordinary users. Such a design has been used in many reputation systems (such as Slashdot) and is in use in many large online communities (notably, Wikipedia, which has a specialized administrator role).

The reputation system does not need as many expert users in order to start working. With the increase of the user community, ordinary users who earn a sufficiently high reputation can be promoted to the expert role. A hierarchical reputation system design is therefore a feasible solution to the cold-start problem.

3.6 Aggregation Algorithms for Credibility Evaluations

The credibility evaluation support system proposed in this chapter bases on the principle of Crowdsourcing. Credibility evaluations are gathered from a crowd of users who utilize the CS system to obtain Web content credibility evaluation, but also post their own credibility ratings. There are many working examples of similar Crowdsourcing systems, and a large and dynamic research community and lots of literature concerning Crowdsourcing system design exist as well.

Once the CS system gathers credibility evaluations, it must aggregate them. There can be at least two goals of this aggregation: to choose a credibility class for an evaluated webpage or statement or to create a ranking of evaluated webpages or statements. Both of these goals can be realized by different types of aggregation algorithms. To avoid confusion, the first type will be referred to as a fusion algorithm. The goal of a fusion algorithm is to aggregate various credibility ratings into a credibility class of evaluated webpages or statements. Importantly, the fusion algorithm works for several webpages or statements at the same time.

The second type of aggregation algorithms will be referred to as a ranking algorithm. The goal of the ranking algorithm is to aggregate various credibility ratings into a ranking of webpages or statements by their credibility. While the CS system proposed in this chapter does not use a ranking algorithm, other types of credibility evaluation support system—for example, a CS integrated with a search engine or webpage directory—could use a ranking aggregation algorithm.

This section first reviews various kinds of fusion algorithms used in Crowdsourcing. Next, a simple fusion algorithm for the credibility evaluation support system proposed in this chapter is described in detail.

3.6.1 Fusion Algorithms for Crowdsourcing

Research on Crowdsourcing has developed many kinds of fusion algorithms, and has studied their properties, especially their ability to remove noise caused by various factors. A very good overview of this topic can be found in [41]. Here, a short overview of the most important approaches will be presented, in order to give a background for the more detailed description of the CS Fusion Algorithm in the next section.

The most basic approach to aggregate ratings and at the same time remove noise is to use majority voting. This approach relies on the increasing amount of votes to bring positive effects. Theoretical perspectives on these approaches are given by Kuncheva et al. [96] and Nowak and Rüger [131]. Note that majority voting will not work well in the case of controversy, as described in Sect. 2.8. In the absence of controversy, the more ratings, the better, although even then the result may be affected by rating bias (see Sect. 2.7). Increasing the number of ratings can be useful even if evaluators are subjective and ratings are noisy [70].

Noise and uncertainty in crowdsourced evaluations may be caused by various factors, such as insufficient information, insufficient expertise, subjectivity, and communication problems [41]. For surface credibility evaluations, a potential source of noise is described by the Prominence-Interpretation theory (see Sect. 2.4.4).

Another important source of noise in credibility evaluations are maliciously motivated evaluators (adversaries). Cheaters, spammers, and malicious evaluators have been encountered and studied in Crowdsourcing research. Research has shown that simply increasing the price paid for evaluations does not lead to a linear increase in evaluation quality (or reduction of noise). Rather, the relationship between price and quality is a concave function, and quality can be maximized by choosing the right price [175]. Deterring cheaters is possible by the right design of the fusion algorithm and Crowdsourcing system in a way that makes cheating more time-consuming than normal evaluation [89]. Many solutions for deterring cheaters and increasing robustness of fusion algorithms have been proposed [31]. Another approach is to develop methods for spam detection [68]. Noise caused by subjectivity is present in many types of Crowdsourcing tasks, not just in credibility evaluation, but also in astronomical or medical tasks [111, 173]. From the point of view of fusion algorithm design, the various sources of noise can be treated in the same manner.

More sophisticated fusion algorithms use the Expectation-Maximization method. This approach has been proposed in the seminal work of Dawid and Skene [24]. Expectation-Maximization fusion algorithms work by estimating the correct evaluation (the result of the fusion algorithm) and the correctness of evaluators at the same time. Correctness of evaluators is used to improve estimation of the correct evaluation (one way of doing this is to still use majority voting, but to weigh each evaluation by the evaluator's correctness). The Expectation-Maximization approach can be used to combat evaluator bias [174]. Also, more complex versions of the Expectation-Maximization algorithm that assume the existence of real, rather than discrete, parameters exist. Such approaches need different optimization methods (typically, gradient descent), but can be used to jointly compute correct evaluations, evaluators' correctness or skill, and the difficulty of objects' evaluation [211]. Such algorithms can be generalized to take into account various features of evaluated objects [210].

3.6.2 Fusion Algorithms for Computing Credibility Distributions

This section describes the Fusion Algorithm of the CS system. This is a central algorithm that integrates information from several other algorithms, such as the Reputation Algorithm, the webpage Analyzer, and the Statement Analyzer, as shown in Fig. 3.1. Figure 3.11 summarizes the input and output of the Fusion Algorithm. The main input are surface credibility evaluations from users. For each user, the reputation algorithm provides a reputation value. The webpage Analyzer computes features of the evaluated webpage. If the evaluation concerns a statement, the Statement Analyzer (see Sect. 3.7) contributes similarities of the evaluated statement to previously evaluated statements. The output of the Fusion Algorithm is a credibility class of the webpage or statement.

The Fusion Algorithm uses a model of credibility evaluations based on the theoretical foundations introduced in Sect. 2.3.4. The definition of credibility used in this book is that of a signal received by evaluating Web users. This signal is a function of information contained in the webpage, as well as meta-information.

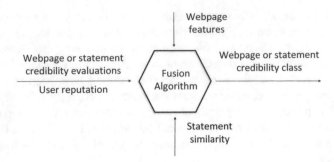

Fig. 3.11 Input and output of fusion algorithm

Ground truth	ω
Signal-based credibility evaluations	α
User skills in credibility evaluation	θ
User honesty of credibility evaluation	ρ

Fig. 3.12 Model assumptions of fusion algorithm

However, the user's own ability to evaluate credibility, as well as the ground truth (in the case when it is available—see Sect. 2.1), influences the signal.

The model assumed by the fusion algorithm is outlined in Fig. 3.12. The main feature of this model is that it differentiates between observed variables and unobserved variables. The only observed variable in the model are signal-based surface credibility evaluations from users, marked in the figure in a blue color. The remaining variables are unobserved, with the exception of the honesty of user evaluations that is approximated by the reputation algorithm of the CS system. This kind of model is similar to the assumptions of fusion algorithms such as Expectation-Maximization [24, 41, 211].

The model is probabilistic in nature. Observed variables are treated as samples of random variables. The goal of the fusion algorithm is to efficiently search for the most probable values of unobserved variables, given the observed input data. Fusion algorithms inspired by Expectation-Maximization use maximum likelihood estimates and optimization heuristics to find locally optimal values of unobserved variables. This is the approach chosen for the fusion algorithm described in this section.

It should be stressed that fusion algorithms based on the assumption of probabilistic user behavior do not take into account the possibility of strategic behavior of users. This is an inherent weakness of such fusion algorithms. On the other hand, the possibility of strategic manipulation is taken into account in the design of the reputation algorithm that is resilient to adversary behavior. This is the reason why these two algorithms are decoupled and integrated by using reputation as an input to the fusion algorithm.

In order to describe the fusion algorithm, some notation is needed. First, a credibility evaluation for webpage or statement p by user u will be denoted by α_{up}. During its operation, the fusion algorithm will maintain a working estimation of the correct credibility rating for each webpage or statement, denoted by β_p. It shall be assumed that a ground truth exists (although it is not known) for the webpage or statement p; recall from Sect. 2.1 that supporting credibility evaluation for information that has no ground truth is synonymous to supporting discussion, and the system can assign a "Controversial" credibility class for such information. The ground truth value for webpage or statement p is ω_p. On the other hand, various webpages or statements may have various difficulties for credibility evaluation. Previous research has shown that taking into account various object difficulties may lead to significant improvements in correctness of a fusion algorithm [211]. Users may have different levels of skill or ability in evaluating credibility. The skill of a user u is denoted by $\theta_u \in [0, 1]$. It is assumed that the level of skill is not dependent on a user's strategic behavior. On the other hand, a user's honesty depends on the user's strategic decisions, and this is captured by the user's reputation calculated by the reputation algorithm. Reputation of user u is denoted by $\rho_u \in \mathbb{R}$.

The fusion algorithm works by estimating the most likely values of the unobserved variables θ and ω. The credibility evaluation skill of each user is estimated by a skill-error matrix that compares the observed user ratings α_{up} to the currently estimated ratings of the algorithm, β_p. A formula shall be given for this error matrix, denoted by $\theta_u(i, j)$, where u is a rating user. For the proposed star scale of Web credibility ratings, $i, j \in \{1, 2, 3, 4, 5\}$ are possible rating values.

Let

$$\eta_{up}(i, j) = \begin{cases} 1 & \text{if } \alpha_{up} = j \text{ and } \beta_p = i \\ 0 & \text{otherwise} \end{cases}$$

Then, the matrix $\theta_u(i, j)$ that models user skills and errors in credibility evaluation is given by the formula

$$\theta_u(i, j) = \begin{cases} \dfrac{\sum_p \eta_{up}(i,j)}{\sum_p \sum_{j \in \{1,\dots,5\}} \eta_{up}(i,j)} & \text{if at least one } \eta_{up}(i, j) = 1 \\ 0 & \text{otherwise} \end{cases}$$

Importantly, the matrix θ_u models both a user's skills (the positions on the diagonal, $\theta_u(i, i)$, represent the correctness of the user's ratings) and errors (the other positions represent the user's rating error tendencies).

The output of the fusion algorithm is based on the distribution of ratings for webpage or statement p that will be denoted by $\mu_p(k)$, where $i \in \{1, 2, 3, 4, 5\}$ is the value of the rating. The estimation of $\mu_p(i)$ can be obtained by the formula

$$\mu_p(i) = \frac{\sum_u [\alpha_{up} = i] \theta_u(i, i) \rho_u}{\sum_u \rho_u \sum_{j \in \{1,...,5\}} [\alpha_{up} = j]} \theta_u(j, j)$$

where $[\alpha_{up} = i]$ is equal to 1 if $\alpha_{up} = i$ and zero otherwise.

The fusion algorithm works iteratively, updating the estimations of $\mu_p(i)$ and using the previous estimations of $\mu_p(i)$ as a basis for the next iteration. The first step of the algorithm is initialization. Here, the values of reputation ρ_u are obtained from the reputation algorithm for each user. Also, the skill-error matrix θ_u is initialized to the identity matrix. This is equivalent to an initial assumption that each user has perfect credibility evaluation skills.

Each step of the fusion algorithm is divided into the E (Expectation) step and the M (Maximization) step.

E step: The E step consists of computing the maximum likelihood estimation of $\mu_p(i)$ for every page p and every $i \in \{1, \ldots, 5\}$, using the skill-error matrix θ_u from the previous iteration.

M step: In the M step, new estimates of correct credibility ratings β_p are computed for each webpage or statement. These estimates are simply the ratings that have the maximum likelihood according to the estimation of $\mu_p(i)$ computed in the E step. The new estimates are therefore given by the formula

$$\beta_p = \underset{i \in \{1,...,5\}}{\operatorname{argmax}} \mu_p(i)$$

Iterations consisting of the E step and M step are repeated until convergence. The fusion algorithm, based on the principle of Expectation-Maximization [24], is only guaranteed to converge to a local maximum. In practice, it is advisable to repeat the algorithm for various sets of initialization parameters, to better approximate the global maximum.

After convergence, the fusion algorithm needs to make a final step. The computed $\mu_p(i)$ is the optimal distribution of credibility ratings on the star rating scale for the webpage or statement p. However, the fusion algorithm outputs a credibility class for the webpage or statement. This credibility class is, as proposed in Sect. 2.8, a function of the distribution of credibility ratings. Therefore, the main goal of the fusion algorithm is to estimate the distribution of credibility ratings after estimating the most likely values for the unobserved variables. Once the distribution is estimated, the algorithm can use the class designs described in Sect. 2.8 to determine a credibility class for an object or webpage. This also means that the Fusion Algorithm can only work if a minimum number of credibility ratings is available (as a rule of thumb, a minimum of 10 ratings is required).

3.7 Using Statement Credibility Evaluations

Many of the features used for webpage credibility classification in Sect. 3.3 have been based directly on the textual content of the webpage and even applied methods of Natural Language Processing (NLP) to this textual content. Moreover, following the design of systems like Snopes or PolitiFact, the user interface proposed for the Reconcile system (see Sect. 3.1) allows the evaluation of credibility of individual statements contained in a webpage.

3.7.1 Systems Supporting Statement Credibility Evaluation on the Web

This idea has also been proposed for other systems. TruthGoggles developed by [159] is a browser extension that scans text on a webpage and identifies phrases present in an external source of fact-checked statements. This source is treated as authoritative and determines whether the phrase is treated as true or false. However, the system performs matching by means of simple string comparison, which results in 100% precision but also very low recall.

Hypothes.is[10] is a project aimed at creating an annotation maintainer, also running as a browser extension. Its goal is to collect comments concerning every single sentence on the Web. It depends not on experts but on crowd annotation and thus simulates the Wisdom of Crowds. No information has been provided about any statement-matching capabilities for Hypothes.is. However, its developers believe that their system will be popular enough to obtain a wealth of data and consequently reasonable recall.

WISDOM, described in [83, 85], is an already-deployed decision support system. It collects pages related to a given topic and then classifies them based on categories of information providers (companies, newspapers, individuals, etc.) and determines the sentiment towards the examined topic. On this basis, WISDOM provides opinion statistics and sample opinions for each class. WISDOM does not attempt to judge information credibility directly, but rather helps users to do so by aggregating and organizing Web information.

Murakami et al. [127] described a vision of a Statement Map Project intended to present facts and opinions concerning a given subject along with logical (agreement, conflict) and epistemic (evidence) relationships between them. The system will retrieve documents related to a query from the Web, split them into statements, and then determine whether these statements are factual or based on opinion and find relationships between them. However, this project, before becoming a reality,

---

[10]www.hypothes.is.

would need advanced NLP techniques still under development, and thus it has not yet achieved the required accuracy.

One of the largest projects that aim to extract factual information from statements on the Web would be the Google Knowledge Vault proposed by Dong et al. [26], an attempt to construct an ever-growing probabilistic knowledge base, organized in the form of RDF ontology triplets, with the aid of relation extraction. Such an approach generates a set of statements with a provided probabilistic measure of its credibility.

3.7.2 Statement Analyzer of the CS System

The basic functionality of the Statement Analyzer of the CS system is to maintain a database of statement evaluations and statement credibility classes. This database can be used to retrieve information about statements contained in a webpage, and to use this information to support the fusion algorithm that has to assign a credibility rating to the webpage.

A conservative design of the Statement Analyzer would only retrieve statement credibility classes for statements that are identical to the ones contained in the webpage. However, by looking at the design and operation of Snopes, it becomes apparent that the same, non-credible statements are repeated on the Web in many minor variations. Human evaluations of statement credibility can, at least, be supported by retrieving statements from the database that are similar to the evaluated statement. Snopes and Reconcile also support another functionality: the summarization of similar statements in a more general, simpler form by a human user. Such summaries could also be referred to as "claims" and can be thought of as a basic form of statements that belong to the same class, when compared using a Semantic Textual Similarity relation. Such claims can also be detected automatically by algorithms that search for important statements of fact in discourses such as political debates [62, 63].

3.7.2.1 Semantic Textual Similarity

The proposed functionality of searching for similar statements brings up the problem of computing Semantic Textual Similarity. This is a well-known research problem in Natural Language Processing.

Several measurements of similarity have been proposed in the literature, that is, by Landauer et al. [97], Mihalcea et al. [119], and Gabrilovich and Markovitch [45], based on surface-level and content features. The concept of Semantic Textual Similarity (STS) has been introduced at the SemEval-2012 conference [3]. The SemEval STS task measures the degree of semantic equivalence. The goal of the task is to create a unified framework enabling an evaluation of multiple semantic components. The participants' aim was to evaluate the similarity between two sentences, resulting in a similarity score ranging from 0 (no relationship) to 5 (semantic equivalence). The construction of this scale is described in detail in the SemEval-2012 STS (17) task [3]. An existing algorithm for computing STS is the DKPro Similarity engine developed by Bär et al. [6].

3.7.2.2 Analysis of Statement Credibility Based on Textual Features

The Statement Analyzer can use textual features to analyze credibility of statements. These features can be divided into two groups: lexical features and structural features. Lexical features range from shallow TF-IDF representations to more advanced semantic modeling through dimension reduction, implementation of dedicated semantic mapping software, or word-to-vector approaches. Structural features are mostly related to syntax. They range from bi-gram analysis, Part-of-Speech analysis, and extraction of production rules from Context Free Grammar (notable example in stylometric research [36, 104]). Sometimes similarities to specific types of discourse (like satire) are used.

Several algorithms and methods for automatic credibility evaluation support of statements have been developed by studying fake online reviews of products or services [36, 44, 64, 104, 125]. These approaches are also sometimes referred to as opinion spam detection in the literature [15, 87, 106, 149].

The ubiquity of such fake reviews has caused commercial review sites such as Yelp or Dianping to develop proprietary fake review filters [105, 108, 126]. Commercial review sites can be the source of large datasets [105]. However, comprehensive approaches for fake review detection do not base only on textual features but also take into account behavioral features and relevant metadata (such as IP addresses and geographical locations).

Textual approaches towards fake review and online opinion spam detection have reached an accuracy of above 80% [35, 44, 104]. Successful approaches typically combine lexical and structural features. Some approaches use semi-supervised learning algorithms (modified PU algorithm) for deceptive opinion detection [44, 151].

Textual analysis of fake reviews can also be used by the reputation algorithm of the CS system. CS system users who wish to earn reputation by reviewing webpages suggested by the Recommendation Algorithm may be required to provide justification. The analysis of such justification may detect fake reviews or spam.

More generally, knowledge gained about fake reviews and opinion spam may be used to detect manipulative statements contained in ordinary webpages, which is one of the goals of the Statement Analyzer. It has been shown that deceptive statements have a different rhetorical structure to true statements [152]. The work of Feng et al. [36] can be considered a classic for the task of deception detection. It uses a hotel review dataset from TripAdvisor and Yelp. The approach is based on stylometry, the quantified analysis of style. The authors generate production rules from a Context Free Grammar Tree, and use them to predict deceptiveness in documents. An accuracy score of 91% is recorded, using a Support Vector Machine (SVM) classification algorithm.

Automatic classifiers developed based on fake reviews or opinion spam may therefore be helpful for supporting credibility evaluations of statements. Another approach towards this goal is automatic fact-checking.

3.7.2.3 Automatic Fact-Checking

Automated fact-checking is an approach that can be directly utilized by the Statement Analyzer of the CS system. It works based on the assumption that the analyzed statement contains a statement of fact [200]. (Therefore, opinions and more complex statements should be treated differently. Statements that contain facts can be detected automatically [62].) Rather than using lexical or structural textual features, automatic fact-checking aims to extract and represent the statement of fact and analyze its factual correctness by comparison to a knowledge base. The Statement Analyzer module should maintain such a knowledge base; however, it is also possible to use external, structured, or even unstructured knowledge bases. For example, successful automatic fact-checking has used the DBpedia [21].

Some approaches to automatic fact-checking are statistical [110], while others are graph-based and require the representation of the knowledge base as a graph (or knowledge network) [21, 165]. It has been shown that even very simple (and computationally fast) algorithms based on the length of the shortest path between a statement and true statements in the knowledge base provide satisfactory results [21]. Of course, the quality of such approaches depends on the quality of the knowledge base. The knowledge base needs not just to contain true statements of fact, but also needs to be comprehensive, in order to cover a lot of potential false statements. This is the reason why DBpedia seems like a good candidate for such a knowledge base, as a structured database of encyclopedic facts (see Sect. 4.3 for a discussion of the credibility of Wikipedia content).

Note that automatic fact-checking can also benefit from algorithms for automatic answering of questions (since any statement of fact X can be transformed into a question: is statement "X" true?). The automatic answering of such a question is equivalent to automatic fact-checking. This is an area that has seen significant advances because of the TREC. A comprehensive review of the area can be found in [91] (see also Sect. 4.2.4).

3.8 Automatic Prediction of Topic Controversy

Section 2.2 discussed what it means to support credibility evaluations on the Web and pointed out the important role of controversy in this process. Distinguishing between information that can have an agreed-upon credibility evaluation from controversial information is an important function of credibility evaluation support. Information is controversial if users cannot agree about this information's credibility. In this section, the notion of controversy on the Web and of controversy detection will be discussed in more detail.

3.8.1   Defining Web Content and Topic Controversy

The first step is to discuss an operational definition of controversy on the Web. The definition proposed in Sect. 2.2 relies on the concept of agreement, which can be understood through the common-sense notion of agreement by "nearly everyone." However, this implies that a substantial number of users must strongly disagree about the credibility evaluation of information, in order for this information to be considered controversial. When the considered information is a webpage or statement, it is unlikely that the credibility evaluation support system will receive credibility evaluation from a sufficiently large number of users, in order to evaluate the information's level of controversy. For this reason, it seems that some aggregates of information should be used when controversy is evaluated. There are two aggregates that could be considered in practical credibility evaluation systems: domains that identify Web portals rather than webpages or search topics (in the case of information retrieval). However, Web portals that are indeed controversial (e.g., portals concerning homeopathy) usually provide information on a controversial topic. For this reason, focusing on the controversy of the topic of information seems reasonable.

This simple definition of controversy also assumes the existence of a single, global community of Web users. The controversy of information can only be evaluated within a certain user community, and the controversy status of information might change from one community to another. Controversies on Wikipedia are a very good example of this situation: the same information may be controversial in one language version of Wikipedia (usually in English) and not controversial in other language versions. This situation can happen for disputed territories like the Falkland or Kuril Islands. In the Japanese view, the Kuril Islands are a "northern territory" of Japan, and this view might not be widely disputed within Japan. On the other hand, in the Russian view, the Kuril Islands belong to Russia. On English language Wikipedia, the Kuril Islands are on the list of controversial topics.[11] For this reason, it is important to obtain evaluations from a global Web user community (which is simplest to do for English language Web content), in order to evaluate controversy.

A more in-depth definition of controversy in Web content can be formulated as follows: Web content is controversial if it concerns a topic that is controversial within a Web users' community. The topic is controversial if Web users from the community cannot agree on the evaluation of credibility of information on that topic.

---

[11]https://en.wikipedia.org/wiki/Wikipedia:List_of_controversial_issues#Politics_and_economics.

The notion of agreement has already been operationalized in Sect. 2.8. The *Con* class has been defined there as a class of rating distributions that are sufficiently close to the extremely disagreeing rating distribution using the EMD. Later, in Sect. 2.8.2.2, this definition has been refined using the Leik coefficient. It turned out that using the Leik coefficient together with the EMD measure resulted in a better fit to controversial clusters discovered in two datasets. However, many other methods can be used for an operational definition of agreement, such as inter-rater agreement measures (e.g., Fleiss' kappa or intra-class correlation coefficient), or dispersion measures of results (e.g., standard deviation). These measures are not suitable for the Likert or star rating scales proposed for credibility evaluation. Other measures that can replace Leik have been proposed by Tastle et al. [189] and Van der Eijk [198]. Using the definition from Sect. 2.8, this discussion can be concluded by a following definition of Web content topic controversy: the topic of Web content is controversial if rating of Web content or statements on that topic obtained from Web users of the CS user community form rating distributions that belong to the *Con* class.

This definition suggests extending the CS with functions of Web content topical classification. Fortunately, this is a subject that already has several working solutions.

It is interesting to note that there exists a way of topical classification on the Web that can make use of existing information on a topic's controversy. This method relies on a similarity mapping of Web content onto Wikipedia articles and will be discussed in more detail below. Next, an overview of approaches that have been used to support controversy detection on the Web will be presented.

3.8.2 Supporting Controversy Detection on the Web

Dori-Hacohen and Allan classified controversy of Internet pages using their similarity to Wikipedia articles with known controversy. Initially basing on a manually annotated set of articles [27], they recently generalized their method for automatic classification [28]. The proposed method works by mapping a webpage onto Wikipedia articles using query generation. The textual content of the webpage is used to define a topical query, and this query is automatically posed to the Wikipedia search engine. Next, the controversy of the found Wikipedia articles is evaluated using several methods that have been proposed in the literature. The controversy scores of the found Wikipedia articles are aggregating using various methods (voting, averages, or maxima). Overall, the proposed method allows for automatic detection of webpage controversy with a precision similar to supervised approaches.

Other methods focus on the controversy of statements. Ennals et al. [33] developed a Dispute Finder browser extension, which finds and highlights text snippets corresponding to known disputes. The database of known disputes is maintained manually and a textual entailment algorithm is used to find snippets corresponding to a known dispute. Initially, the database was populated from PolitiFact and Snopes, and subsequently in [33] developed a method of finding disputes on the Internet using English language text patterns typical for disputes.

Kawahara et al. [84] focused on recognition and bird's-eye presentation of contradictory and contrastive relations between statements related to a topic (search query) and expressed on webpages (search engine results). The method builds upon predicate-argument language structures in Japanese; however, it is believed to be adaptable to other languages.

Finding contradictions with the help of sentiment expressed by viewers was attempted by Tsytsarau et al. in [194]. It is required that a topic in question has a number of online reviews or opinions, from where a sentiment can be first aggregated and then used for identifying the controversy.

Yamamoto [220] developed a Web query support system by collecting disputed sentences about queries from the Web and then suggesting some of the most typical and relevant disputed sentences to the user in order to enhance user's awareness of suspicious statements.

However, more problems arise with the attempt of providing assistance to users of search engines on controversial queries and controversial results. There are challenges regarding scope and context of queries, scientific correctness versus popular beliefs, requirement of moral judgment to several possible correct answers, and dependence on cultural and social setting of the information-seeking person, as described by Dori-Hacohen et al. in [29].

3.8.3   Controversy Tagging in the Credibility Evaluation System

In Sect. 3.1.1.2, it was mentioned that the design of the Reconcile prototype CS system allows users to tag Web content as controversial. This method is considerably faster than methods that rely on an analysis of rating distributions, since only a single tag (or a few tags from various users) would be enough to change the controversy status of a webpage or statement. However, when a user is asked to evaluate the controversy of a webpage, she or he may overestimate the popularity of her or his own opinion in the community or follow the *availability heuristic* when imagining the opinion of a typical community member. Both potential sources of errors may be somehow controlled by asking many people instead of single individual.

Nevertheless, the tagging of controversy may serve as an early warning for CS system users. It is also possible to combine the user tagging approach with other approaches. For example, the automatic controversy detection approach can be used to automatically turn on the controversy tag for Web content that is evaluated as controversial by the algorithm. On the other hand, Web content should only be assigned to the "Controversial" class on the basis of evaluation of a rating distribution. Also, considering topics rather than single webpages or even statements allows to aggregate more ratings, leading to a more reliable diagnosis of the controversy status of Web content on that topic.

3.9   Presentation of Credibility Evaluations and Its Influence on Users

As described in Sect. 3.1, a credibility evaluation support system is designed to present credibility evaluations to users as they browse the Web, through the capabilities of a Web browser extension. The CS can present warnings when users browse non-credible pages, present short summaries of credibility evaluations in a browser's toolbar, and augment search results with visual icons that summarize the retrieved webpages' credibility. Moreover, they can present more information through a specialized Web portal, allowing users to participate in discussions, browse credibility information, etc.

One of the earliest systematic efforts to support Web content credibility evaluation comes from Japan. The WISDOM project [83, 85] aimed to create a decision support system for Web search that would also support credibility evaluation. The user interface of the proposed system was highly complex, suitable for a separate Web portal (see Fig. 3.13). The proposed interface works like a search

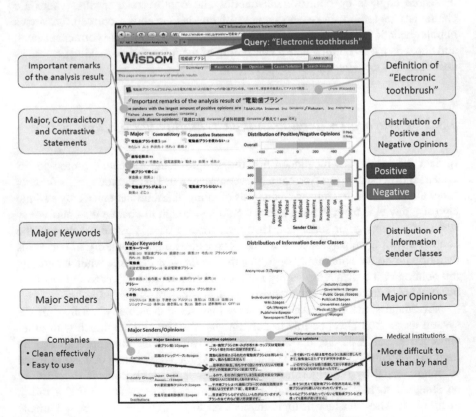

Fig. 3.13 Credibility evaluation support by WISDOM system. Source: [83]

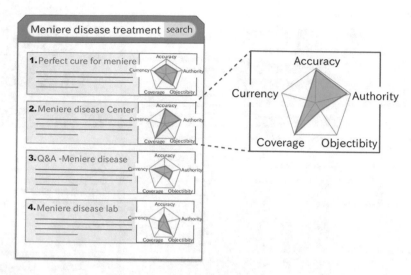

Fig. 3.14 Search result enhancement using credibility radar charts. Source: [223]

engine interface, but supplements ordinary search results by several other results such as definitions of concepts, results of sentiment analysis, information regarding topic controversy, major keywords, as well as information regarding the identity of content providers about the subject.

One can view the work of the WISDOM project as the proposal for the design of a Web search engine or meta-search engine. Another view is that of a decision support system; however, the main goal of the system is to organize search results and support credibility evaluation.

Another Japanese approach originated from Kyoto University [222–225]. The group's research focused on discovering additional information to support credibility evaluation on the Web and to present this information in an ergonomic and persuasive manner. A method of presenting information about various dimensions related to credibility evaluation of Web content was by radar charts (see Fig. 3.14). These charts could be placed next to search results, and a user could click on them to enlarge and see values for five dimensions: accuracy, authority, objectivity, coverage, and currency.

Not only search results but also webpages have been augmented using information for supporting credibility evaluation. Authors of [160] have proposed to augment a webpage by information about its popularity and temporal and geographical usage statistics (see Fig. 3.15). This augmentation, according to authors, has a strong effect on the accuracy of credibility evaluation by users. However, the authors' study was based on 21 webpages and 26 users, which is too small a sample to draw conclusive results. Moreover, the study was based on an infrequently used and incorrect definition of credibility that was presented to users before credibility evaluation. This definition states: "A credible webpage is one whose information one can accept as the truth without needing to look elsewhere. If one can accept

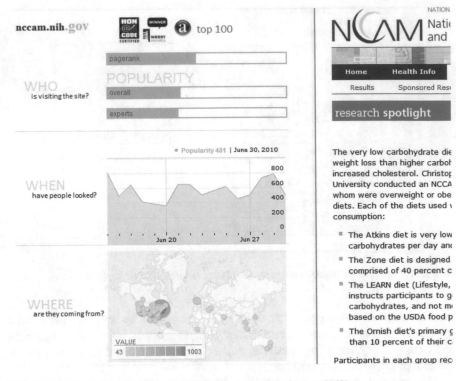

Fig. 3.15 Webpage augmentation for credibility evaluation. Source: [160]

information on a page as true at face value, then the page is credible; if one needs to go elsewhere to check the validity of the information on the page, then it is less credible." Not only is this information suitable only for surface credibility (for earned credibility, more information is necessary for evaluation), but it can also be expected to be strongly correlated with the popularity information visualized together with the webpage. If a lot of people visit the webpage and deem it authoritative (as evidenced by popularity, PageRank, and expert popularity), then other users will feel less motivated to look elsewhere for more information.

The Reconcile CS prototype's interface, as described in Sect. 3.1, consists of a Web browser extension and a dedicated CS portal. The portal can display more detailed information about a webpage than the browser extension (see Fig. 3.16), which mainly presents a traffic light icon (green for the Highly Credible class, yellow for the Neutral class, or red for the Highly Not Credible class) on the Web browser's toolbar. The portal displays a distribution of all ratings and allows users to browse evaluations of statements contained in the webpage (if any evaluations are in the database) and participate in a discussion about the webpage's credibility. Still, the Reconcile's CS portal has a much simpler interface than, for example, the

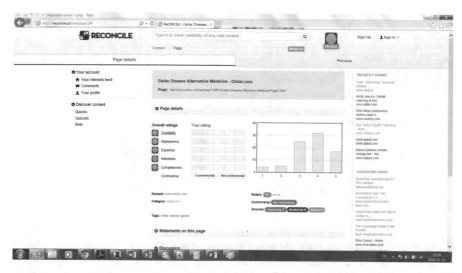

Fig. 3.16 Reconcile CS portal presentation of webpage with neutral credibility class

WISDOM system. This is because Reconcile CS focuses on credibility evaluation, while WISDOM, as well as other CS systems, offers additional functionality.

3.9.1   CS System Persuasiveness

In this section, the effectiveness of presenting information about Web content credibility to users is examined. The main goal of presenting information about Web content credibility is to influence the behavior of users, allowing them to make the right judgment about the truth of Web content. As discussed in Sect. 2.2, the objective of credibility evaluation is to propose evaluations that are closer to (one of two kinds of) truth: scientific truth or post-structuralist truth. This section aims to estimate whether the CS system's credibility evaluation would be taken into account by its users. To evaluate the effectiveness of various methods of presenting information about Web content credibility by a prototype CS, an experiment concerning medical Web content has been carried out. The content used in the experiment belongs to the factual, specialist category.

The evaluation presented in this section is based on an experiment [1]. A single task in this experiment consisted of evaluations of three websites drawn randomly from a corpus of 190 webpages on nine health-related topics. Websites are chosen using most popular, and those increasing the most in popularity, medical searches performed on Google from the USA in 12 months preceding the study and chose nine topics. Corresponding search phrases were formulated, each aimed at finding both credible and not credible information. Random websites were selected from those that were shown on the first results pages (as searched for in the USA), and

Table 3.3 Summary of Web content used for evaluating CS

Topic	No. of webpages	No. of evaluations
Twitch eye treatment	24	1143
Whooping cough treatment	24	1152
Celiac disease treatment	23	1112
Diabetes treatment	22	1023
Hormonal contraception	21	979
Norovirus treatment	21	979
Heart disease treatment	19	901
West Nile virus	19	913
Depression treatment	17	776

Source: [1]

those that did not contain any meaningful content that could be subject to credibility evaluation were filtered out. The list of medical topics used in the study together with the number of webpages and the number of lay user evaluations for each topic is presented in Table 3.3.

A prototype CS developed as part of the Reconcile project was used in the study. Two types of users took part in the study: lay users recruited via Amazon Mechanical Turk and medical experts from the Medical University of Warsaw. The medical experts took part in the study during two medical congresses and from their houses. Based on their evaluations, each website was assigned one unique expert rating that was a result of experts' consensus. The lay users were mTurk workers from English-speaking countries (mostly the USA). All users were paid accordingly for their participation in the study.

The lay user data presented in this section is based on three experimental treatments that were part of the experimental study [1]. Participants were assigned to the treatments randomly. In each case, they were asked to evaluate three websites with respect to six dimensions: credibility, expertise, intentions of the authors, completeness, controversy of the information provided, and appearance of the website. For all the dimensions except for controversy, a 5-point ordinal scale was used with labeled choices (e.g., 1 completely not credible, 2 mostly not credible, etc.). Controversy was measured using the binary tag of the Reconcile prototype CS (controversial versus not controversial).

The experimental scenarios were as follows:

- NH (no hints) scenario: in this case, participants were asked to evaluate the webpages without any external support.
- EH (expert hint) scenario: in this case, the Reconcile interface was used to present the suggested evaluations of the webpages. The suggested evaluations were based on previously gathered expert ratings of the given page and were presented in a form of a traffic light (e.g., green corresponded to credible and red to not credible content) next to the field where the user was submitting his own evaluation.

- RE (reversed expert) scenario: this case was identical to the EH scenario except for the fact that the suggested ratings were exactly opposite to the ratings provided by the experts. One hundred fifty-eight webpages were chosen—ones that received expert credibility ratings other than 3 (the middle of the scale) and marked the credible websites as not credible and vice versa.
- Full scenario: in this case, the users had access to all information presented by the Reconcile Web portal, including distributions of all ratings, comments, etc.

To avoid letting users learn that the system suggestions are misleading in RE scenario, this scenario and the EH scenario were joined. The participants were served either three webpages in the EH scenario or two pages in the EH scenario and one (the last in the package) in the RE scenario. In all the scenarios, the subjects' activity, that is, page clicks, time spent on each task, going back and forth within the quest, etc., was tracked and recorded.

The effectiveness of the CS in supporting credibility evaluation is evaluated by the agreement of ordinary users' evaluations and expert evaluations. In other words, the experiment evaluated the "persuasiveness" of the CS, or its ability to intervene and adjust ordinary users' credibility evaluations.

There are clear limits to the ability of the individual ordinary users to discern the valuable and trash health information on the Web. When no support is provided, only 27.72% of all their evaluations are exactly the same as expert evaluations of the given webpages, while 49.72% are higher. The main problem is therefore a tendency to overestimate the credibility of the medical information encountered on the Internet. Taking into account the fact that both values 4 and 5 indicate credible content while choosing ratings between 1 and 3 indicates various amounts of doubt, the problem becomes much less dramatic. For the following analyses, all the ratings were divided into positive (4 or 5) and negative (other values). In this case, 62.53% of the lay evaluations are the same as expert evaluations, that is, both groups think the content as (generally) credible or both group consider it (generally) not credible. The share of overly positive ratings equals 23.43% and the share of overly negative ratings equals 14.03%.

The situation improves even further when relying on the Wisdom of Crowds. Under this approach, individual lay ratings are aggregated to produce a group-based evaluation that in theory should be more accurate as it eliminates the individual biases. As [184] suggests that when imperfect judgments are aggregated in the right way, the collective intelligence is often excellent. To test this supposition, median lay ratings were computed for each page. Two facts became clear. First, the share of accurate lay ratings did indeed increase from 62.53% to 70.52%. Second, the share of overly optimistic ratings remained practically unchanged and equaled 23.68%. In other words, while the wisdom of the crowds approach can help to evaluate accurately the websites that the individual users tend to unjustifiably see as not credible, it does little to identify the content that is seen as credible and is in fact treacherous. This is due to a clear positive bias in lay evaluations.

Can the CS improve ordinary users' evaluations accuracy by offering simple suggestions in the form of traffic lights (showing whether the evaluation is positive or negative)? In general, the answer is positive. The share of ordinary users' evaluations that are exactly the same as the expert evaluations rises by almost 10% points (from the previously mentioned 27.72% to almost 37%). Unfortunately, the share of overly positive ratings falls only slightly (from the 49.72% to 46.22%). When looking at binary credibility classes (4–5 credible, 1–3 not credible), the share of accurate ratings equals 74.51% and the overly positive ratings amount to only 17.63% of all the ratings. When the Wisdom of Crowds approach is used (aggregating all ordinary user's evaluations), an impressive 87.9% of the webpages are generally classified adequately. The remaining 12% are however still overrated.

3.10   Essential Elements of a CS System's Design

This chapter discussed the design of a CS system, elaborating on several algorithms and methods that could be used in CS systems, as well as discussing the integration of these algorithms into one system. The reference model of a CS system introduced in Sect. 3.1 described several modules: the reputation algorithm, the fusion algorithm, the webpage and Statement Analyzers, as well as the webpage recommendation algorithm. Last but not least, the user interface of a CS system has been discussed in detail in this chapter.

What follows is a summary and specification of the most important modules of a CS system, as well as of findings regarding their effectiveness. The first issue is resistance to adversaries. The reputation algorithm and recommendation algorithm of the CS system can jointly increase resistance to adversaries. The main idea behind their combined use is that the CS system, using the recommendation algorithm, would pick webpages to be evaluated by users. For evaluating webpages chosen by the recommendation algorithm, users would be able to score the most reputation points. The result of this approach is presented in Sect. 3.5.1: the CS system becomes resilient even to an especially difficult type of adversary—the imitating attacker. However, this approach should be resilient to any adversary strategy that relies on the adversary's ability to strategically select webpages for evaluation.

The design of the user interface of the CS system is clearly of high importance. The first function of the user interface is to effectively elicit ratings of webpages and statements, making the rating process easy and intuitive. On the other hand, it is not enough to merely ask users to rate objects on a star rating scale. It is important to get information about factors that influence a user's credibility evaluation. Several user interface designs for the CS system were discussed, for example, the WOT browser extension that has an easy-to-use interface for rating webpages.

Reputation can also be used to enhance the fusion algorithm. The algorithm described in Sect. 3.6 makes use of reputation in order to weigh user evaluations. Evaluation from users with high reputation has a larger impact on the aggregated credibility rating. On the other hand, the credibility evaluations of an adversary who has a low reputation will have a low impact on the aggregated credibility rating.

The second function of the user interface is to present the CS system's credibility evaluations to users. In Sect. 3.9.1, it was shown that a simple form of presentation—the traffic lights metaphor, with a green light signifying high credibility and a red light signifying low credibility—can effectively persuade users by changing the distributions of their credibility evaluations.

Chapter 4
Credibility of Social Media

Gossip, as usual, was one-third right and two-thirds wrong.
Lucy Maud Montgomery, Chronicles of Avonlea

Whoever is careless with the truth in small matters cannot be trusted with important matters.
Albert Einstein

This chapter describes methods of supporting credibility evaluations on Twitter, in online Q&A systems (on the Stack Exchange platform), and on Wikipedia. This is the focus of a large body of research, including the recent EU Pheme project. The chapter will include description of experiments that gather data to train classifiers of tweet credibility, as well as research on the role of credibility in information propagation. The chapter will also discuss the role of credibility in Question and Answer (Q&A) services, as well as the credibility, quality, and controversy of Wikipedia articles.

In general, the main difference between credibility evaluations of Web-based social media content and ordinary Web content (pages or statements) is the easy access to information about the identity of the content's author. Social media are built on user contributions, and no user wants to hide his or her authorship (nor are they allowed to, by most platforms). Even if these identities are transient pseudonyms, they can be a starting point for source credibility evaluation.

Section 2.3 contained the information that source credibility is a relational concept. It is always evaluated by a user, the trust giver, who is regarding another user, the trust receiver. Source credibility is equivalent to trust in two contexts: the veracity and the expertise of the trustee. Supporting source credibility evaluation can be done by aggregating source credibility evaluations from several users (in one or both of the relevant contexts) and presenting an aggregated evaluation of the trust receiver's trustworthiness or expertise. However, whenever a user wishes to evaluate the credibility of information on social media, she or he is back in the relational context.

The question regarding credibility evaluation support for social media is whether or not information about source credibility is enough. Going beyond this

© Springer International Publishing AG, part of Springer Nature 2018
A. Wierzbicki, *Web Content Credibility*,
https://doi.org/10.1007/978-3-319-77794-8_4

information is usually difficult. For many kinds of social media (such as Twitter), the information available in a single piece of content (tweet) is very little and hard to base upon. Here, techniques described in Sect. 3.7 can be useful, unless the shared social media content contains a webpage URL, in which case the CS system for ordinary Web content can be used directly.

However, another important advantage of social media is that they usually generate behavioral data that is evidence of user's credibility judgments, and can be used to estimate the Wisdom of Crowds. For example, retweets on Twitter are usually evidence of positive credibility judgments; so are upvotes of answers in Q&A systems. For credibility evaluation of traditional Web content, these queues are usually lacking and have to be constructed through the user interface of a CS system.

4.1   Credibility of Tweets and Twitter Users

Twitter is one of the most popular social media services today. Invented as a simple application of the mobile Short Messaging Service, it has since developed into a global information sharing platform. It allows users to post and share short textual messages (at most 140 characters long) called tweets. Tweets can be sent over e-mail, SMS, or from several mobile applications. This means that Twitter enables global information sharing in real time. For this reason, it has been used to disseminate time-critical information about important events. This information is often posted directly from the source (e.g., a news agency, popular politician, celebrity, or authority figure) and gets shared (retweeted) by users worldwide.

Twitter is often called a micro-blog, but it can also be thought of as an online social network and is treated as such by its experienced users. This means that Twitter users are aware of their social network environment, for example, their number of followers, as well as the popularity and influence of people they decide to follow on Twitter. The news-sharing behavior on Twitter, for this reason, can be thought of as information propagation through social networks. Viral news are shared globally, while less popular news propagate through small parts of the network and die out. Unfortunately, non-credible rumors along with credible information can both be widely propagated [55]. Some false rumors even turn viral and can cause significant harm, although rumors are being questioned by users, and aggregate rumor propagation on Twitter differs from the propagation of credible news [116].

For this reason, the subject of credibility evaluation on Twitter has received significant research attention. Similarly to research on ordinary Web content credibility support, research on credibility evaluation on Twitter can be divided into the following categories: research that aims to characterize and model how users evaluate credibility on Twitter and research that aims to design credibility evaluation support (CS) systems or algorithms for Twitter.

4.1.1 Characterizing Credibility Evaluations on Twitter

One of the first studies of credibility evaluations on Twitter dates from 2010 to 2011 [16, 116]. These studies have found that generally, credibility evaluations on Twitter can be described similarly to evaluation of ordinary Web content. Credibility on Twitter is evaluated by considering source credibility and message credibility. Due to the ease of identifying the source on Twitter, source credibility plays a larger role. However, message credibility is important, as well, and can affect user decisions on whether or not to retweet the message. On the other hand, even though Twitter messages are short, the sheer volume of these messages makes it difficult to evaluate earned credibility of each message, which brings the discussion back to evaluating surface message credibility most of the time.

Apart from similarities between credibility evaluation of ordinary Web content and credibility evaluation on Twitter, Twitter has several special characteristics. These are especially network characteristics of users (number of followers, number of retweets) and special characteristics of messages (Twitter hashtags, special language used on Twitter). These special characteristics also affect credibility evaluations on Twitter.

Later studies [133, 163, 170, 171] have confirmed and extended the findings of Castillo et al. [16]. Another special characteristic of Twitter is that it is frequently used to share important or even dramatic news, as well as additional information related to important events. This behavior of users can be thought of as participating in crisis management, or at least assisting in sharing information about crises. However, researchers who have investigated 14 high-impact events discussed on Twitter [55] found that only 17% of tweets related to the event contained credible situational awareness information.

According to Mendoza et al. [116], Twitter is more effective than traditional communication channels in the later stages of natural disasters or other catastrophic events. In the first two stages, warning and threat, traditional media are more effective. However, starting from the impact stage, traditional media become too slow, or their coverage can be damaged. Twitter can work using the SMS service,[1] which is a low-bandwidth service of the GSM network that is usually the most resilient even during network outages. The asynchronous and delay-tolerant nature of the SMS service makes it also more suitable to situations with intermittent network connectivity. In the study of the earthquake in Chile in 2010, researchers found that Twitter works as a collaborative filter that can select true news with high accuracy— over 95% of tweets related to true news were affirmative, while almost 40% of tweets related to false rumors were denying. However, still about 45% of tweets (the majority) related to false rumors were affirmative. The conclusion from this study is that Twitter users behave differently when propagating information about false rumors and true news. Twitter users do a good job of evaluating the credibility of true news, but a much worse job of evaluating credibility of false rumors.

---

[1] https://support.twitter.com/articles/14014.

4.1.2 Supporting Credibility Evaluation on Twitter

One of the first problems of supporting credibility evaluation on Twitter is determining what the information is. As it was mentioned in Sect. 2.3, the type of information determines what truth model to apply and what kind of credibility evaluation support can be applied. Twitter is a medium for exchanging news, but also for ordinary conversations about people who partied too long and have a hangover. It is also often used to express emotions by its users. Another problem is to determine whether the shared information is likely to be shared further (or even turn viral) and therefore is a significant target for credibility evaluation support, or whether it is dying out.

There already exist automatic tools that deal with detecting emerging viral information on Twitter and can determine the topic of this information. One such tool is TwitterMonitor[2] [113]. It is an example of automatic event detection on Twitter. TwitterMonitor works by first detecting sharp increases of keyword occurrence in tweets. For each such case, TwitterMonitor then constructs a query that characterizes the event, using conjunctions (obligatory terms) and disjunctions (optional terms). Such a query represents a topic of emerging news or conversations on Twitter. These queries can serve as aggregates for tweets, making it easier to recognize how the crowd of users evaluates the topic and providing more information than for a single tweet.

Castillo et al. [16] report an experiment that applied Crowdsourcing to evaluate the newsworthiness and credibility of Twitter topics, identified using TwitterMonitor. The researchers used Amazon Mechanical Turk and asked users to evaluate credibility of topics identified by TwitterMonitor. Each topic was presented using keywords and ten example tweets. In a first Crowdsourcing task, users were asked to identify the type of information: news or chats. Chat credibility was not evaluated; only topics that were identified by users in the previous task as news were submitted to credibility evaluation in a next task. Users evaluated credibility using three classes: "Almost certainly true," "Likely to be false," and "Almost certainly false." Another class was "I can't decide." Each topic was evaluated by seven users, and at least five out of seven needed to agree in order for the class to apply. Interestingly, in a preliminary test, the class "Likely to be true" was used as well; however, almost all users chose to use this class. In order to get rid of this bias, the class was removed, forcing users to choose one of the remaining classes. Less than 20% of about 750 evaluated topics did not result in consensus; remaining topics were divided into over 40% "Almost certainly true," over 30% "Likely to be false," and only 8.6% "Almost certainly false." This means that a similar evaluation bias was observed for Twitter topics, as for ordinary webpages and statements (see Sect. 2.8).

The resulting dataset [16] was used to train machine classifiers of Twitter topic credibility. The tweets and topics were used to determine features that could be used

---

[2]www.twittermonitor.net.

for classification, similarly to the approach discussed in Sect. 3.3. These features were divided into four types:

- Message-based features. These features were based on a single tweet. Some of them were based only on the tweet's content, such as the number of exclamation or question marks, word with positive or negative sentiment, etc. The list of such content-based features for tweets is much shorter than for ordinary webpages (see Table 3.2), because tweets are very short. Other features were Twitter specific, such as whether the tweet contains a hash (a hashtag used on Twitter) or whether the tweet was a retweet.
- User-based features. These are features specifically aimed at estimating a Twitter user's trustworthiness or expertise. However, Twitter only has a number of rather general features about its users, such as the number of followers, followees ("friends" on Twitter), time since registration, or number of tweets or retweets made by the user.
- Topic-based features. These are aggregates of the two previous types for the entire topic.
- Propagation-based features. The propagation of messages on Twitter occurs via retweets, and a propagation tree may be constructed of messages belonging to a topic. The depth of this tree, for example, is a measure of the messages' importance (the greater the depth, the more "viral" the message). Also, the total number of initial tweets (the degree of the root of the propagation tree) is another important factor. It is important to notice that propagation-based features are also related to the topic, not just to an individual tweet.

The classifier used in [16] was a binary J48 decision tree. It achieved an impressive accuracy of 86%. This is higher than the machine classifiers of webpage credibility. The reason for this success is the existence of topic-based and user-based features. Topic-based features express, as a whole, the behavior of a significant group of users, who all needed to make at least a surface credibility evaluation of the retweeted news. The aggregation of their behavioral indicators turns out to approximate the Wisdom of Crowds. This fact is apparent when we consider the main propagation-based feature: the depth of the retweet tree. This is a simple indicator of how many times Twitter users have made a positive evaluation of surface credibility.

Additionally, user-based features are what's missing in webpage credibility evaluation: an estimation of source trustworthiness and expertise. While this estimation is based on simple user-based features, the authors of [16] notice that credible news will be retweeted by users who have previously written a large number of messages and have many followers. This is proof of their expertise in evaluating news quality on Twitter, for which they need to have both high domain expertise and be highly trustworthy.

When considered separately, the various types of features (text-based, user-based, and propagation-based) have various importance for credibility evaluation. In their study, the researchers have trained classifiers separately on each of these groups of features. The group that achieved the highest accuracy was the group of

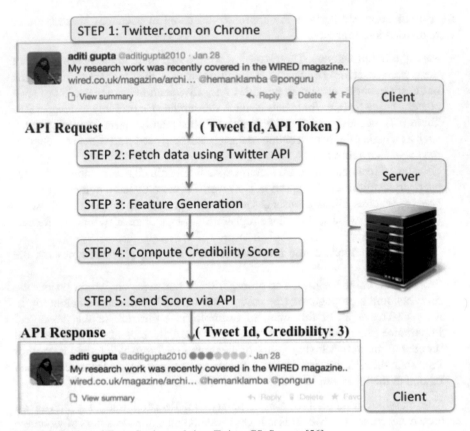

Fig. 4.1 Design of TweetCred, a real-time Twitter CS. Source: [56]

propagation-based features. Again, this seems to be related to the repeated positive surface credibility evaluations that a news message has to pass in order to propagate far on Twitter.

One of the challenges for credibility evaluation support on Twitter is that Twitter is a real-time service. Twitter users take a very short time to read a tweet and react (make a surface credibility evaluation, ignore, retweet, or choose another action). Recent work [56] has developed a working credibility evaluation support system for Twitter called TweetCred. TweetCred works in real time and gives automatic evaluations of every tweet using a machine classification algorithm.

The design of TweetCred is shown in Fig. 4.1. The browser extension works as a client for the TweetCred server and uses an API to forward an identifier of the tweet to be evaluated, along with a Twitter API token. This token allows the server to call the Twitter API and request information about the tweet and its source. This information is used by the server to compute tweet features used by the machine classifier. The result of the credibility classification of the tweet is returned by the server using TweetCred's API to the client (browser extension). The response time of the TweetCred service is under 10 s for 99% of the users in the tests reported in [56].

The machine classification algorithm for tweet credibility used by TweetCred uses features different than these used in [16], because of the restrictions imposed by TweetCred's real-time operation. It is not possible to calculate, for example, the propagation features used in [16] in a mere few seconds. On the other hand, the most important features used by TweetCred are related to the tweet itself (whether or not the tweet contains a URL, how long is the tweet, tweet age, number of retweets, etc.) and to the user that sent the tweet (whether the user has a profile, ratio of number of friends/number of followers, ratio of number of status change notifications/number of followers). The majority of the top features for assessing credibility of Twitter content were tweet-based features, rather than user features.

4.1.2.1 User Interface for a CS System for Twitter

Following the reference design of a credibility evaluation support system (see Sect. 3.1), a new user interface needs to be implemented for Twitter. One of the ways of doing this is through the creation of a bot account on Twitter. Such a bot account can reply to a user's request by a "Follow" action. The bot will then receive any tweet that the user makes. The bot can then use the Web Service interface to the CS and forward the tweet to the CS for credibility analysis. The tweet will then be treated like a statement, unless it includes a URL (then it is treated like a webpage). After receiving the results of the credibility analysis, the Twitter bot can reply to the user using a "Direct Message."

Another possibility is to use a browser plug-in, similarly to the browser plug-ins for evaluating webpages. The plug-in can display tweet credibility in a browser's toolbar or augment the Twitter interface. An example of such an approach is Tweet-Cred [56]. The user interface of TweetCred is shown in Fig. 4.2. The TweetCred CS displays automatic credibility evaluations for every tweet, on a 1–7 star scale, in real time.

The creators of TweetCred have evaluated their system with real Twitter users. When users were presented with an automatic credibility evaluation for a tweet done by TweetCred, they could choose whether they agreed or give their own evaluation of the tweet's credibility. Similarly to the experiments described in Sect. 3.9.1, TweetCred authors found that users only agreed with TweetCred's credibility score in about 40% of the cases. In the remaining 60%, Twitter users typically thought that the TweetCred score was too low. This once again demonstrates the existence and durability of a positive bias in credibility evaluation. Only 11% of the users thought that TweetCred's score should be lower, while 48% thought it should be higher.

Fig. 4.2 User interface of TweetCred, a real-time Twitter CS. Source: [56]

4.1.3   Controversy on Twitter

As it was mentioned in Sect. 2.2, an important function of credibility evaluation support is distinguishing between information that can have an agreed-upon credibility evaluation from controversial information. Moreover, information that does not have a verifiable ground truth (human beliefs that are not verifiable through everyday facts or specialist knowledge) can only be treated by credibility evaluation support tools similarly to controversial information. The only way to support credibility evaluation for controversial information or human beliefs without a ground truth is by supporting debate. For better or for worse, such information abounds on social media, especially on Twitter.

Controversies can receive wide coverage on Twitter very quickly. However, Smith et al. found in [172] that Twitter is primarily used for spreading information to like-minded people rather than debating issues. This demonstrates that there exists a pressing need for information technology for supporting debate, despite the popularity of social media. Users are quicker to rebroadcast information than to address a communication by another user. Individuals typically take a position on an issue prior to posting about it and are not likely to change their opinion. Yardi and Boyd [226] observed group dynamics on Twitter between pro-life and pro-choice groups related to a certain event and discovered both homophily and heterogeneity in conversations about abortion. People are exposed to broader viewpoints than they were before, but are limited in their ability to engage in meaningful discussion.

Researching controversies involving known entities in Twitter, Pennacchiotti and Popescu [141] used timely and historical controversy scores to classify controversy. They found that most controversies in Twitter refer to micro-events (e.g., TV shows, award shows, or sport events).

Recently (2015), Garimella et al. [47] used social media network structure on Twitter to invent a network-based controversy measure and showed that content features are less helpful in this task.

4.2 Credibility and Quality of Answers in Q&A Systems

Question and Answer (Q&A) systems, also referred to as Community-Based Q&A systems, are another type of Web-based social media that is clearly in need for credibility evaluation support. Q&A systems have certain special characteristics that make them a very attractive target of research on Web content credibility.

Compared to ordinary (Web 1.0) webpages, Q&A systems have the benefit of more structure and better focus. The content of Q&A systems is either a question or an answer. Moreover, good answers should be relevant to the question and therefore should not contain much unrelated content, which is a typical problem of credibility evaluation support for ordinary webpages. Last but not least, similarly to other social media, it is simple to identify the source of the content on Q&A systems and to compute the source's reputation (reputation is, in fact, a feature of most Q&A systems today).

Users of Q&A systems may have less motivation for deliberately falsifying answers. Compared to ordinary webpages, Q&A systems contain less spam. Recall from the definition of source credibility that it is a characteristic of the source that has two dimensions: a user's trustworthiness in the context of veracity and a user's expertise. Most research on Q&A systems has focused on evaluating the expertise of Q&A users.

Research on Q&A systems that is related to the problem of evaluating the credibility of an answer can be grouped into three categories, depending on the research problem. The three research problems considered in the literature have an increasing difficulty and can be described as follows:

1. Q&A Research Problem 1: Answer Credibility Ranking. Given a question and a set of relevant answers to that question from a Q&A system, rank the answers by their credibility.
2. Q&A Research Problem 2: Answer Relevance and Credibility Ranking. Given a question and a dataset of all questions and answers in the history of a Q&A

system, find the most relevant existing answers to the question, and rank them by their credibility and relevance.

3. Q&A Research Problem 3: Automatic Answer Construction. Given a question, a dataset of all questions and answers, and the entire Internet, formulate a credible answer to the question automatically.

Out of the three research problems, the first one is most closely related to Web content credibility evaluation. On the other hand, in the literature, the term "answer credibility" is rarely used, and "answer quality" is used instead. This may be due to a lack of terminological distinction and clarity in the research area. Since this book has introduced a precise definition of credibility, this term will be used instead of quality, as the credibility of an answer is clearly a dominant factor of answer quality.

The second research problem is related to the reuse of existing answers and is also an information retrieval problem. This problem has been recognized and studied in the IR research community for several years, also at TREC (1999–2006). The goal has always been to create a ranking of answers that would integrate relevance and quality (credibility). For this reason, an overview of this work will be given in this section.

The third research problem seems, on the surface, to be unrelated to Web content credibility evaluation. However, it is important to recognize that there exists an interesting (and up till now, unexplored) link between automatic question answering and credibility evaluation. The reason for this is that if there is a good algorithm for automatically answering a question, credibility evaluations of answers submitted by users of a Q&A system to that question can be carried out by comparing user-generated answers and the automatically generated answer. The existence of this link justifies an overview of the research on automatic question answering in this section, especially as this research has achieved impressive results (at TREC in 2007–2009, the accuracy of automatic question answering has reached 70%).

4.2.1 Ground Truth of Credibility Evaluation Support in Q&A Systems

Research on credibility evaluation support in Q&A systems has often used the fact that in these systems, answers (and questions) are evaluated by users. Typically, there are at least two ways in which a Q&A user may evaluate an answer. The asking user can mark an answer to his question at the "Best Answer." In addition, other users can upvote or downvote answers and questions.

However, while this feature is clearly a source of useful data, it raises questions regarding the ground truth of the credibility of answers. In the discussion of this topic, a point made in Sects. 2.3.4 and 2.1 is relevant—that the actual truthfulness of an answer may be distinct from the answer's credibility. From this point of view, user evaluations of answers are good material for ground truth of (surface or earned) message credibility evaluations, while they may be insufficient for evaluating an answer's objective truth (if this is theoretically possible). The main concern here can be stated as follows: are users who do not know the answer to a question themselves likely to give correct evaluations of answer veracity? This concern applies especially to the "Best Answer" evaluation. For some questions, this is clearly not the case (e.g., questions and answers on medical topics). On the other hand, for other types of answers, the verification of answer correctness may actually be quite simple and quick (such as for questions about programming on StackOverflow).

For this reason, in cases which require ground truth about the veracity of an answer, another approach must be used. This is the case, for example, for evaluating correctness of answers to factoid questions. Such an evaluation requires manual tagging of answers by experts. Datasets of questions with correct and incorrect answers exist, for example, the datasets from the TREC factoid question answering track.

"Best Answers" are a solid empirical foundation for modeling and predicting credibility of answers. Research has shown that past best answers to questions from various domains are frequently evaluated as best answers again, by new users [166]. This property can be exploited to improve Q&A systems by automatically replying to new questions with past best answers to similar questions. Q&A systems do not allow users to ask identical questions repeatedly (such questions are typically removed by the system or its administrators). Users are encouraged to search and read for answers to their question before posting it. However, this does not mean that similar questions are not asked repeatedly. The fact that the same best answer is evaluated as a best answer to a similar question shows that users' decisions are repeatable, and thus predictable.

On the other hand, users systematically evaluate answer credibility higher than experts. Evidence of such credibility bias has been found in the health domain [134]. This bias is quite similar to the bias of credibility evaluations of medical webpages, as demonstrated in Sect. 2.7. It turns out that at least in the medical domain, experts are much more critical than ordinary users in credibility evaluation not just for webpages but also answers to questions in Q&A systems. Positive bias of evaluations is, however, a general phenomenon on the Web [79, 92].

The actual veracity of answers to simple factual questions has also been evaluated by researchers who studied Q&A systems [140]. For this type of questions, users have a relatively high correctness of about 80% (however, the reference level is 50%, since simple factoids are either correct or incorrect). This finding confirms the value of Q&A systems, but also shows that there exists a scope for their improvement. It should also be stressed that the correct answers are not necessarily produced by a single user. When a question is asked, it frequently first receives answers that do not provide any arguments for or against a claim, or answers that do not resolve the issue. This is especially the case for questions on controversial topics, where first answers do not resolve the question in over 70% of the cases [157]. Subsequent answers are given by users who have read the previous answers, which means that they can take these answers into account. Even for non-controversial topics, the quality of individual answers varies significantly, even though the quality of answers is good on average [73, 180].

4.2.2   Answer Credibility Evaluation and Ranking

Investigations of answers to a single question point to the conclusion that both answering the question and evaluation of answers are collaborative processes. The final choice of a "Best Answer" is therefore not just dependent on the judgment of the asking user, who may, for example, take into account the number of upvotes of an answer, or simply compare the answers to one another. Even so, many factually irrelevant factors have significant positive impact on the credibility perception of Q&A system users. One such factor is timeliness: earlier answers have significantly higher probability to be chosen as "Best Answers" [166]. Other factors are politeness and confidence, which have been found important in the medical domain [134].

Even factors such as wit may have impact on "Best Answer" selection. Consider the following question from a real Q&A system: "What is the solution to the equation $x^2 - 4x + 5 = 0$?" The asking user received many factually correct replies, but selected the following "Best Answer": "I think you should figure it out for yourself. When people give you the answer it's called cheating, love."

In order to predict answer credibility, measured by presence of "Best Answer" labels, supervised machine learning approaches have been used. Many different features, both textual and non-textual, have been proposed to evaluate answer quality. The significant features of an answer include [9, 191]:

1. Textual overlap or similarity of question and answer
2. Number of comments for answer
3. Number of upvotes and downvotes for answer
4. Simple statistical features, such as length and counts of parts of speech
5. NLP features such as readability and sentiment polarity

However, answer credibility may also be predicted by the source credibility of the answering user. The following features are significant for user source credibility in Q&A systems:

1. Number of answers posted
2. Number of best answers
3. Upvote/downvote ratio
4. Indegree and outdegree in answering graph, where a link between users u_1 and u_2 exists if user u_2 answered a question of user u_1
5. HITS hub score and authority score in answering graph
6. Number of questions asked by the user

The last feature, number of questions asked by the user, is related to learning that also occurs in Q&A system communities. By asking questions and receiving answers, users learn from each other; therefore, a user who has asked many questions can have a significantly higher source credibility when she will be giving an answer. Evidence of learning behavior in Q&A systems has been demonstrated in recent research [197].

Because answering a question is a collaborative process, the quality of the answer will also depend on question features:

1. Subject length
2. Question length
3. Time of posing
4. Number of stars
5. Number of answers

Several approaches have been proposed to predict answer credibility. One of the most successful was an approach that has used hierarchical classifiers [191]. In the proposed approach, the first stage was the classification of the question type. Six question types have been considered: Definition, Factoid, Opinion, Procedure, Reason, and Yes/No. Using lexical features and syntax-driven semantic features, questions were assigned to one of these classes. In each class, a separate classifier attempted to predict answer credibility for a question.

Answer types were classified into two classes, Good or Bad, using simple statistical or NLP answer features and similarity between question and answer, but without using source credibility features of answering users. The achieved accuracy varied depending on the question type, but on average was approximately 80%. The worst two classes were the Factoid and Yes/No classes. This is not surprising since the classifiers relied only on answer features, and answers in these two categories were most likely short and hard to evaluate using NLP or statistical answer features.

4.2.3   Finding the Most Relevant and Credible Answers

Research on retrieving the most relevant and credible answers is significantly older than research on evaluating an answer's credibility. First research on this question dates back to 1999, when the Text REtrieval Conferences (TREC) have started a track on question answering[3][201].

An interesting approach to this problem, which can also be used for evaluating answer credibility, has been proposed by Bian et al. [9]. Recognizing the fact that because of user collaboration and learning, answer credibility is actually linked to question quality, the researchers have proposed a reinforcement algorithm that simultaneously estimates four values: answer quality, question quality, reputation of a user in the context of answer quality, and reputation of the user in the context of question quality. The four values are defined as follows [9]:

1. Answer quality: a summary of accuracy, comprehensiveness, and responsiveness of an answer
2. Question quality: the ability of a question to attract high-quality answers

---

[3]http://trec.nist.gov/data/qa.html.

3. Reputation in the context of answer quality: user reputation that indicates the expected quality of an answer from that user
4. Reputation in the context of question quality: user reputation that indicates the expected quality of a question from that user

The reinforcement algorithm works by assuming that answer reputation can be calculated from answer qualities, and question reputation can be calculated from question qualities. Logistic regression is used to predict the quality of an answer or question based on above mentioned answer and question features, as well as the reputations of the users. Next, the reputations are calculated, and another iteration of the algorithm starts. Iteration continues until all values converge.

The algorithm has been shown to perform well for predicting question quality (manually labeled). The algorithm's performance for retrieving high-quality answers has been evaluated using TREC datasets. Precision of retrieving a best answer in the top five answers drops to 50%. As it was mentioned, solutions to the first Q&A research problem of evaluating answer credibility have achieved an 80% accuracy for binary answer credibility evaluation. If there was a good algorithm for selecting relevant answers, the probability of correctly classifying credibility of three out of five most relevant answers would be about $0.8^3 = 0.512$, a value close to the results achieved by the reinforcement algorithm.

4.2.4   Automatic Answering of Questions

The problem of automatic answering of questions has been considered in Information Retrieval research since the 1960s [91], but it has gained in popularity in 2007, when the TREC introduced a special track on the subject. A comprehensive review of the area can be found in [91]. Various methods of this area can be jointly described as a series of steps:

1. Natural language question processing to form a query representation
2. Document processing into knowledge representation stored in a knowledge base
3. Querying of knowledge bases using structured or logical queries obtained from the natural language question
4. Ordering of retrieved knowledge by relevance to query using a relevance function
5. Formulating the answer in natural language

Various approaches differ by their knowledge and query representation, from simple representations such as a bag of words to complex ones such as a semantic Web representation. Vector space models, probabilistic models, SQL models, and logical models are different examples of knowledge representation used in automatic query answering.

Research on question answering follows a perspective that centers on information retrieval. An assumption is made in this research that makes it independent of credibility evaluation: that the knowledge base consists of only credible information.

Once this assumption is made, the problem reduces to a problem of determining the relevant information, as well as processing natural language (interpreting the question, constructing the answer).

The difference between automatic answer construction (Q&A Research Problem 3) and answer relevance and credibility ranking (Q&A Research Problem 2) lies in the knowledge representation. In the case of answer ranking, knowledge is simply represented as answers to questions, and the goal is to find an answer constructed by a human that matches as new question. For automatic answer construction, knowledge is usually represented in a more complex way, and a ready answer created by a human may not be available. Therefore, after the most relevant knowledge is retrieved for a new question, the answer must still be constructed in natural language.

The type of knowledge representation and semantic analysis used to retrieve relevant knowledge depends on the type of the question. For factual questions, representations of questions and potential answers can capture rather shallow semantics (e.g., using named entity recognition). On the other hand, for questions that inquire about procedures ("How" questions) and questions that inquire about reasons ("Why" questions), knowledge related to events and discourse should be extracted and represented. Special representations may be required to answer temporal and spatial questions—in these cases, representations may use specialized logics.

As mentioned above, automatic answer construction methods might be of use for credibility evaluation of new answers in a Q&A system. Automatically constructed answers, or even intermediate knowledge retrieved for a new question, may be compared to new answers in order to evaluate their credibility. Such an approach is a promising direction of future work.

4.2.5   Summary of State of the Art in Q&A Credibility Evaluation

Because of its unique context, the question-answer relation, as well as an increased significance of expertise evaluation, Q&A credibility evaluation poses unique research problems. However, this problem also has similarities to credibility evaluation of other social media, as the identity of the source is more easily established, and more information on the source is available. This fact increases the importance of reputation systems that can be used to evaluate a Q&A system's user expertise and source credibility.

Exploiting the semantic similarity of questions and answers, as well as the possibility of using more Question and Answer-related metadata, improves the ability to evaluate answer credibility. Nevertheless, there still remains a lot of room for improvement of current systems. On the other hand, algorithms for retrieving or even automatically constructing an answer to a question exist and have been researched since the 1990s. Unfortunately, these algorithms all rely on the assumptions that they are using only credible information. Therefore, it is not clear at present how research on answer retrieval or construction can be reused to evaluate answer credibility.

4.3   Quality, Credibility, and Controversy of Wikipedia Articles

For many Web users, Wikipedia is the starting point of search for factual or encyclopedic information on the Web. As the largest, multilingual, continuously updated online encyclopedia, Wikipedia is one of the most important information sources on the Web. For this reason, the credibility of Wikipedia content is a subject that cannot be ignored by credibility research.

Moreover, Wikipedia is a Web 2.0 (social) medium. It is created, updated, maintained, and managed by a community of users. The Wikipedia knowledge community has been an inspiration for entrepreneurs, practitioners, and managers worldwide [216]. This community can be considered the most developed and mature Web 2.0 community and is, therefore, the object of intense study conducted by researchers wishing to learn how to improve the designs of socially centered Web platforms. The Wikipedia knowledge community is one of the best examples of how collective intelligence can be achieved on the Web [102]. Much of this research is relevant towards an understanding of how the community of Wikipedia users evaluates and improves the credibility of Wikipedia content.

4.3.1   Ground Truth for Wikipedia Article Credibility

Wikipedia credibility is a subject of ongoing controversy since the increase of the popularity of Wikipedia. In a famous study in 2005, the journal *Nature* compared the accuracy of scientific articles from Wikipedia and from the Encyclopaedia Britannica.[4] The study used a blinded review of articles from the two sources on the same subject. The results were that the number of serious factual errors identified in the two sources was similar. While the *Nature* article was criticized by Britannica, *Nature* rebutted the objections and did not retract the article.

Since then, the accuracy of Wikipedia articles has been tested in several domains. Wikipedia itself takes its own correctness very seriously, and several efforts have been made by the Wikipedia community (and Wikimedia foundation) to evaluate reliability of Wikipedia articles.[5]

---

[4]http://www.nature.com/nature/journal/v438/n7070/full/438900a.html.

[5]https://en.wikipedia.org/wiki/Reliability_of_Wikipedia.

Wikipedia is a Web 2.0 medium and a knowledge community. This community has established its own rules and procedures of Wikipedia article evaluation. These procedures are continually evolving, but they can be used to establish ground truth of Wikipedia article credibility.

Currently, the most reliable procedure for Wikipedia article quality evaluation is the community's own classification. Each article on the English Wikipedia can be assigned by community members into one of several classes[6]: Stub, Start, C, B, or A. The highest class, A, means a complete article with encyclopedic quality. A separate assessment procedure that requires an external review can give an article a "good article" (GA) or "featured article" (FA) grade. According to Wikipedia, in March 2017, there were 4970 featured articles on English language Wikipedia (about 0.1%).[7] The number of good articles is larger, around 25,000 (about 0.5%).

Another, discontinued method of evaluating Wikipedia article quality was the Article Feedback Tool (AFT).[8] This tool followed an approach used in many types of credibility evaluation support systems. Article readers could rate the article using one of several criteria: trustworthiness, objectivity, completeness, and quality of writing. The evaluation used a star rating (see Sect. 2.5.1). The data gathered using the AFT is still available for research, even though the use of the AFT has been discontinued.

4.3.2   Modeling Wikipedia Article Credibility

The Wiki editing model has a strong impact on the quality of the produced content. Wikipedia has a set of standards and rules that govern how the Wiki editing model should be utilized to maintain its reliability and integrity. There have been some attempts in assessing the source credibility of information by analyzing edit histories of articles written by particular authors.

One of the most popular reputation systems basing on Wikipedia edit history is WikiTrust [2], a system for assessing the credibility of content and author reputation. It enables users of MediaWiki software (which runs Wikipedia) to get information about an origin, author, and reliability of each fragment of article text. It basically works by promoting stable content, the fragments of text which stay unmodified across edits of an article. Such article edits are regarded as "reviews." Authors of stable article content are further promoted by assigning them higher reputation score, which in turn gives better scores for the reviewed content, and so on. There has been some criticism [117] whether such an approach measures credibility, mainly because this simple algorithm is easy to exploit and it strongly discourages authors from participating in writing on controversial topics.

---

[6]https://en.wikipedia.org/wiki/Wikipedia:WikiProject_assessment.

[7]https://en.wikipedia.org/wiki/Wikipedia:Featured_articles.

[8]https://en.wikipedia.org/wiki/Wikipedia:Article_Feedback_Tool.

Other, similar system called *QuWi* has been proposed by Cusinato et al. [23]. It is a framework for quality control in Wikipedia basing on the proposal of Mizzaro [122], a method for complementing peer review in scholarly publishing. They adopted the method to the Wiki system, with particular attention to the fact that authors contribute identifiable pieces of information that can be further modified by other authors. Similarly to WikiTrust, the algorithm assigns quality scores to articles and reputation to contributors. The articles' ranks may be used, for example, to let the reader know how reliable is the text he or she is looking at, or to help contributors in identifying low-quality articles to be enhanced. The users' reputation measures the average quality of their contributions and can be used, for example, for conflict resolution policies based on the quality of involved users. The proposed algorithm is further evaluated by analyzing the obtained quality scores on articles for deletion and featured articles, also on six temporal Wikipedia snapshots. The results show that this algorithm seems to appropriately identify high- and low-quality articles and that high-quality authors produce more long-lived contributions than low-quality authors.

Wöhner and Peters [218] proposed a different approach to solve the problem of assessing quality. Instead of evaluating the source credibility, they have looked at the edit histories of featured articles and articles marked for deletion. They examined the entire life cycle from its creation to the moment of assigning one of the quality measures. To simplify the model, the authors looked at the articles' revisions in monthly intervals. They have found metrics, which classify well the content quality basing on the persistence of contributions. High-quality articles have significantly higher persistence of revisions (the higher number of changes that persist between the examined revisions). The article metrics found as best in quality evaluation are as follows:

- Maximum persistent contributions
- Mean persistent contributions
- Sum of numbers of persistent contributions from the last 3 months
- Article length

Additionally, the authors discovered that the number of edits (both persistent and transient) is significantly higher in 3 months before nomination for featured article. In the case of worse-quality articles, usually no significant peaks in the number of edits were observed.

4.3.3   Modeling Wikipedia Article Controversy

The very first paper devoted to the problem of cooperation and conflict between editors on Wikipedia was published in 2004 by Viégas et al. [199]. Authors developed a tool for visualizing the patterns of conflict using history of edits. Based on similar meta-information (i.e., number of edits, unique editors, and anonymous edits), Stvilia et al. [179] measured articles' quality. Buriol et al. [14] studied conflicts in Wikipedia focusing on reverting edits between authors.

Wikipedia edits are organized around the concept of "revision." Editors make changes in an article and publish a new version (aka revision). Current revision may always be reverted (by everyone). The whole history of revisions is accessible on Wikipedia. Repeating mutual reverts leads to edit wars and usually indicates existence of controversy (or at least argument about some facts). Edit wars were in-depth studied by Sumi et al. in [181] and [182]. Not all edit wars are non-constructive. Yasseri et al. [227] identified mutual reverts that lead to consensus and those remaining in permanent controversy.

A broad spectrum of accessible meta-information about editors' behaviors may be used for detecting which article is controversial. Vuong et al. proposed two controversy ranking models for Wikipedia articles drawing from the history of collaboration and edits [204]. Kittur et al. [88] proposed a very good method based on edits dynamics and talk pages. Recently, Rad and Barbosa [146] compared different methods for detecting controversy (some of them are based on properties of collaboration network). This work has been extended by Jankowski-Lorek et al. [72].

Sentiment analysis has proven to be very efficient in many applications, including predicting outcome of political elections [156, 195, 208], stock companies valuation [34], or e-commerce review analysis [129, 206], but is not very common in Wikipedia research. Among over 2000 articles focusing on the Wikipedia, Okoli et al. [135] identified only few that apply sentiment analysis. Wikiganda [19] looked for propaganda in controversial Wikipedia articles by measuring sentiment in single revision of articles. Ferschke et al. [37] analyzed sentiment of talk pages of Simple English Wikipedia for dialog acts, with the goal to identify successful patterns of collaboration which increase the article quality. Laniado et al. [98] focused on analyzing the emotional styles of Wikipedia editors. Finally, Dori-Hacohen and Allan [27] used sentiment as a baseline for detecting controversy on the Web and compared these results with method based on tagged corpus of articles from Wikipedia. Wikipedia has received a lot of attention from the researchers especially in the field of social behavior and content quality. In contrast to studies about conflicts, Borzymek et al. [13], Turek et al. [196], and Wierzbicki et al. [214] studied collaboration and teamwork based on Wikipedia social network.

Wikipedia has previously been successfully used as a data source for semantic information retrieval to improve the results from search engines and to create categorization of texts. The Wikipedia category graph (WCG) was used in researches to improve an ad hoc document retrieval [81], identifying document category [158], and acquiring knowledge [128]. Medelyan et al. [115] published an extensive overview of researches that mines Wikipedia. In 2006, Voss [202] called the category structure a collaborative thesaurus. The structured form of Wikipedia categories allowed for automated learning of ontology [228]. Kittur et al. [90] used WCG to detect contentious topics in Wikipedia using annotated data. Recently, Biuk-Aghai et al. [10] made an attempt to visualize human collaboration in Wikipedia. They visualized WCG subtrees by transforming them into simple trees.

In search for controversial topics inside Wikipedia articles, Borra et al. [12] developed a tool called Contropedia. A controversy score is assigned to every Wiki link and then is presented graphically as controversy dashboard, showing both the score of the Wiki link and the associated timeline of edits. The method is language agnostic.

4.4 Fake News Detection in Social Media

The problem of fake news detection is probably as old as human civilization, but has gained in prominence since the 2016 American presidential election. Following the election, many media experts and political commentators have expressed the belief that Donald Trump would not have been elected president were it not for the influence of fake news [4]. The difference lies not in the use of fake news, but in the massive proliferation and strong influence of fake news on Internet-based social media. There, most popular fake news are more widely shared than in mainstream media. Also, they tend to influence opinions of news consumers as strongly (or stronger) than news propagated using mainstream media [4, 167].

This situation demonstrates the pressing need of developing technical means for the detection of fake news on social media. The problem of fake news detection is another instance of the problem of Web content credibility evaluation support. In other words, a system for fake news detection would be a credibility evaluation support (CS) system. However, the problem of fake news detection has its own special characteristics and significantly raises the difficulty of ordinary credibility evaluation support.

In order to understand the reasons for the difficulty of fake news detection, let us begin with a definition of fake news. While many definitions of fake news have been used in the literature [188], Shu et al. propose the following definition [167]:

Fake news is a news article that is intentionally and verifiably false.

Notice that the insistence on the possibility of verifying fake news (in other words, the requirement of ground truth existence and availability) limits the scope of Web content and social media messages that can be considered as fake news. For instance, conspiracy theories are not considered fake news, because they cannot be verified. (On the other hand, fake news may be related to a conspiracy theory, such as fake news related to "Pizzagate"—see Sect. 1.2.2.) This distinction is similar to the distinction of types of information that are associated with different concepts of truth in Sect. 2.2. On the other hand, the definition of fake news requires that the fake news be "intentionally false." This implies the existence of an adversary, a content producer (and distributor) who intends to disseminate fake news because it fulfills his objective. This situation has already been discussed in Sect. 3.2 that dealt with adversaries of CS systems.

Fake news detection is a research area that has recently gained in popularity. Approaches used today are similar to approaches discussed in this book. They can be divided into two groups, based on news content features and social context features [167]. Previous research on detecting fake reviews and opinion spam has resulted in textual methods that have an accuracy of over 80%. Such methods have been reviewed in Sect. 3.7, together with automatic fact-checking methods. The reader may also recall methods for automatic answering of questions discussed in Sect. 4.2.4 that are relevant for automatic-fact checking, as well. Many of these methods have been applied for fake news detection [22].

On the other hand, social context features depend on the meta-information available on social media, as discussed in Sect. 4.1. User-based, post-based, and network-based features can be extracted from meta-information on Twitter or Facebook and can significantly aid in fake news detection [187]. However, they are a double-edged sword.

The real difficulty of the problem of fake news detection lies in the fact that it needs to be done quickly. Consider fake news spreading on Twitter. If we allow news to reach thousands of Twitter users, the pattern of their retweets and associated meta-information will enable us to reach a decision whether the news is fake or not [219]. Behavior of users during the proliferation of fake news leads to behavioral patterns that are easy to detect, such as conflict or controversy [74].

However, it may be too late. When fake news reaches a significant number of social media users, it becomes amplified due to an "echo chamber effect": users who agree with the fake news tend to follow each other and will continue to discuss and share this fake news frequently. Based on the frequency heuristic, users naturally favor news that they hear frequently, even if it is fake. This leads to a positive bias in the evaluation of fake news' credibility. Psychological studies have shown that presenting convinced users with factual information that contradicts fake news may not reduce, but sometimes even increases fake news credibility, especially in ideological groups [132].

Therefore, fake news detection on social media should be fast, preferably in real time (as soon as fake news occurs). Researchers have observed that on Twitter, the time between the proliferation of fake news and the moment when debunking information based on fact-checking starts to spread is from 10 to 20 h [162]. This means that any automatic solution that wishes to improve the current situation should work faster than that.

Fast reaction to fake news on social media can be achieved based on news content features. These can be linguistic or even stylometric [22, 153, 167] (see Sect. 3.7). Analysis of title structure and linguistic traits of fake news has discovered notable patterns: fake news has sensational titles, but repetitive content that is more similar to satire than real news [66, 153]. On the other hand, some evidence suggests that stylometric methods are effective for detecting partisanship, but less effective when detecting fake news [145].

Several approaches attempt to use knowledge-based analysis of news content, in order to detect contradictions with established knowledge bases [21, 58, 165]. The problem, then, becomes reduced to the establishment and maintenance of a high-quality knowledge base. This problem is not yet solved today, although several approaches exist, such as DBpedia and the Google Relation Extraction

Corpus (GREC). As a matter of fact, using Wikipedia itself seems like a promising approach towards fake news detection in the future. As discussed in the previous section, Wikipedia credibility is continuously evaluated by Wikipedia users, editors, and admins using several established procedures. There also exist many tools that support Wikipedia article credibility evaluation. Moreover, Wikipedia (unlike traditional encyclopedias) is updated very quickly, especially concerning newsworthy subjects (e.g., the news of Michael Jackson's death was reported on Wikipedia less than 2 h after the event [9]).

A fast method that bases on content is so-called "clickbait" detection. This method relies on the fact that fake news typically have headlines or titles that provoke readers to click on them. However, these titles or headlines often have little to do with the rest of the news content. Rather, they are designed to generate reader interest. The dissimilarity between the heading and the content and a "tabloid style" of the heading are symptoms of "clickbaiting" that can be exploited for fake news detection [18, 20, 51, 162].

The observed accuracy of fake news detection methods depends on the dataset used for evaluation (see Sect. 2.6.5 for an overview of fake news datasets). For expert-based datasets such as LIAR or FakeNewsNet (obtained from PolitiFact), accuracies of state-of-the-art algorithms are between 84% and 89% [168]. However, this high accuracy is obtained using a combination of content features and social context features (including behavioral features from Twitter). Methods that use only content features (and are therefore capable of real-time operation) have a much lower accuracy: 60–70%.

Methods based on automatic fact-checking are harder to evaluate because of the lack of non-credible fact examples. For example, Ciampaglia et al. use a graph-based algorithm based on a knowledge network from DBpedia to verify correctness of statements from the Google Relation Extraction Corpus (GREC) [21]. The performance of their algorithm is evaluated by rank-order correlation coefficients between scores assigned by reviewers for the GREC and algorithm output. The Kendall and Spearman correlation is non-zero, but quite low (9–17%). Other automated fact-checking algorithms have used rumors from Snopes.com as negative examples and have collected external information using Google [144]. The authors reported an accuracy of 80% of their algorithm.

A benchmark for fake news detection does not currently exist. The closest to a benchmark could be a SemEval-2017 task[10] [25] or the Fake News Challenge.[11] However, the latter has only published one task so far (in 2017), which was the task of stance detection. Compared to this, the SemEval-2017 task "RumourEval" had two parts: one of stance detection and the other of rumor veracity. The results of the latter part of the SemEval-2017 task are quite disappointing. None of

---

[9]http://moz.com/blog/a-bad-day-for-search-engines-how-news-of-michael-jacksons-death-traveled-across-the-web.
[10]SemEval-2017 Task 8: RumourEval: Determining rumour veracity and support for rumours.
[11]http://www.fakenewschallenge.org/.

the participating teams reached the baseline accuracy. However, only one team participated in the open variant of the task that could use external resources (all other teams only participated in the variant that used only resources provided by SemEval).

To summarize, fake news detection on social media is an emerging research area that can benefit from previous research on Web content credibility evaluation support. The significance of the problem of fake news detection highlights the overall importance of research on Web content credibility evaluation. Many approaches have been proposed for fake news detection; however, while progress has been made, a satisfactory solution is not yet available.

Chapter 5
Theoretical Models of Credibility

As far as the laws of mathematics refer to reality, they are not certain, and as far as they are certain, they do not refer to reality.
Albert Einstein

This chapter describes a theoretical model of Web content credibility evaluation, based on game theory and the notion of a signal. The chapter describes the analysis of the game-theoretic model and its later extensions that are studied using social simulation. Extensions include considering reputation of content providers for credibility judgments and the phenomenon of learning that affects the accuracy of consumer's credibility judgments. The introduced models are used to study the global effect of credibility evaluation support on strategies of content producers and consumers.

Research on supporting Web content credibility evaluation requires models for evaluation and study of adversary strategies. Such models overcome certain disadvantages of empirical evaluation of credibility evaluation support methods. Models can consider diverse what-if scenarios, such as adversary strategies against credibility evaluation methods. Models also remove limitations of scale and allow to study global impact of credibility evaluation support. An example of a new feature of textual Web content being empirically found to improve the correctness of credibility evaluations by 30% can be set forth. Researchers would in such a case be faced with the following questions: What would be the impact of the improved credibility evaluation on the behavior of content producers? Would the possible changes in content producer behavior be sustainable? Such questions are another example of a what-if scenario that cannot be studied without models of credibility evaluation.

A model of credibility evaluation should achieve the right balance between generality (simplicity) and detail. A model that is unable to express important aspects of the problem will not be suitable. Aspects that should be captured include properties of content, for example, quality of presentation or degree of language persuasiveness, economic incentives of adversaries, and credibility

© Springer International Publishing AG, part of Springer Nature 2018
A. Wierzbicki, *Web Content Credibility*,
https://doi.org/10.1007/978-3-319-77794-8_5

assessment capabilities of Web content users. These properties are not captured by models typically used to study trust management or reputation systems (which are frequently based on game theory, such as the Prisoner's Dilemma [5]).

On the other hand, multi-agent models that are often used for studying the behavior of adversaries may be too detailed and are often designed specifically to study a particular algorithm or method. The goal of this chapter is to present a comprehensive yet general and flexible model of how Web content credibility is determined by Web content producers and evaluated by Web content consumers. This model is based on game theory, allowing to find analytical solutions to its simpler versions. When required, the model can be used as a basis of a multi-agent simulation that allows to study evolutionarily stable equilibria [155].

The most related work in game theory concerns persuasion games [50, 164]. Earlier work used the Prisoner's Dilemma to model credibility [57]. Persuasion games can be thought of as models for a situation when one agent tries to convince the other to make a certain decision by communicating certain information about the states of the world that will affect a receiver's decision. The receiver (listener) must have his own rule for making a decision based on the statements. It has been shown that in the theoretical model, optimal and deterministic persuasion rules can be found [50]. However, persuasion games do not take into account any properties of the communicated information that may affect the decision of the receiver. These games also do not sufficiently express the preferences of the sender (speaker) regarding the receiver's decisions. For example, it is not possible to differentiate between an honest and dishonest sender.

For these reasons, the model presented in this chapter bases on a new kind of game called the Credibility Game. The model's design follows the basic structure of Shannon's Information Theory [161]: the game is played by two asymmetric players, a sender and a receiver. The sender communicates information, and the decision that the receiver has to make is whether to accept or reject this information. In this aspect, the Credibility Game is simpler than persuasion games where the receiver's decision concerned an action, and the outcomes of this action could depend on complex states of the world. The main difference, however, lies in the ability of our model to take into account various properties of the communicated information that will affect both the receiver's decision and the outcome of this decision.

The Credibility Game is a signaling game. This means that the receiver will be able to evaluate received information without knowing its properties (which are known to the sender), by examining a signal that depends on the properties of information but includes random noise. This approach, frequently used in game theory, is another basic type of model that can be also used for credibility evaluation. In short, every credibility evaluation can be modeled as the evaluation of a signal. This also means that credibility is modeled by the signal. For this reason, before introducing the Credibility Game, the next section of this chapter deals with signal-based credibility models. Section 5.2 introduced the Credibility Game and presents results of its analysis. An economic model of a Web content producer is presented that is the basis of the payoffs of the game. In Sect. 5.3, the Credibility Game is extended with reputation. The resulting model is studied using a multi-agent simulation, enabling to discover the model's evolutionary equilibria. Section 5.5 presents a modified version of the iterated Credibility Game where players have two roles (both of a producer and consumer of information). This modified version is used to model online knowledge communities where information is shared (such as in online Q&A systems). Using this modified model, it is possible to study how credibility evaluation influences the global learning processes of the community.

Before describing the Credibility Game, in the next section, a simpler model of surface message credibility is presented that is in complete agreement with the definition of credibility proposed in this book. In Chap. 2, the definition of message credibility was proposed for the sake of this publication: message credibility is a signal. In the next section, a mathematical model of this signal is presented; moreover, this model can be fitted to empirical data. This ability gives further support to the usefulness of the concept of signal in modeling credibility. Next, this concept will be used in signaling versions of the Credibility Game.

5.1   Signal-Based Credibility Models

Surface credibility (see Sect. 2.3.3) is one of the most important types of credibility in credibility research. The reasons for this fact are simple: many online systems for Web content quality or credibility evaluation work based on voluntary ratings from ordinary Web users. These users usually do not spend much time on credibility or quality evaluation. Reminding the definition of surface credibility, "Surface credibility is derived from a superficial examination of the message by the receiver. It is a first impression of message credibility. Evaluating surface credibility requires little time and effort on behalf of the receiver." This definition fits, to a large degree, the evaluations obtained from a crowd of volunteers in a credibility evaluation service such as WOT or others.

It is frequent to assume that ratings given on a selected scale need to be aggregated from many users in order to achieve a single result. However, this raises methodological concerns: various users may have a different understanding of the evaluation scale (and hence, differing skews in their evaluation). In this section, an alternative, theoretical approach will be presented—one that makes a basic assumption that users make superficial evaluations of Web content based on a *signal*. This assumption fits surface credibility evaluation.

Signal-based models do not assume that the signal is on a single, predefined scale for all evaluators. The values of the signal from two different users are never compared directly. Rather, a single user will compare signal values for two different webpages. Based on this comparison, the user will be able to tell which webpage is more credible (on the surface) than the other. Signal-based models aim to approximate the distribution of a signal for a single webpage. These distributions can then be used to predict results of comparisons among webpages with a certain probability. The results presented in this section are based on [94].

Signal-based credibility models have a powerful expressive capability. The signal can reflect several features of the webpage that a user can take into account in surface credibility evaluation. Moreover, signals of various users can differ depending on user characteristics, such as credulity or expertise. These abilities of signal-based credibility models will be exploited further in the next section of this chapter.

This section aims to define a signal-based credibility model and to show to what extent empirical data of credibility evaluations can be used to estimate the signal. The ability to do so is important, because it means that algorithms and methods for credibility evaluation support can be evaluated based on a credibility model that can be fitted to real empirical data.

5.1.1   Normalized Random Utility Signal Model

The signal model of surface credibility introduced in this section is based on the Normalized Random Utility Model (NRUM) with varied variation [139]. In NRUM, each choice of a participant among two objects is expressed as using two random variables from two normal distributions (one for each compared object) and making decision according to which of the random variables has a greater/lower value. Normal distributions are defined by mean and standard deviation and are assigned to each object. In this study, each webpage will be described using such a model.

The signal can be situated on a different scale for each user, and is influenced by all webpage features that can have an impact on user's evaluation, as well as by user's characteristics. In this section, a method of estimating such a signal from crowdsourced evaluations is described. The estimated signal can be used for predicting new evaluations to achieve better results compared to several benchmarks.

Fitting of a signal-based model to crowdsourced evaluation results allows for a better understanding of the evaluation process. In other words, it is possible to discover what is behind the ratings in order to better describe objects (webpages). The estimated signal for each webpage not only allows for better comparison but can be used to study the degree of uncertainty or disagreement generated by the webpage or to estimate webpage features that have an impact on users' evaluations (Fig. 5.1).

Random Utility Models are economic models [114, 190] also used for choice and preference problem [139]. They model situations of choice or user preferences using random variables from two distributions, one for each compared object.

Two traditional Random Utility Models are Plackett-Luce RUM [143, 176] and **Normal RUM**. Within Normal RUM, some methods use the same variation for all normal distributions [109, 190], while others allow the variation to differ [139]. In this section, the latter approach will be employed.

The NRUM expresses the signal for each webpage as a random variable from the normal distribution $N(\mu_i, \sigma_i)$, where:

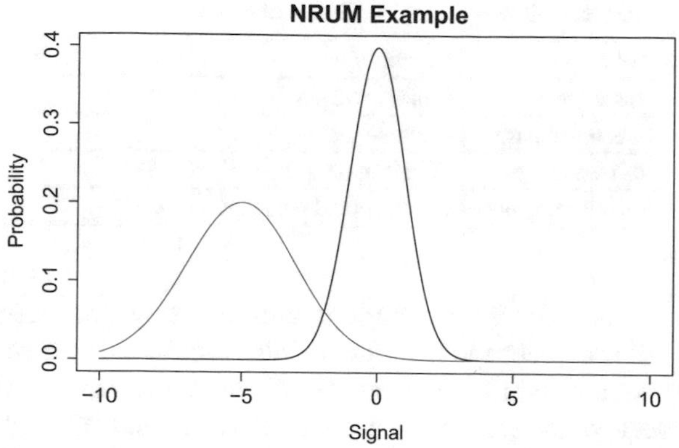

Fig. 5.1 NRUM example with differing variances. If it is assumed that the respondent chooses an object with a signal that has a higher mean (x-axis), the object modeled by the black signal distribution has a higher probability of being chosen than the object modeled by the red signal distribution. Source: [94]

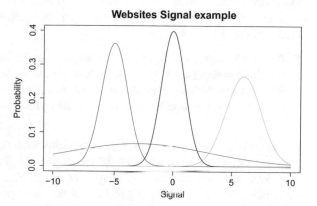

Fig. 5.2 Signal probability distributions for four artificial webpages

- μ_i is the mean of signal for the webpage i. In this model, the signal mean is affected only by the surface credibility of the webpage.
- σ_i is the standard deviation of signal for the webpage i, which can be affected by evaluation uncertainty, difficulty, or webpage controversy.

Therefore, such a model describes webpages with two values—their mean surface credibility and the standard deviation of surface credibility.

5.1.1.1 NRUM Signal Model Example

A simple example serves to visualize this model and to display the model's applications:

there are four webpages—Black, Green, Red, and Purple. An evaluation must be provided for these websites with no knowledge about them. Crowdsourcing users are asked to rate these webpages (using a 5-point scale). Next, the NRUM signal model is fitted to the obtained evaluation data, which leads to the signal distributions for each webpage shown in Fig. 5.2.

Table 5.1 Signal models for four artificial webpages

Color	Description	Mean (credibility)	St. deviation (uncertainty)
Black webpage	Neutral webpage	0	1
Green webpage	Credible webpage	6	1.5
Red webpage	Mendacious webpage	−5	1.1
Purple webpage	Controversial webpage	−3	6

The "Green" webpage is almost always preferred over the "Red" one. The "Black" webpage is in the middle (usually getting worse ratings than the "Green" one and better than the "Red" one) and the "Purple" webpage is receiving very varied ratings—it wins even versus the "Green" webpage sometimes, but is generally worse than the "Black" webpage (Table 5.1).

The webpages in this example may be categorized with regard to surface credibility in the following way:

- **Neutral webpage**, some regular webpage from the Internet
- **Credible webpage**, a highly rated webpage that is known for its credibility
- **Mendacious webpage**, an obvious scam or false information
- **Controversial webpage**, with very varied opinions—like alternative medicine, etc.

This model is useful especially for describing such "Controversial" webpages—they can receive better scores even for webpages commonly known as credible, but only from some specific group of people (or on the other hand, some webpages can be credible for the majority of people, but for some groups are not). Aggregating such ratings by mean or median will describe them as similar to "neutral" webs, and this valuable information about them will be lost.

5.1.1.2 Fitting the NRUM Signal Model to Credibility Evaluation Data

One of the advantages of the NRUM signal model for surface credibility is that it can be fitted to experimental data. Given a dataset of user credibility evaluations of webpages, a signal can be approximated for each webpage. Since it is assumed that each webpage is evaluated based on its signal, it is possible to calculate the probability that one webpage will be evaluated higher than another. This probability can be compared with the empirical probability from the data. A joint error function that is a sum of errors for all webpages can be calculated. This function can be minimized using a gradient descent method.

Briefly, there are N normally distributed random variables given (where N is the number of webpages in the dataset): $X_1 \sim N(\mu_1, \sigma_1)$, $X_2 \sim N(\mu_2, \sigma_2)$, ..., $X_N \sim N(\mu_N, \sigma_N)$. The goal is to estimate the parameters of these distributions. For some, not all, pairs of the webpages, empirical frequencies $r_{i,j}$ of how frequently webpage j was evaluated not worse than another webpage i are given. These empirical frequencies can be compared to the theoretical probabilities, resulting in a set of equations for various pairs i, j:

$$P(X_i \leq X_j) = r_{i,j} \tag{5.1}$$

If the webpage evaluations in the dataset are on an ordinal scale (like in the C^3 corpus), then for each evaluating user, the $r_{i,j}$ frequencies can be updated under the assumption that the user compares the webpage j that he or she is currently evaluating to previously evaluated webpages. This means that if the user evaluated webpage i before, his or her evaluations for webpage j and webpage i can be directly compared, leading to a modification of the frequencies $r_{i,j}$ (which is calculated for all users). A variant of this procedure uses a "memory assumption": that the user can only remember a fixed number of k webpages. The evaluation of webpage j is therefore only compared to the user's previous k evaluations of other webpages.

The searched values are $\mu_1, \sigma_1, \ldots, \mu_N, \sigma_N$, minimizing the error function:

$$E = \sum_{i,j} \chi(i, j)(P(X_i \leq X_j) - r_{i,j})^2 = \tag{5.2}$$

$$= \sum_{i,j} \chi(i, j)(\Phi\left(\frac{-\mu_i + \mu_j}{\sqrt{\sigma_i^2 + \sigma_j^2}}\right) - r_{i,j})^2 \tag{5.3}$$

where $\chi(i, j) = 1$, if the pair i, j has a defined frequency $r_{i,j}$ in the dataset, and $\chi(i, j) = 0$ otherwise. $\Phi(z) = \int_{-\infty}^{z} \frac{1}{\sqrt{2\pi}} \exp\left(\frac{-x^2}{2}\right) dx$ is the cumulative density function of the standard normal distribution. The error function can be minimized using a gradient descent method [94].

5.1.2   NRUM Evaluation

The NRUM can be used as a predictive model, which opens up the possibility of the model's evaluation. Given a dataset of webpage credibility evaluations that is split into two parts—the training and validation part—the NRUM can be fitted for each webpage using the training part, and then can be used to predict user evaluations for the validation part. Moreover, several alternative prediction procedures may be used as benchmarks. The goal is to verify whether or not the NRUM signal model is well suited to user evaluations.

The evaluation of the NRUM has been carried out on a subset of the C^3 dataset that contained 180 medical webpages. The dataset contained 3823 evaluations (over 20 evaluations for each page). The dataset was split into a training part that contained about 30% of the evaluations and a validation part that contained the remaining 70%

of validations. The NRUM was estimated for each webpage using the procedure described in the previous section and the evaluations from the training dataset. Next, the estimated distributions for each webpage were used to predict how often the evaluators would give a webpage j a better rating than for webpage i. This prediction was compared against three alternative methods:

- **Random signal**. This method uses the assumption that users use a signal that is pure random noise. This means that the probability of preference of any webpage over any other webpage is constant: $r_{i,j} = 0.5$. Such a solution can be good in minimizing prediction error, but does not give any information about evaluated webpages at all.
- **Random prediction**. In this method, for each pair of webpages i, j, the prediction of the value $r_{i,j}$ is drawn from a uniform random distribution (from interval $< 0, 1 >$).
- **Mean evaluation comparison**. For each pair of webpages, this method compares the means of user ratings and predicts that a webpage with a higher mean will always receive better evaluations than webpages with lower means (and returns $r_{i,j} = 0.5$ if the means of evaluations for webpages i and j are equal).

Table 5.2 shows the mean absolute, median absolute, and mean square errors of the NRUM signal model predictions. The NRUM signal model is calculated in two variants, without memory (any webpage's evaluation is said to have been compared with all previous evaluations of the user) or with memory of eight webpages (any evaluation is only compared to eight previous evaluations). It is clear that the NRUM performs well when compared to the benchmarks, even if the overall mean error is not low enough to guarantee a good prediction. This, however, was not an objective: the goal was to demonstrate that the NRUM signal model is suitable for modeling surface credibility evaluations. The results of the experiment confirm this, indicating also the possibility for improvements, as the signal model with memory clearly performs better than the memoryless one.

Table 5.2 Prediction errors for NRUM signal model and benchmark methods

	Mean error	Mean square error	Median error
Random signal	0.234	0.082	0.250
Random prediction	0.331	0.165	0.331
Mean evaluation comp.	0.268	0.120	0.250
Signal model	0.206	0.068	0.170
Signal model (memory)	0.193	0.060	0.193

Fig. 5.3 Signal model for
five selected webpages.
Source: [94]

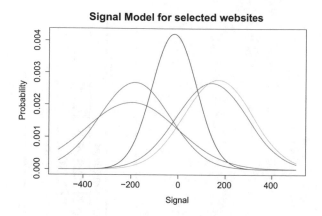

5.1.2.1   Selected Examples

To show how the NRUM signal model works, five "distinctive" webpages have been
selected from the dataset. These were the two most credible ones (with high and low
standard deviation, respectively), two least credible, and one from the middle.

The results and sources are shown in Fig. 5.3 and Table 5.3. In addition, Table 5.3
contains a rating on the same, 5-step credibility evaluation scale, given by medical
experts (PhD students of a medical degree).

Clearly, the results for those "most obvious" webpages are quite similar to expert
ratings. "Not credible" webpages concern, for example, "what doctors don't tell
you"—aromatherapy (red) or advocating use of coconuts to heal virus symptoms,
without citing medical sources (purple). The "Purple" webpage has a higher (the
highest from all results) standard deviation, probably because the advice contained
in the page might work, leading to a disagreement among evaluators. This example
illustrates how such cases can be spotted using the NRUM signal model.

Keeping in mind the possibility of modeling surface credibility evaluations as
random variables from a distribution that is specific to a webpage, one can now turn
to a more complex model of information credibility. This game-theoretic model will
also use the concept of a signal.

5.2   The Credibility Game

The signal model of the previous section is a basic model of message credibility
that gives a mathematical form to the definition of credibility proposed in Chap. 2.
This model can also be fitted to empirical data and used in algorithm design. On
the other hand, the signal model does not express or explain the behavior of the
sender and receiver of the message. This means that the signaling model contains no
information on the impact of credibility evaluation support methods or CS systems

Table 5.3 Selected websites with estimated signals and expert ratings

Color	Mean	Standard deviation	URL	Expert rating
Red	−183.08	148.46	http://www.wddty.com/alternative-ways-to-prevent-or-treat-whooping-cough.html	1
Purple	−196.46	193.31	http://www.healthboards.com/boards/west-nile-virus/392259-natures-viral-cures.html	1
Black	−17.04	94.67	http://www.southernnevadahealthdistrict.org/west-nile/symptoms-treatment.php	3
Green	169.48	143.90	http://www.webmd.com/a-to-z-guides/noroviruses-norwalk-viruses-topic-overview	4
Blue	142.19	149.40	http://www.patient.co.uk/health/Norovirus.htm	4

on sender and receiver behavior. The need for such a model is obvious, for example, for the validation of CS systems. However, such a model needs to be significantly more complex than the signal model.

5.2.1 Model Requirements

When designing a complex model, it is useful to list all requirements for this model in advance, because frequently satisfying all of them will be hard. The requirements list can serve as a critical checkpoint in the model's evaluation.

A model of Web content credibility (and more generally, quality) evaluation should fulfill the following requirements:

1. Use asymmetric roles for users who can produce or consume information.
2. Explicitly model the quality of information produced and consumed by users.
3. Model the preferences and economic incentives of information producers and consumers.
4. Model the consumer's ability and methods of evaluating information credibility.
5. Model diverse strategies of information producers and consumers.
6. Allow to take into account the use of credibility evaluation support methods and to study their impact on the model.

In the Credibility Game, there are two players: the *content producer* (CP) and *content consumer* (CC). This may seem limiting, as in a Web 2.0 setting a user can have both of these roles (be a *content prosumer*). However, the prosumer model can be achieved by iterating an asymmetrical model and letting players take turns and act using various roles in each turn (this approach is described in Sect. 5.5). In an encounter, CP produces and CC consumes information (Web content), fulfilling requirement 1. The entire context of the encounter is fixed for the duration of the game, and this content includes the topic of the information (so information concerns a single topic). This simplifying assumption does not limit the generality of the model, as one can imagine concurrent encounters that have various contexts (or topics of content). Notice also that while it is assumed that one CP interacts with one CC in the game, it is possible to iterate the game, and a single CP may interact with multiple CCs in several iterations (to model a typical one-to-many relation as exists in the current Web between content producers and consumers).

The truthfulness (or quality) of produced information will be explicitly modeled as properties of the information, fulfilling requirement 2. The truthfulness property introduces a ground truth into the model, enabling to evaluate the correctness of credibility evaluation support methods. It can be safely assumed that consumers will prefer to accept truthful information. On the other hand, producers may prefer that consumers accept false information. This type of producer preference can be modeled in various ways. The simplest approach is to create two types of producers in the game, such as an honest and dishonest CP. A more complex approach would explicitly model the economic incentives of a producer (allowing also to express varying degrees of honesty or dishonesty). The strategies of producers will determine the choices of the properties of produced information. On the other hand, the strategies of the consumer will consist of credibility evaluation methods. In the simpler versions of the game, the consumer will be limited to using a signal and his choice will concern the threshold for this signal. More complex strategies may use CP's reputation (Sect. 5.3).

Credibility evaluation support methods may be simply modeled as ways of improving the signal for the consumers who use these methods.

5.2.2   Basic Model

In the basic version of the Credibility Game, information has two properties: truthfulness (TF) and presentation or persuasiveness (L) with $TF \in [0, 1]$, $L \in [0, 1]$. Initially, assume that TF and L are binary. As mentioned before, TF models the ground truth concerning evaluated information, while L models presentation quality of Web content (or persuasiveness of language).

CC's actions are binary: he or she can either accept or reject produced information. On the other hand, CP's actions consist of choosing combinations of the two properties of information, and therefore CP has four actions.

The preferences of CC regarding accepted information are simple and depend solely on TF: he or she prefers accepting information with $TF = 1$ to $TF = 0$. On the other hand, CP's preferences are more complex. In the basic model, CP can be of two types: honest (CP-H) and dishonest (CP-L). Then, CP-H will have preferences consistent with CC with respect to TF. However, CP-L will prefer that CC accepts information with $TF = 0$ to $TF = 1$.

Preferences of CP regarding the L property will depend on whether CC accepts or rejects the information. Increasing L can be thought of as being associated with a cost or effort on behalf of CP. However, a higher L increases the likelihood that CC will accept the produced information. The CP will incur a loss if CC rejects information with $L = 1$. If CC accepts the information, CP will prefer that CC accepts information with $L = 0$ regardless of the CP's type.

The four combinations of produced information in the basic Credibility Game may be simply summarized as BF (bad looking falsehood, $TF = 0$, $L = 0$), GF (good looking falsehood, $TF = 0$, $L = 1$), BT (Bad Looking Truth, $TF = 1$, $L = 0$), and GT (Good Looking Truth, $TF = 1$, $L = 1$). In the basic model, these are also the four actions available for CP. Additionally, these four combinations are the four producer strategies in the basic Credibility Game (partially fulfilling requirement 5).

The payoffs of the Credibility Game are obtained by players after they choose their actions. As usual in game-theoretic models, it is assumed that CP and CC choose their actions without knowing the actions of the other player. However, the actions are not simultaneous: rather, CP chooses a version of the information first.

Next, CC obtains a signal that depends on the information version chosen by CP. Finally, CC chooses whether to accept or reject the offered information.

In the basic model, one CP interacts with one CC. In iterated versions of the model, the choice of an action by the consumer may be preceded by the choice of one of many producers, for example, based on reputation (see Sect. 5.3).

5.2.2.1 Payoff of Basic Credibility Game

The payoffs of the basic version of the Credibility Game model the preferences of the CC and of two types of content producers: CP-H (honest or altruistic CP) and CP-L (dishonest or strategic CP). This fulfills requirement 3 for a model of credibility evaluation.

Payoffs of CC: CC is indifferent in case of rejection.

$$CC_{BFR} = CC_{GFR} = CC_{BTR} = CC_{GTR} = 0$$

CC's payoffs in case of acceptance depend only on TF.

$$CC_{BFA} = CC_{GFA} = -2 < CC_{BTA} = CC_{GTA} = 2$$

Payoffs of CP-L: In case of rejection, CP's payoffs depend inversely on L and increase with TF.

$$CP^L_{GFR} = -3 < CP^L_{FR} = -2 < CP^L_{GTR} = -1 < CP^L_{BTR} = 0$$

In case of acceptance, CP^L's payoffs depend inversely on TF and on L.

$$CP^L_{GTA} = 1 < CP^L_{BTA} = 2 < CP^L_{GFA} = 4 < CP^L_{BFA} = 5$$

Payoffs of CP-H (honest content producer): In case of rejection, CP-H has the same payoffs as CP-L. In case of acceptance, CP^L's payoffs depend inversely on L and increase with TF:

$$CP^H_{GFA} = 1 < CP^H_{BFA} = 2 < CP^H_{GTA} = 4 < CP^H_{BTA} = 5$$

The payoffs of CP-L in the basic version of the Credibility Game are designed so that if the game is iterated and the players can switch roles (the CC becomes CP-L in the second iteration, and vice versa), then the combined payoffs for the most cooperative and most non-cooperative actions fulfill the assumptions of a generalized Prisoner's Dilemma (see Sect. 5.5). The same is not true for CP-H: in an iterative version of a game of CP-H and CC with role switching, the Nash equilibrium is cooperative and Pareto-optimal.

Table 5.4 Basic game of CP-L and CP-H versus CC

CP-L vs CC:

	A	R
BF	-2 / 5	0 / -2
GF	-2 / 4	0 / -3
BT	2 / 2	0 / 0
GT	2 / 1	0 / -1

CP-H vs CC:

	A	R
BF	-2 / 2	0 / -2
GF	-2 / 1	0 / -3
BT	2 / 5	0 / 0
GT	2 / 4	0 / -1

5.2.3 Economic Model

The payoffs of the basic Credibility Game as defined in Table 5.4 are a special version of a more general, economic model of the content producer. This extension of the basic model that fulfills requirement 3 is no longer tractable using game-theoretic methods, but can be conveniently used in simulation. This model also extends the Credibility Game model in another way: by allowing the TF and L properties to have continuous (rather than binary) values.

The model considers the total utility of a content producer from the production of content that depends on the number of consumers that have accepted this content. This utility expresses the situation of the content producer in an iterated Credibility Game with multiple consumers.

The utility of the CP is given by

$$U(I) = kG(TF) - C(TF, L)$$

where k is the number of consumers who have accepted CP's content, G is a function that describes the gain of the CP, and C is a function that describes the cost of information production. Note that G is a function of TF, not L. This utility function models the fact that the *marginal cost of producing information is zero*: the CP bears only a fixed cost of production that does not depend on the number of consumers.

The gain of the content producer is given by

$$G(TF) = \alpha TF + \beta$$

$\alpha > 0$ for an honest producer (CP-H) and $\alpha < 0$ for a dishonest producer (CP-L).

The cost of the content producer is given by

$$C(TF, L) = \gamma TF + \delta L + \epsilon$$

where $\gamma < 0$ models that increasing the truthfulness of the produced information reduces the cost of its production (the cost is determined by cognitive effort for manufacturing a falsehood). $\delta > 0$ models that improving the look increases the cost. $\epsilon \geq 0$ models a fixed cost.

If CP-L has the following parameters,

$$\alpha = -5, \beta = 7, \gamma = -2, \delta = 1, \epsilon = 2$$

the resulting utility function is given by

$$U^{CP-L}(I) = \begin{cases} 3TF - L + 5 & \text{if } k = 1 \\ 2TF - L - 1 & \text{if } k = 0 \end{cases}$$

This utility function produces the payoffs for CP-L for the basic Credibility Game for binary values of TF and L.

Analogously, consider the following parameters for CP-H:

$$\alpha = 1, \beta = 4, \gamma = -2, \delta = 1, \epsilon = 2$$

The resulting utility function produces the payoffs for CP-H for the basic Credibility Game.

The cost functions for CP-H and CP-L do not differ. For this reason, in order to study the sensitivity of strategy stability to payoffs, it is sufficient to study a variation of the coefficients α and β. This kind of sensitivity analysis can only be carried out using simulation (see Sect. 5.3).

Using the economic model, it is possible to use continuous values of the two parameters that model information properties: TF and L. This also means that the model can express an infinite variability of producer strategies, fulfilling requirement 5 with regard to producer strategies.

5.2.4 Equilibrium Analysis

The equilibrium analysis of the Credibility Game model proceeds in three steps:

1. Analysis of Credibility Game without signal and with fixed CP strategies
2. Analysis of Credibility Game with signal and with fixed CP strategies
3. Analysis of Credibility Game with signal and with dynamic CP strategies

The first two steps are tractable using mathematical (game-theoretic) methods. The last step can be analyzed using computer simulation.

5.2.5   Analysis of Credibility Game Without Signal

The initial assumption is that consumers do not receive a signal, but can directly observe a producer's type. On the other hand, for this preliminary analysis, it can be assumed that the producer's type does not determine the producer's strategy. Producers can choose a strategy regardless of their type, for example, CP-L can choose to produce content with $TF = 1$ (BT or GT). Notice that strategies could be *mixed*, in the sense that CP chooses an action (BT, GT, BF, GF) with a certain probability.

5.2.5.1   Game-Theoretic Analysis of Credibility Game Without Signal

The analysis presented in this section follows the reasoning from [138].

For CP-L   Under the above assumptions, the Credibility Game has a unique Nash equilibrium in mixed strategies (and no equilibrium in pure strategies; a pure strategy is a strategy when the same action is chosen by CP with probability 1). For simplicity, reference will be made to a pure strategy that chooses an action (e.g., CP-L chooses action F with probability 1) with the same name as the action (in our example, "strategy F"). First, note that for CP-L the strategy GF is dominated by F and strategy T is dominated by BT. This implies that it is only necessary to consider mixed strategies that will choose actions F or BT. The probability that CP-L chooses action F by x should also be noted. This means that CP-L chooses the action BT with probability $1 - x$. The probability that CC chooses action A (accept) will be denoted by y. This means that CC chooses action R with probability $1 - y$.

The unique Nash equilibrium for mixed strategies is given by $x = \frac{1}{2}$ and $y = \frac{2}{5}$.

An evolutionarily stable strategy (ESS) is a strategy which, if adopted by a population in a given environment, cannot be invaded by any alternative strategy that is initially rare. An ESS is an equilibrium refinement of the Nash equilibrium. In order to determine the equilibrium solution that is evolutionarily stable, the replicator dynamics equations [155] can be used requiring the partial derivatives of action choice probabilities x and y to be zero. This condition is expressed by

$$\frac{\dot{x}}{x} = 5y - 2(1 - y) - [x(5y - 2(1 - y) + (1 - x)2y] = 0$$

$$\frac{\dot{y}}{y} = -2x + 2(1 - x) - [y(-2x + 2(1 - x)) + (1 - y)0] = 0$$

$$(5.4)$$

After some algebra, two solutions are obtained, $x = 1$, $y = 1$ and $x = \frac{1}{2}$, $y = \frac{2}{5}$. However, the solution $x = 1$, $y = 1$ is just a fixed point and not evolutionary stable strategy (ESS), since it is not a Nash equilibrium; an ESS must also be a Nash equilibrium. Therefore, the only ESS of the game is $x = \frac{1}{2}$, $y = \frac{2}{5}$.

For CP-H The game has 1 equilibrium in pure strategies and 0 Nash equilibrium in mixed strategies. Observe that for CP-H the strategy BT is dominant. Anticipating this, CC's best response is the strategy A. Therefore, (BT,A) is the subgame-perfect equilibrium of the game.

Since (BT, A) is a subgame-perfect equilibrium, it is also an evolutionarily stable equilibrium.

5.2.6 Analysis of Credibility Game with Signal

The next step is to consider the situation in which consumers receive the signal. Contrary to the assumptions in the preliminary analysis, CC cannot observe CP's type anymore. On the other hand, the type of CP determines the value of TF for information produced by that CP. In other words, a CP can choose among two strategies that are: for CP-L, GF or BF; for CP-H, GT or BT. CPs can also use mixed strategies, as before.

Introducing the signal into the model has important consequences. Recall the requirement 4 for a model of credibility evaluation: to model the ability of the consumer to evaluate credibility. This requirement can be fulfilled using a definition of the signal received by CC. The signal will be a random function of properties of the information, TF and L. Increasing the impact of TF on the signal can model an improvement of the abilities of CC to correctly evaluate credibility. A perfect credibility evaluation would be achieved by CC if her signal would depend solely on TF (without random noise). On the other hand, naive consumers would only take into account the presentation quality L instead of the truthfulness TF. In between these two extremes, several versions of the signal can be created that depend jointly on TF and L (and include random noise). Using a similar reasoning, it can be shown that the introduction of the signal fulfills requirement 6: the ability to model credibility evaluation support techniques. The use of a service for credibility evaluation support by the CC can be modeled by an improvement of the signal received by the CC.

CC can use the received signal in their choice of whether to accept or reject information by simply comparing the signal to a threshold. If the signal is above the CC's threshold, she will accept the version of I produced by CP. This simple strategy is quite flexible, as threshold values can adapt over time and become the subject of evolution (learning). Also, the use of the signal increases the variety of possible consumer strategies, fulfilling requirement 5 with regard to the consumer.

Since for this analysis it was assumed that the producer's type determines the value of TF of information produced by him, the producer's choice is limited to whether or not he or she is to make a costly effort to improve the presentation of the produced information. CP-H can produce information versions T, BT by deciding whether to invest in presentation quality ($L = 1$) or not. Similarly, CP-L can produce information versions GF or F.

CC is randomly matched with a CP of certain types, chosen from a population that has a fixed proportion r of honest producers. In game-theoretic analysis, this assumption is called a choice by nature which in this case randomly selects a CP from the population. The payoffs of the players are described in Table 5.4. Recall that the investment into making information look nice subtracts 1 from the producer's payoffs.

5.2.6.1   Analysis of Credibility Game as Signaling Game

The strategic form of this signaling game is shown in Fig. 5.4. The analysis presented in this section follows the reasoning from [138].

It is assumed that in the FALSE information set, CP plays Not Invest (i.e., Bad Look, $L = 0$) with probability x_1, while he invests ($L = 1$) with probability $1 - x_1$. Also, in the TRUE information set, CP plays Not Invest (i.e., Bad Look, $L = 0$) with probability x_2, while he invests ($L = 1$) with probability $1 - x_2$. On the other hand, in the Bad Look information set, CC plays Accept with probability y_1, while in the Good Look information set, he plays Accept with probability y_2.

In the TRUE information set, CP-H should be indifferent in terms of expected payoffs between investing or not on high-quality presentation; therefore, it should

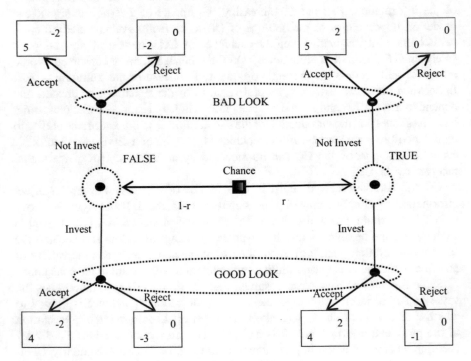

Fig. 5.4 The signaling game of credibility. Source: [138]

be for CP-H that

$$x_2(5y_1 + (1 - y_1)0) = (1 - x_2)(4y_2 - (1 - y_2)) . \tag{5.5}$$

In the FALSE information set, CP-L should similarly be indifferent between investing or not on high-quality presentation, and thus it should be for CP that

$$x_1(5y_1 - (1 - y_1)2) = (1 - x_1)(4y_2 - 3(1 - y_2)) . \tag{5.6}$$

Regarding the CC strategies, forward induction is employed as follows: The unconditional probability that the game reaches the right node of the Bad Look information set is x_2r, while for the left node it is $x_1(1 - r)$. At the right node of Bad Look, CC would always play Accept (A), while at the left node of the same information set, he would always play Reject (R). Thus, after observing the Bad Look, the conditional probability that CC assigns of being to the right node should equal its probability y_1 of playing Accept in this information set, that is, it should be that

$$y_1 = \frac{x_2r}{x_2r + x_1(1 - r)} . \tag{5.7}$$

Reasoning similarly for the Good Look information set, the probability y_2 of playing Accept is given by

$$y_2 = \frac{(1 - x_2)r}{(1 - x_2)r + (1 - x_1)r} . \tag{5.8}$$

The solution to the system of Eqs. (5.5), (5.6), (5.7), (5.8) for $r=1/2$ is given by $x_1=0.0283$, $x_2=0.2176$, $y_1=0.8846$, $y_2=0.4460$. This is an assessment (or perfect-Bayesian) equilibrium of this game.

Two special cases will now be studied: of a completely naïve consumer and of an expert consumer. The following issue will be that of how a producer could use information about customers' expertise.

The Naïve Consumer The completely naïve consumer accepts information based solely on the presentation quality. This means that CC receives a signal that depends only on the L property of produced information. Such a CC will play Accept with probability $y_1 = 0$ in the Bad Look information set, while she plays Accept with probability $y_2 = 1$ in the Good Look information set. Anticipating this, the dominant strategy for both CP-L and CP-H is to invest in presentation quality, that is, $x_1 = x_2 = 0$.

The Expert Consumer If the CC is a highly skilled expert, he or she can correctly assess the credibility of information and determine the type of the CP regardless of the presentation quality of the information. In other words, whether in Bad Look or in Good Look, CC knows if he or she is at the right or the left node of the respective information set and plays accordingly. A highly skilled expert CC would play Accept (A) when matched with CP-H and Reject (R) when matched with CP-L. Anticipating this, neither CP-H nor CP-L has any incentive to invest on high-quality presentation against an expert CC, that is, $x_1 = x_2 = 1$.

Anticipating Consumers' Expertise If the CC population consists of a fraction f of highly skilled experts, while the rest are totally naïve, CP would not know in advance the type of the CC that he is matched with. Then, reasoning similarly to the equilibrium analysis above, CP-H would always play Invest ($L = 1$) if $f < 0.8$, otherwise Not Invest. CP-L would always play Invest if $f < 6/7$, otherwise Not Invest.

In general, there can be CCs with various levels of expertise according to which CC assigns a conditional probability to encounter a CP-H or a CP-L given a certain presentation quality (i.e., Good Look or Bad Look information sets). These conditional probabilities determine y_1, y_2 with whom CC plays Accept in the Bad Look and the Good Look information sets respectively and the x_1, x_2 are then derived by Eqs. (5.5) and (5.6).

5.2.7 Studying Impact of Consumer Expertise

In the previous section, completely naïve and perfect expert consumers were considered. However, such consumers would rarely exist in practice—they are merely an abstract model of an extreme situation. In order to study the impact of consumer expertise, a more subtle model is needed. Fortunately, the simple extension of the Credibility Game with a signal is sufficient to greatly enhance the model of consumer expertise.

The Credibility Game with signal can be used to investigate an important hypothesis concerning the relationship between consumer expertise (in evaluating information credibility) and producer equilibrium strategies. The hypothesis can be formulated as follows: in the Credibility Game with signal, dishonest content producers will change their strategy depending on the amount of experts in a population of content consumers. Specifically, a dishonest CP will choose the Good Looking False (GF) strategy if there are few expert consumers, while he will switch to a Bad Looking Truth (BF) strategy if there are many expert consumers.

The reasoning behind the hypothesis is as follows. Dishonest CPs get a higher payoff if the CC accepts a falsehood (for the GF or BF strategy). However, if the CC uses a signal, she will not accept produced information if the signal is below a threshold. Therefore, the dishonest CP will improve the signal by improving the look of produced information and will choose the GF strategy.

On the other hand, an expert CC receives signal that has a low variance and depends mostly on TF, not on L. Generally, the composition of a signal can be controlled by a weight that controls the impact of TF (and L) on the signal. The signal is a random variable $S(\mu, \delta)$ which has a normal distribution $N(\mu, \delta)$ with mean $\mu \in [0, 1]$ and standard deviation $\delta \in [0, 1]$. The mean can be a function of the properties of produced information, TF and L:

$$\mu = w_{TF}TF + (1 - w_{TF})L$$

An expert consumer can be modeled by a consumer who has high w_{TF}. The value of δ can be fixed or can also depend on a CC's expertise (expert consumers can have a lower standard deviation of the signal).

Since the expert consumer receives a signal that does not depend strongly on L, the dishonest CP's strategy of improving the signal using L will not work. Therefore, when faced with a population in which there are many expert CCs, the dishonest CP can only switch to a strategy which has $TF = 1$ (BT or GT). However, since for the expert CC's the value of L does not improve the signal, and producing information with high L is costly for the CP, the dishonest CP will choose the Bad Looking Truth (BT) strategy.

In this analysis of the signaling Credibility Game, it was assumed that expert consumers would always know the TF value of the produced information. This is equivalent to setting $w_{TF} = 1$ and $\delta = 0$. Without this assumption, it is not possible to verify the initial hypothesis using mathematical analysis. Simulation must be used instead. A simulator of the Credibility Game has been developed. Here, simulation results that can be used to verify the hypothesis discussed above are presented.

5.2.7.1 Credibility Game Simulator Design

The simulator described in this section has been used to analyze the impact of consumer expertise and also the impact of reputation (see Sect. 5.3). This section contains a brief overview of simulator design. For a more detailed description of simulator design, readers are referred to [215].

Each simulation run involves several basic steps, namely, initializing the populations of producers and consumers, performing a certain number of interactions between each consumer and the chosen producer, evaluating payoffs, and changing the properties of both types of agents. The entire simulation procedure is described below, along with some important parameters that need to be set:

1. Generate initial population of N producers and M consumers.
2. For each *generation* $\in 1 \ldots G$ do

    (a) For each *iteration* $\in 1 \ldots I$ do

        (i) Each producer produces one piece of information according to his strategy

        (ii) Each consumer:

            (A) chooses one producer from the population according to the producer choice strategy

        (B) evaluates the producer's information and decides whether to accept it or not

        (C) modifies gain depending on the accepted/rejected information features and payoffs

        (D) rates the producer according to his or her rating strategy (this action concerns the use of the reputation system described in Sect. 5.3)

    (iii) Gains are modified for all producers depending on their $type \in honest, dishonest$, and on features of produced information (truthfulness and look) and its acceptance rate, based on the $payoffs$ simulation parameter.

    (iv) The original producers ratings are updated taking into account the evaluations from this iteration.

  (b) Producers evolve (modify the TF and L properties of the information produced in the next generation).

  (c) The initial ratings of all producers are reset.

  (d) Consumers evolve (modify their acceptance thresholds for both signal and reputation).

Producer Strategy

In the simulations described in this chapter, producer's strategies are limited to choosing among the available actions BF, GF, BT, and GT. However, the simulator allows to define and study more complex strategies, for example, choosing TF and L directly and using the economic model to determine the payoffs.

Consumer Strategies

The first consumer strategy concerns producer choice. The simulator implements two possible strategies regarding the choice of the producers for interaction from the entire population. The first one allows to choose one producer at random. The second one randomly picks three candidates and then chooses the one with the highest reputation. However, this predefined set can easily be extended to model more sophisticated strategies.

    The second consumer strategy is used to accept or reject information offered by a chosen producer. Currently, there are two factors that can be taken into account by consumers while deciding whether to accept information or not. These are acceptance by signal (using the signal threshold) and acceptance by reputation (using the reputation threshold). One may choose to use only one of them; however, it is also possible to incorporate logical alternative or conjunction of both. The type of strategy is predefined for all the consumers at the beginning of the simulation. However, the thresholds of a chosen acceptance strategy evolve at the end of each generation.

Evolution of Agent Strategies

Evolution of the producers' strategies involves altering the truthfulness and look of the generated content. The Stochastic Universal Sampling technique is applied to select the strategies potentially useful for recombination, using payoffs as a fitness metric. This method allows to avoid genetic drift [215]. Producers can only copy strategies from other producers of the same type (honest or dishonest). The detailed procedure consists of the following steps:

1. Divide the population into groups of honest and dishonest producers
2. For each group

   (a) Use Stochastic Universal Sampling to select strategies that are going to be copied
   (b) For each producer in the group, copy the truthfulness and look value from the selected strategy

3. Alter the look strategy of 1% of randomly chosen producers to a random value (0 or 1)

For consumers, only the acceptance strategy can evolve. This involves altering signal and reputation thresholds by copying strategies of the best consumers and adding small mutation to it. Consumers can only copy strategies of other consumers within the same type (with the same expertise). The detailed procedure has similar steps as for the evolution of producer strategies.

5.2.7.2 Impact of Consumer Expertise on Producer Equilibrium Strategies

Using the simulator based on the Credibility Game with signal, it is possible to investigate the impact of consumer expertise on producer equilibrium strategies.

In the simulation, the expertise of consumers is modeled as follows, using the parameters of the signal: w_{TF} (weight of TF in the signal mean) and δ (standard deviation of signal). Extreme cases are $w_{TF} = 0$. However, intermediate cases are also considered. Consumers that prefer good-looking information regardless of its truthfulness have $w_{TF} = 0.33$, while expert consumers who are more aware of the information's truthfulness are modeled by $w_{TF} = 0.66$. Similarly, expert consumers have a lower standard deviation of the signal: $\delta = 0.05$. Non-expert consumers have a high standard deviation of $\delta = 0.66$. The proportion of expert consumers can be varied in the simulation; all non-expert consumers have the lower value of w_{TF}.

Simulations are initiated with a population of consumers that is varied by the proportion of experts (given a particular setting of parameters for expert and non-expert consumers). In all simulations, there are 80% dishonest producers. This models a situation when most producers have a clear incentive to produce false information. Simulations are used to test the hypothesis whether the evolutionarily

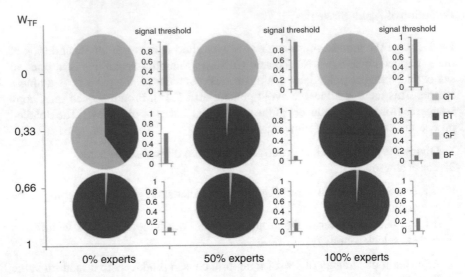

Fig. 5.5 Stable producer strategies in varying populations of expert and non-expert consumers. Source: [215]

stable strategies of these dishonest producers would change depending on the presence of experts in the consumer population.

The results of the simulation experiment are shown in Fig. 5.5. The figure presents the percentages of strategies (GT, BT, GF, and BF) in the population of producers in the evolutionary equilibrium (averages for ten simulation runs). The values are shown against different populations of consumers, where two parameters are varied: the w_{TF} value for experts and the percentage of experts in the consumer population.

Simulation results indicate that the composition of signal has a crucial impact on the signal's ability to alter the dishonest producers' behavior and provide incentives to submit true information. In an environment with only less experienced consumers, who exhibit preference for look (0% experts, $w_{TF} \in 0, 0.33$), dishonest producers will choose the GF (Good Looking False) strategy in an evolutionary equilibrium. On the other hand, if there are at least 50% experts who receive a signal with $w_{TF} \geq 0.33$, then these same dishonest producers will switch to the BT (Bad Looking Truth) strategy in the evolutionary equilibrium, to avoid rejections by consumers.

The effects shown by the simulation analysis are not always stable, as in the less extreme simulation settings some simulation runs show varying behavior. However, the results clearly support the hypothesis that dishonest experts' behavior depends on customer expertise in the extreme settings (all simulation runs show the same outcome).

This hypothesis was additionally evaluated by performing two-sample t-test with unequal variances, investigating the statistical significance of the difference between the behavior of dishonest producers in an environment with 0% expert consumers and 50% expert consumers ($w_{TF} = 0.33$). The tested hypotheses were defined as follows: h0: The same number of dishonest CPs choose to produce true information in an environment with 0% expert consumers and in an environment with 50% expert consumers (difference=0). ha: More dishonest CPs choose to produce true information in an environment with 50% expert consumers, than in an environment with 0% expert consumers (difference>0)

Assuming the significance level equal to 0.05, there is sufficient evidence to reject the null hypothesis ($p = 0.0026$).

This simple simulation experiment shows the profound impact of signal and signal composition on the behavior of information producers. This leads to the conclusion that credibility evaluation can affect the global equilibrium of information producers. Furthermore, methods (technical or social) that can improve credibility evaluation can have a large, positive impact on the global equilibrium. Consider the case of a population of inexperienced consumers that regularly accept false information—for example, Web content that promotes an alternative medicine or unconfirmed therapy for a disease. Imagine that in such a situation, a watchdog organization (such as Health on the Net) appears and starts to review information on the Web about the effectiveness of the alternative medicine or therapy. Assuming that the results of the watchdog's monitoring can reach sufficiently many consumers (which could be supported by technical means, such as the browser extension used by the WOT service), the effect could be that the false information is no longer profitable to produce and publish online (in other words, the alternative medicine producer would go out of business).

Still, the condition that all produced information will be evaluated by consumers who have sufficiently high expertise (a good signal composition) is hard to meet in practice. Moreover, in reality, consumers of information use several heuristics that do not depend directly on the produced information (message) to evaluate information credibility. One of such heuristics is source credibility evaluation. This heuristic can also be modeled using an extension of the Credibility Game with signal—the Credibility Game with reputation.

5.3 Credibility Game with Reputation

The Credibility Game is able to model two important aspects of message credibility: surface credibility and earned credibility. After it is extended with reputation, it becomes able to model an additional aspect: reputed credibility. As described in Sect. 2.3.3, there are four aspects of message credibility, summarized in the table below (Table 5.5).

Surface credibility is derived from a superficial examination of the message by the receiver. Results of empirical studies that have attempted to measure surface credibility have usually showed that users spend little time on this evaluation (an order of minutes at most). Moreover, surface credibility is easily influenced by Web

Table 5.5 Aspects of message credibility modeled by Credibility Game with reputation

Aspect of message credibility	Element of Credibility Game model
Surface credibility	Signal
Earned credibility	Payoff
Reputed credibility	Reputation
Presumed credibility	

content presentation and several other factors. Because of these properties, the signal in the Credibility Game is the best suited element to model surface credibility.

On the other hand, earned credibility refers to the evaluation of message credibility based on a more detailed investigation or personal experience. This aspect is best modeled by the payoff of the Credibility Game. Using personal experience to verify the veracity of information requires acting on the basis of this information, which can only be done if the information has not been rejected in the encounter.

Last but not least, reputed credibility is an important aspect related to the source of the message. As the name suggests, this aspect of credibility is best modeled by the source's reputation. As one can recall from Sect. 2.3.1.1, reputation is subjective and context dependent. In this case, the context is established by the examination of the truthfulness of received information, or by the examination of the signal by the consumer. The Credibility Game allows to consider both contexts, creating a unique opportunity of modeling reputation that is based on an examination of earned credibility (payoff) or surface credibility (signal).

As it was mentioned in Sect. 2.3.1.2, reputation is subjective (or local), meaning that it concerns a pair of agents (in this case, a content producer and a content consumer). Each consumer could have his own view of a producer's reputation. However, a variant of reputation frequently used in practical systems is global reputation that can be thought of as an aggregation of local reputation into a single value that is associated with an agent (the producer). The Credibility Game allows to use either of the two types of reputation, depending on the algorithm used to calculate reputation (e.g., a distributed algorithm would calculate local reputation, while a centralized algorithm could calculate global or local reputation). This section shall consider the case of global reputation and use simple, centralized reputation algorithms. This will allow to focus on a comparison of the two types of reputation that can be based on signal or payoff.

5.3.1 Reputation System for Credibility Game

The reputation system used in this study is similar to the ones utilized by many existing Web services and news aggregators. Consumers can leave feedback by voting up or down, which corresponds to adding or removing one point of reputation from the CP's score. Total reputation score is a plain sum of the votes. The reputation system is asymmetric: it maintains the reputation of content producers, not content consumers.

In order to better understand the impact of the reputation system, the methods of modeling an imperfect reputation system were also considered. The decision was made to model a typical adversary attack—the whitewashing attack. This attack is simple to use in a reputation system that does not use strong identities and does not have a reward for keeping the identity [203]. Using a whitewashing attack, an agent that has earned a bad reputation can simply switch his identity and start anew with a higher (default) reputation. In the simple reputation system used in our analysis, such an attack would be effective and would result in a decreased ability of the reputation system to identify misbehaving agents.

5.3.2 *Role of Reputation in Strategies of Content Consumers*

The role of reputation in strategies of content consumers is twofold. Firstly, reputation has been incorporated into the consumer's acceptance strategy. Four possibilities were investigated: strategies based solely on signal, solely on reputation, as well as the logical alternative and conjunction of the two. Therefore, in the proposed extension of the Credibility Game, CC's strategy consists of a pair of thresholds: one for signal and one for reputation. There are four possible simple acceptance strategies for consumers:

1. Acceptance *by signal*
   Information I is accepted by CC, if signal generated by I exceeds CC's signal threshold.
2. Acceptance *by reputation*
   Information I produced by CP is accepted by CC, if CP's reputation exceeds CC's reputation threshold.
3. Acceptance *by signal and reputation*
   Information I produced by CP is accepted by CC, if signal generated by I exceeds CC's signal threshold AND CP's reputation exceeds CC's reputation threshold.
4. Acceptance *by signal or reputation*
   Information I produced by CP is accepted by CC, if signal generated by I exceeds CC's signal threshold OR CP's reputation exceeds CC's reputation threshold.

The second role of the reputation score is related to the selection of the content producer by CC. Two matching rules were examined. The first one is simply a random choice of the producer. The second approach starts with a random selection of three producers from the entire population. Among these three producers, the one with the highest reputation score is then chosen by CC. In this way, the model was created that mirrored how CC makes a selection using some independent criteria (such as relevance) and then using reputation to select the best CP.

5.3.3   Signal-Based and Payoff-Based Reputation

In the proposed extension of the Credibility Game, two voting rules that determine how consumers evaluate producers are investigated. The first one is based on signal. It models a situation where a consumer leaves feedback immediately after the initial evaluation, relying on his or her first impression. In this case, CC votes the producer up whenever the information signal exceeds the threshold and votes down whenever it does not. The other examined voting rule is based on game payoffs. This one illustrates the behavior of consumers, who after choosing to accept or reject the information are able to verify whether relying on the information has been beneficial or not, and can leave feedback dependent on this verification. For example, if the produced Web content contains the description of a treatment for a disease, a signal-based rating is produced when a consumer finds the content to be credible without trying the treatment, while a payoff-based rating is produced if the consumer tries the treatment and reports the results to the reputation system. In the case of simulation, the consumer rates the producer only if the interaction alters his payoff. If the payoff increases, the feedback is positive. If the payoff decreases, the feedback is negative.

5.3.4   Impact of Reputation on Credibility Evaluation

In the previous section, it was shown that when consumers lack expertise, dishonest producers tend to exploit them and to provide false but well-presented information. This phenomenon might actually be a problem in a real-life system, as it is very likely that a large fraction of users, who seek information on the Internet, are not the most experienced ones [59], and therefore can only evaluate content basing on the first impression. However, a great variety of the existing Web services allow the community members not only to post information, which is the activity of content producers in the presented model, but also to leave feedback for other users. The latter is a crucial extension of the consumer's strategy, which can have a significant influence on equilibrium behavior.

The Credibility Game has been extended with reputation to investigate the impact of reputation on CP's behavior. This extension was used to examine several hypotheses regarding the influence of reputation on the community, where the fraction of expert consumers is extremely low (namely, 10%) and information look is very important for all consumers ($w_{TF} = 0.33$). Such a scenario can be plausible for many publicly available services, as it might be difficult to provide experts with incentives to actively participate in such a community. The main goal was to investigate whether different acceptance and voting rules can effectively improve information truthfulness against populations of mostly honest or mostly dishonest producers. Additionally, the aim was to examine the influence of reputation whitewashing on the results.

The Credibility Game extended with reputation is no longer tractable using mathematical analysis. Instead, like in the previous section, simulation was used to determine evolutionarily stable equilibria under various parameter configurations. The simulator design has been described in Sect. 5.2.7.1.

For consumers, only the acceptance strategy can evolve. This involves altering signal and reputation thresholds by copying strategies of the best consumers and adding small mutation to it. The Stochastic Universal Sampling technique is applied to select the strategies potentially useful for recombination, using payoffs as a fitness metric. It is important to notice that consumers can only copy strategies of other consumers within the same type (namely, with the same expertise level). The detailed procedure has similar steps as for the evolution of producer strategies.

The simulation analysis described in this section involves four settings. All settings had in common the population of consumers, composed of non-expert consumers (10% experts, $w_{TF} = 0.33$), and the population of producers: 80% honest and 20% dishonest.

1. Setting 1: 80% honest producers. Signal-based reputation. No whitewashing.
2. Setting 2: 80% honest producers. Signal-based reputation. 80% producers white-wash their reputation.
3. Setting 3: 80% honest producers. Payoff-based reputation. No whitewashing.
4. Setting 4: 80% honest producers. Payoff-based reputation. 80% producers whitewash their reputation.

The four settings allow to study the impact of two variables: basing the reputation on signal or payoff and the impact of whitewashing which is a control variable that affects the overall efficacy of the reputation system. A detailed comparison of all settings is described in [215]. (There, four additional settings with 80% dishonest producers are described that serve as a pessimistic condition. However, results for 80% honest and 80% dishonest producers were mostly similar.) The results of the four settings will be described in two groups: settings 1 and 2 for the signal-based reputation system and settings 3 and 4 for the payoff-based reputation system.

For all four settings, results were compared with data generated in a reference setting that did not involve reputation at all (also referred to as reference results). In this scenario, consumers accepted information solely based on signal and chose the producers for interaction at random. For such a setting, it was observed that all of the honest producers not only decided to generate true information but also to invest in presentation (choosing the GT strategy). On the other hand, all of the dishonest producers invested in presentation; however, they had no incentive to provide truthful information, thus choosing the GF strategy. These results were 100% compatible with theoretical predictions based on signal properties.

5.3.4.1   Signal-Based Reputation System

Setting 1: Signal-Based Reputation, No Whitewashing

Recall that the consumer in the Credibility Game with reputation can use one of four acceptance strategies: by signal, by reputation, by signal OR reputation, or by signal AND reputation (see Sect. 5.3.2). Regardless of the acceptance rule, reputation provides an incentive for dishonest producers to switch to the GT strategy (which according to their payoffs is less profitable in case of acceptance, but safer in case of rejection), if reputation is taken into account, while choosing the producer for interaction (see Fig. 5.6).

The average number of consumers, who were given the GF information for evaluation in the first generation of the reference results, is about 26% of the entire population, while after changing the producer choice strategy to the reputation-based one, this number increases to about 39%, which is caused by filtering out some of the weakest (in terms of signal properties) strategies, namely, BF and BT. This suggests that even with a relatively small number of experts in the community and the emphasis on presentation in the signal properties, dishonest producers do have incentive to produce true information, if they are exposed to the consumers' evaluation frequently enough. Moreover, only four generations were required to entirely eliminate the GF strategy from the population of producers (both honest and liars).

The generalized results of the final simulation outcome are as follows: When reputation is taken into consideration, while choosing the producer for interaction, all the producers choose GT regardless of the acceptance strategy. When the producers are chosen at random, the results depend on the acceptance strategy:

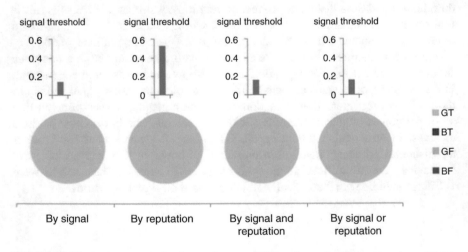

Fig. 5.6 Stable producer strategies in varying populations of expert and non-expert consumers. Source: [215]

- Acceptance by signal only (reference results), acceptance by reputation or signal

  - GT is chosen by all the honest producers.
  - GF is chosen by all the dishonest producers.

- Acceptance by reputation only, acceptance by reputation and signal

  - GT is chosen by all the producers.

The results confirm the effect of reputation on the stable strategies of content producers but also point out the impact of how reputation is used by consumers. In particular, the most effective way to use reputation is not for evaluating a single producer, but for comparison of various producers to select the most reputable one. Even a modest level of choice (choice from three candidate producers, as in our simulation) is enough to make reputation effective.

The same results (namely, choosing the GT) can be observed for the random producer choice, if the acceptance strategy is based solely on reputation or on reputation and signal. On the other hand, the results for a random producer choice and the acceptance strategy based on signal or reputation are similar to the reference results (where the acceptance strategy is based solely on signal and the choice of a producer for interaction is 100% random). In this case, it is not profitable for the dishonest producers to generate true information, as they can exploit signal properties to increase their acceptance rate and, according to payoffs, the profits from a single interaction with one consumer are (in case of acceptance) four times larger for the GF strategy than for the GT strategy.

A more thorough analysis of the results was performed focusing on two acceptance strategies: acceptance by signal AND reputation and acceptance by signal OR reputation. The investigation of the consumers' strategies in the last generations is shown in Table 5.6.

The acceptance strategy based on signal or reputation seems to be less restrictive; however, the final results of the simulation reveal that it results in a slightly higher overall signal threshold (while significantly higher for the minority of experts) and an extremely high reputation threshold. On the contrary, consumers whose acceptance strategy is based on the theoretically more restrictive logical and operator end up with lower signal and reputation thresholds. This phenomenon is probably caused by frequent errors in the early-stage generations and the consumers' payoffs setting. The logical and operator applied to the acceptance by signal and by reputation

Table 5.6 Consumer acceptance strategies in last generation

Acceptance strategy	By signal AND reputation	By signal OR reputation
Average expert's signal threshold	0.35	0.77
Average signal threshold	0.15	0.21
Average reputation threshold	325	1619
Average reputation	810	714

results in only 25% chance of accepting the processed information (there are four possible configurations and only one of them yields the overall acceptance), while at the beginning of the simulation 50% of strategies generate true information. This, along with the low expertise of the consumers, probably results in the high rejection rate of true information, which does not allow the consumers to increase their payoffs. Thus, the ones with the lower thresholds are preferred in the evolutionary process, as they have a better chance to increase their payoffs. On the contrary, the logical or operator nurtures high acceptance rate at the beginning of simulation and therefore allows the consumers to learn by "punishing" the acceptance of false information. This results in a dramatic increase of both threshold values (reputation threshold in particular). Interestingly, in this scenario, the final results indicate that the inflated reputation threshold did not provide dishonest producers with an incentive to generate true information. By the end of the simulation, dishonest producers all chose the GF strategy, while in the previous setting with the lower final reputation threshold they decided to alter their behavior and produce accurate content. This suggests that when the reputation threshold of the consumers passes some critical value, it becomes extremely difficult for the producers to get accepted by reputation, and therefore they choose to comply with the signal properties. Moreover, the GF strategy is, according to payoffs, more beneficial for them in case of acceptance.

Setting 2: Signal-Based Reputation, 80% Whitewashing

The results described in the previous section are obtained for a perfectly working reputation system with no adversaries. In order to consider a pessimistic case, in the next setting, reputation whitewashing was allowed. If not discouraged, whitewashing can become a fairly common practice for dishonest producers to abandon their discredited identities and take on new ones. This behavior can potentially lead to substantial lowering of reputation system efficiency.

To model the phenomenon of reputation whitewashing, the producers were allowed to randomly reset their reputation at the end of each iteration. The probability is specified by an additional parameter (it is 80% for the described scenarios with whitewashing). The degree to which this phenomenon affects simulation outcome was examined.

When the acceptance strategy was based only on signal and the matching rule was based on reputation, the results were exactly the same as the reference results. This is surely caused by the producer choice randomization which constitutes a direct effect of 80% whitewashing. The results for the acceptance strategies based on reputation and signal, and on reputation only, seem to be a little bit surprising. Regardless of the matching rule, 80% whitewashing did not remove the incentive to produce true information (in case of random producer choice it even provided the motivation to do it). However, it did remove the incentive to invest in presentation (for both producer types). In-depth analysis of the final population reveals that the dominant strategy chosen by almost all producers of both types has a 0% acceptance rate, as an average rating of about 4 at maximum never gets close to the average threshold. This low acceptance rate explains the strategy choice because, according to payoffs, only producing BT information allows the producers not to lose anything.

The results for the by signal or by reputation type of strategy are the same as the reference results. This is not particularly surprising when compared with the same setting without whitewashing. In that case, reputation was practically irrelevant for the dishonest producers' evolution, because it was more beneficial for them to remain compliant with the signal properties. Therefore, even 80% chance of whitewashing has no influence on the final population.

5.3.4.2   Payoff-Based Reputation System

The results presented above were based on the assumption that producer ratings are based on consumers' evaluations of the signal derived from produced information. In other words, the CC voted the CP up whenever he or she would have accepted information based on signal and voted CP down whenever she or he would have rejected the information based on signal. In case of reputation-based acceptance strategies, this leads to simple aggregation of signals from several consumers. This, in fact, turns out to be beneficial and effective, because signal is a random variable—aggregating several signals reduces the standard deviation. However, it can be argued that consumers should rate producers only when they have firsthand experience with the reliability of a given information piece, that is, they accepted it and know how it changed their payoffs. One reason for this hypothesis is that aggregating various signals will not remove the signal's bias. This section contains an analysis of payoff-based reputation and verifies the validity of the hypothesis that payoff-based reputation will be superior to signal-based reputation.

The reference results for the two settings discussed in this section are the same as for the previous two settings. If reputation is not used, all honest producers choose the GT strategy, while all dishonest ones choose the GF strategy.

Setting 3: Payoff-Based Reputation, No Whitewashing

In general, the results of Scenario 3 indicate a stronger preference for the BT strategy, regardless of producer type (when choice of the producers for interaction is 100% random) in comparison with the signal-based rating system (Scenario 1). A stronger preference can be observed for generating true information, which seems to be a natural result of a more accurate feedback based on the actual interaction results and not on the first impression. Figure 5.7 shows the stable producer strategies for Scenario 3 (right hand) and Scenario 1 (left hand) when consumers used a random producer choice and acceptance by reputation. The effects of payoff-based reputation are shown in Table 5.7. The table shows the percentage of producers in the last generation of the simulation that have used the strategy in the first column, while consumers used various acceptance strategies and various kinds of reputation.

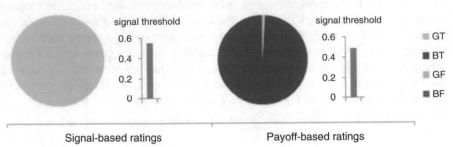

Fig. 5.7 Comparison of stable producer strategies for consumer acceptance by reputation, random producer choice. Source: [215]

Table 5.7 Impact of payoff-based and signal-based reputation on stable producer strategies

	Signal-based reputation		Payoff-based reputation	
	Random	Best reputation	Random	Best reputation
CP strategy	CP choice (%)	CP choice (%)	CP choice (%)	CP choice (%)
GT	100	99	1	1
BT	0	1	99	99
GF	0	0	0	0
BF	0	0	0	0

It is clear that all producers (honest and dishonest) switch from using the GT strategy (investing in presentation) to the BT strategy (maximizing payoffs by not incurring costs for improving presentation). Importantly, in the reference scenario with no reputation, 80% of honest producers would use the GT strategy, while 20% of dishonest producers would use the GF strategy.

If consumers use more complex acceptance strategies ("signal AND reputation" or "signal OR reputation"), not all producers switch to the BT strategy, because improving the signal still plays an important role in increasing consumer acceptance. It is important to remind that when the "signal OR reputation" acceptance strategy is used, some dishonest producers may still choose to use the GF strategy, since some consumers may still accept GF information if they receive a sufficiently high signal value.

Overall, the conclusion is that in realistic cases, when consumers base their acceptance on a conjunction of signal and reputation, it still pays for producers (honest and dishonest alike) to invest into presentation of information. However, if consumers base their reputation ratings on payoffs, producers have a stronger incentive to produce truthful information and may decide to reduce their investment in presentation of information. If consumers base their reputation ratings on signal (first impression), all producers will choose to produce truthful information and still invest into presentation (leading to a suboptimal payoff for producers).

5.4 Sensitivity Analysis to Changing Payoffs

The Credibility Game simulator introduced in the previous section has been validated by comparing simulation outcomes to equilibrium strategies predicted by game-theoretic analysis. On the other hand, it enables to extend analysis of the Credibility Game to settings that cannot be analyzed mathematically. In this section, the payoffs of the Credibility Game are considered. As it was mentioned, they have been specially designed to model preferences of the content producers and content consumers and to make an integrated Credibility Game with switched player roles equivalent to a Prisoner's Dilemma (Sect. 5.2.2.1). Moreover, the discrete Credibility Game payoffs are determined by a continuous economic model.

Using the economic model of payoffs introduced in Sect. 5.2.3, a sensitivity analysis of the evolutionary equilibria to the game payoffs was carried out. It should once more be mentioned that in order to study the sensitivity of strategy stability to payoffs, it is sufficient to study a variation of the coefficients α and β of the content producer's utility function. It was done in the range of $-10 < \alpha, \beta < 10$. For each combination, a simulation was conducted until a stable strategy emerged for the producer depending on its type. Simulation was set up for population of 100 CP and 1000 CC. Since honest producer strategy is quite straightforward, the decision was made to use 80:20 mix of types where CP-L are 80% of producer population.

This created a matrix of 400 simulation results, showing strategy distribution at the end of simulation. In almost all cases, a single dominant strategy was found for each type of the producer (CP-H and CP-L). Using simulation results, maps were drawn showing dominant strategies for the investigated range of utility function coefficients. Figure 5.1 depicts map of stable strategies for each type of content producer. On each axis of the figure, the values of α or β are shown. Each box has a width of 1 (starting from -10 and ranging to 10).

On each map, it is possible to distinguish two intersecting lines that are boundaries of areas that promote good-looking strategy versus bad looking strategy (this boundary shows coefficients range where payoffs render investment into presentation of information non-profitable) and boundary between truthful strategy and false strategy. Note that there exist ranges of coefficient where the stable strategy is to lie even for honest producers and similarly to tell truth by liars.

The analysis shows that there exists a region (cone) of α and β where for both types of producers, the stable strategy is GT (this is the intersection of the two GT regions on the two sides of the figure), and another region, where the stable strategy is BF. In these two regions, studying phenomena such as the influence of expertise or reputation becomes impossible. The coefficient values chosen for the version of the Credibility Game studied in this section do not lie in these regions and, therefore, a mixture of strategies for the two types of CP can be expected to emerge from the simulations, depending on additional parameters (Fig. 5.8).

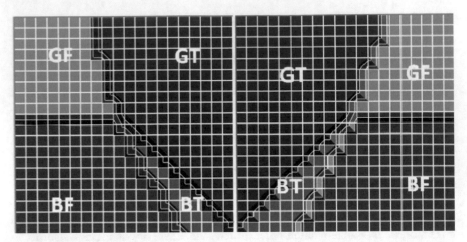

Fig. 5.8 Stable strategies for CP-H (right) and CP-L (left) as parameter of alpha (x-axis) and beta (y-axis) coefficients. Source: [215]

5.5   Modeling Web 2.0 Content Credibility Evaluation Using Symmetric Credibility Game

The Credibility Game may be applied as a model for another situation: the interaction of prosumers in a knowledge community. A practical example of such a situation are the popular Question and Answer (Q&A) systems. In a Q&A system, users interested in a topic form a community (typically using a platform such as Quora[1] or Stack Exchange[2] which has multiple separate instances for various topics, including the most popular StackOverflow[3] site for programmers). Any user may ask questions or answer them (becoming a content producer). A user that has asked a question may accept the answer (becoming a content consumer). However, the crucial feature of knowledge communities is that users are prosumers: they may both consume and produce information. Another feature is that users may learn or improve their knowledge, leading to an improved ability to answer questions. The results presented in this section are based on [93].

Section 4.2 contained the information that numerous attempts have been made to model and predict credibility of answers in a Q&A system. However, these attempts used machine learning to predict answer credibility measured by the "Best Answer" tag. Such attempts do not take into account user learning [166] and also do not allow to investigate the question: does a whole Q&A user community learn by improving its global ability to answer questions? This question is related to another

---

[1] www.quora.com.
[2] https://stackexchange.com.
[3] https://stackoverflow.com.

one: how resilient is a Q&A user community to credible but incorrect information (answers)? Such and like questions can be answered by using a model derived from the Credibility Game.

Interestingly, the extension of the Credibility Game discussed in this section is particularly suitable to the modeling of fake news dissemination in social media. This situation can also be described as a prosumer situation: each Twitter user can be both a news consumer and a news provider.

In an attempt to model the credibility of answers on a Q&A forum, it is necessary to consider the ability of the basic Credibility Game model to express properties of such information. The basic Credibility Game has been designed for webpages. Two properties of information, truthfulness (TF) and look (L), have been used to model Web content. The TF property seems quite suitable for modeling veracity of answers to a specific question. After all, the correctness of an answer is definitely one of the most important criteria of its credibility. However, correctness may not be the only property of an answer that would cause a user to accept the answer to his or her question. Another such property could be the overall persuasiveness of the answer. Consider the following examples of questions and answers:

- Question: "What is a good treatment for a strong headache?"
- Answer: "Aspirin is the best way to stop a headache. It is also effective against flu, and even protects against heart attacks and strokes. Aspirin is inexpensive and has few side effects, especially if you use an enteric-coated pill."

This answer, even though it is truthful, contains several embellishments and a lot of additional information that serves to persuade the asking person to use aspirin. It is an example of Good Looking Truth ($L = 1$, $TF = 1$). More examples demonstrate other combinations of information properties:

- ($TF = 0$; $L = 0$): "Put some Olbas oil on your forehead."

  - This solution is wrong (or at the very least, not very effective) so $TF = 0$. The author does not make an additional attempt to convince the reader to accept the answer, therefore $L = 0$.

- ($TF = 0$; $L = 1$) : "Do not take an aspirin, because it is an acid and can damage your stomach. Put some Olbas oil on your forehead and rest in a dark room. This will stop almost any headache."

  - $L = 1$ because the answer contains a lot of additional information to persuade the asking person. This persuasion can be based on a negative motivation (fear of damaging the stomach). $TF = 0$ because Olbas oil is not effective against headaches.

- ($TF = 1$; $L = 0$): "Take an aspirin."

  - This solution is correct ($TF = 1$), but the author does not make any attempt to convince the reader ($L = 0$).

In the fake news dissemination scenario, it is even simpler to see the role of persuasiveness. Fake news are often accompanied by catchy or even sensational headings (sometimes referred to as "clickbait"). These headings attract the attention of social media users.

Even though the basic version of the Credibility Game (Sect. 5.2.2) is capable to express crucial properties of Q&A content, it is not suited to model Q&A knowledge communities or fake news dissemination on social media, since it assumes that each user can only be a CC or a CP. However, this assumption may be relaxed in an iterated version of the Credibility Game if the players are allowed to switch roles. This version shall be referred to as the *Symmetric Credibility Game*. This extension of the basic version is not complicated to understand. In a single iteration of the Symmetric Credibility Game of two players, each player first chooses the content producer role and produces information. Next, each player chooses the content consumer role and decides whether to accept or reject the information produced by the other player. Each of the two interactions follows the rules of an ordinary Credibility Game (possibly extended with signal or reputation). An additional assumption is made that the two instances of the Credibility Game are "simultaneous": the players cannot change their strategies in the second Credibility Game depending on the strategy chosen by the other player in the first one.

Players add their payoffs obtained using both roles. These payoffs of the Symmetric Credibility Game have an additional property for one of the possible types of the CP role: the dishonest producer CP-L.

5.5.1   Payoffs of Symmetric Credibility Game

In the Symmetric Credibility Game, players can choose any combination of the actions available for the CC and the CP, namely, BF+R, BF+A, GF+R, GF+A, BT+R, BT+A, GT+R, and GT+A. The payoffs of the Symmetric Credibility Game are simply the sums of payoff for the CP and CC roles (see Sect. 5.2.2.1). This section will show that these payoffs (if the CP is of the dishonest type) resemble the classic symmetric game used in most research on reputation systems: the Prisoner's Dilemma.

5.5.1.1   Symmetric Credibility Game with Dishonest Producer Is a
Prisoner's Dilemma

For the sake of this analysis, focus is placed on a combination of the most non-cooperative and most cooperative behaviors of both players. These are the combinations: BF+R (most non-cooperative) and GT+A (most cooperative). For simplicity, these actions will be called: D=BF+R, C=GT+A.

The payoff table for such a limited Symmetric Credibility Game can be constructed by adding the payoffs of the CC and the CP (keeping in mind that the

Table 5.8 Payoff of Symmetric Credibility Game for extremely cooperative and extremely non-cooperative actions played using CC and CP-L roles

CC+CP-L	C=GT+A	D=BF+R
C=GT+A	3,3	−3,5
D=BF+R	5,−3	−2, −2

player plays both roles at the same time, so he receives one payoff as a CC and one as a CP). The CP type needs to be fixed. The initial assumption is that it is CP-L (a dishonest producer).

The payoff table looks as follows (Table 5.8).

The game is now symmetric. Let us denote the payoffs (C,C) by R: $R = 3$ and for (D,D) by P: $P = -2$. Finally, **denote** the payoff of the first player for (C,D) by S: $S = -3$, and the payoff of the second player for (C,D) by T: $T = 5$.

This game fulfills the assumptions of the generalized Prisoner's Dilemma [5]:

$$T = 5 > R = 3 > P = -2 > S = -3$$

and

$$(T + S)/2 < R$$

This means that the Symmetric Credibility Game played by CC and CP-L (limited to the most cooperative and most non-cooperative combinations of CC and CP actions) is a Prisoner's Dilemma. The same does not apply, in case of combining Credibility Game played by CC and CP-H. Then, the Nash equilibrium of such game constitutes the combination of the most cooperative actions: GT+A.

5.5.2 Modeling Agent Learning and Knowledge

Each player in the Symmetric Credibility Game has the ability of taking both the roles of the CP and CC from the ordinary Credibility Game. Apart from these roles, players in the Symmetric Credibility Game do not have any special characteristics that could impact their strategies or behavior. However, since the intention is to use the Symmetric Credibility Game to model prosumers interacting through a Web 2.0 (Q&A) portal, an additional model requirement must be fulfilled. Players of the Symmetric Credibility Game should be able to learn and use the results of their learning to produce better information. There exists solid evidence for the existence of learning phenomena of Q&A users [166].

Social media users who receive fake news may also be able to learn about their factual correctness. Evidence about fake news dissemination on Twitter [162] shows that it is usually followed by debunking news published by fact-checkers. Ordinary social media user can learn from these more critical users.

The Symmetric Credibility Game with signal is almost sufficient to model the learning phenomenon. First assumption is that an agent (player) will have two additional parameters called *experience* and *knowledge*. Experience $\eta \in [0, 1]$ is a real number that will be increased by a constant increment each time the agent accepts truthful information (with $TF = 1$) in the CC role. On the other hand, each time the agent accepts untrue information, his or her experience will decrease by the same constant increment.

Knowledge $\kappa \in [0, 1]$ is the result of learning from successful trials. The learning process can be modeled by a standard S-Curve function [99].

$$\kappa = \frac{1}{1.582(1 - e^{-\eta})} \tag{5.9}$$

where η is the experience of the agent (the constant 1.582 in the denominator is included for normalization).

The two parameters will impact an agent's decisions in the Symmetric Credibility Game in two ways. First, when an agent takes the CP role and produces information, the produced information may depend on the agent's knowledge. For example, if the agent is an honest producer and wishes to produce truthful information, the probability that he or she will succeed can be equal to κ. (If the economic payoff model is used that allows TF to be a continuous value, knowledge could determine TF directly: $TF = \kappa$.)

Second, when the agent takes the CC role, his or her ability to evaluate information (its expertise) should depend on knowledge. In the Credibility Game, an agent's expertise was modeled using the signal. In particular, signal was determined using two parameters: w_{TF}, the weight of TF in the mean of the signal, and δ, the standard deviation of the signal. In the Symmetric Credibility Game with learning, $w_{TF} = \kappa$ and δ is a constant. This assures that agents with higher knowledge become experts in credibility evaluation.

5.5.3 Consumer Acceptance in the Symmetric Credibility Game with Learning

Players in the Symmetric Credibility Game accept information in the CC role using acceptance strategies similar to the strategies of the Credibility Game. They can use signal (as described above, signal can depend on an agent's knowledge) as well as reputation. In the remainder of this section, it will be assumed that players use payoff-based reputation to select content producers (selecting the CP with the highest reputation from three randomly chosen CPs, as described in Sect. 5.3.2) and to accept information. Information acceptance is based on signal only, in order to better study the impact of knowledge on agent behavior. In other words, CC chooses producers based on reputation, but accepts the information from a selected producer based on signal.

5.5.4 Simulation of Symmetric Credibility Game with Learning

Like in the analysis of Credibility Game with reputation, the Symmetric Credibility Game with learning can be analyzed using simulation. The same simulator as described in Sect. 5.2.7.1 has been used in the analysis described in this section. Agent strategies in the Symmetric Credibility Game are the strategies related to both the CP and CC roles. These strategies evolve separately in the simulation, until an evolutionary equilibrium is reached. However, agent experience and knowledge does not evolve, but rather is incremented/decremented during the entire simulation depending on the agent's acceptance decisions in the CC role.

It is important to note here that the Symmetric Credibility Game used in the simulations is an iterated game with several (in the reported simulations, 100) agents. This means that a single iteration of the Symmetric Credibility Game looks as follows: all agents first choose the CP role and use their strategy to produce information. Next, all agents choose the CC role and choose one of the other agents (with an exception of itself) as a producer to interact with. This means that agents do not necessarily interact two times with one another (once in the CP role and once in the CC role) as in the Symmetric Credibility Game with two players, although such an interaction is possible. Random choice in the simulation has an impact on the choice of agent pairs. It is also possible that an agent in the CP role who has a low reputation will not be chosen by any other agent in the CC role, and will therefore have zero payoff for this instance of the Credibility Game.

In the simulations reported in this section, 100 agents have been used who could take both CP and CC roles. The payoffs of the Symmetric Credibility Game have been described above. Each experience gain (or loss) of an agent was equal to 0.01 (in other words, after accepting truthful information 100 times, an agent's experience would rise from 0 to 1). Initial experience/knowledge was randomized using a normal distribution. The mean and variance of this distribution were simulation parameters.

5.5.5 Hypotheses Regarding Learning Knowledge Communities and Credibility Evaluation

The Symmetric Credibility Game with learning can be used to model credibility evaluation in a variety of Web 2.0 communities (especially knowledge communities, such users of thematic fora or Q&A sites, but also Twitter users who receive fake news) and to study various phenomena that are related to credibility evaluation. This section sets out to study a few hypotheses related to user communities of Q&A sites and the spreading of fake news.

The following hypotheses will be evaluated in this section:

1. The community will be able to learn (the average knowledge in the community will rise).

2. Increased persuasiveness ($L = 1$) is harmful for the community.
3. The community will be able to resist adversaries who wish to promote incorrect answers or fake news.
4. Reputation is helpful for resisting adversaries by the community.

5.5.6   Speed of Community Learning

The first hypothesis has been tested using a simulation scenario that included only honest agents (agents that could take the honest producer role). However, the initial knowledge of these agents was varied, resulting in behavior that could be similar to dishonest producers (honest agents with low knowledge would often produce information with $TF = 0$).

Figures 5.9 and 5.10 demonstrate that the validity of Hypothesis 1 depends on the initial conditions: the initial level of knowledge in the community. If this level is too low, then the average knowledge in the community will not only not increase but rather decrease and stabilize at a very low value. In such conditions, almost all agents will increase the persuasiveness of generated content ($L = 1$). On the other hand, if the initial knowledge is average (mean of the knowledge distribution equal

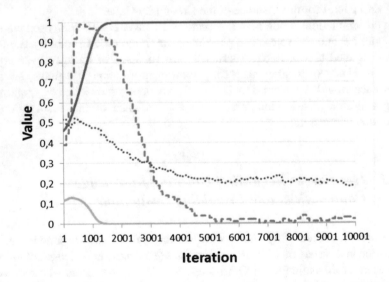

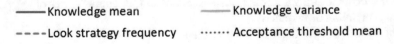

Fig. 5.9 Average knowledge scenario results (mean $= 0.5$, std.dev $= 0.2$). Source: [93]

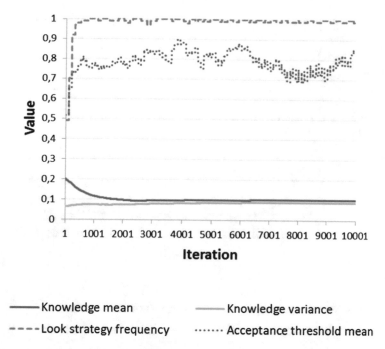

Fig. 5.10 Low knowledge scenario results (mean = 0.2, std.dev. = 0.2). Source: [93]

to 0.5 with low standard deviation), then the average knowledge of agents in the community will rise until it reaches the highest value (1). At the same time, the frequency of investing in persuasiveness will decrease.

The conclusion about the lack of community learning in a low knowledge scenario is pessimistic with regard to fake news dissemination on social media. The initial knowledge of ordinary social media users with regard to manufactured fake news can be assumed to be low. This highlights the role of experts and fact-checkers in the community: without them, community learning is unlikely to take place, and fake news can dominate the community opinion.

Since the initial conditions of the simulation seem to have a high impact on the equilibrium, it is necessary to investigate the sensitivity of the equilibrium to initial conditions further. This can be done by changing the parameters of the initial distribution of knowledge. In particular, it is important to investigate the impact of initial knowledge variance on the equilibrium. The results of this analysis are shown in Figs. 5.11, 5.12, and 5.13. In particular, the varied knowledge scenario can be thought of as a model of a situation when ordinary users and experts are present in a community.

The results demonstrate that while increasing the mean of the initial knowledge distribution will speed up reaching the equilibrium, increasing the variance of this distribution will increase the time needed to reach an equilibrium. This result explains the long duration of fake news spreading on social media. Despite the

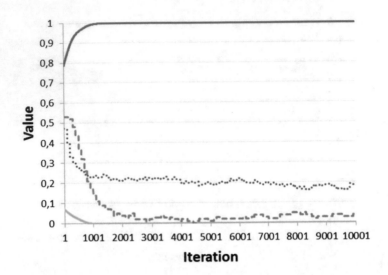

Fig. 5.11 High knowledge scenario results (mean = 0.8, std.dev. = 0.2)

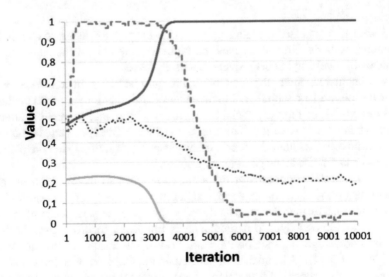

Fig. 5.12 Varied knowledge (mean = 0.5, std.dev = 1). Source: [93]

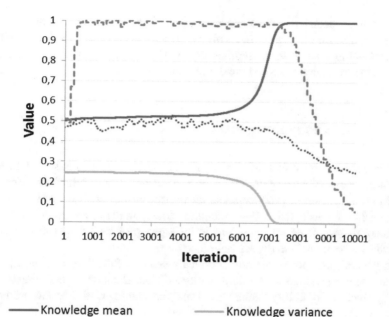

Fig. 5.13   Polarized knowledge (mean = 0.5, std.dev = 99). Source: [93]

presence of experts and fact-checkers, it may take a long time for the community to learn and debunk fake news.

The polarized knowledge scenario can model a situation when two partisan groups exist in social media that have different prior credibility evaluations of fake news. From Fig. 5.13 that concerns the polarized knowledge scenario, it can be observed that there seems to be a phase transition of average knowledge from the mean of the initial distribution to 1. Increasing the variance of the initial knowledge distribution does not affect the equilibrium, but only the time needed to reach the equilibrium. This is an interesting result that suggests that learning communities with similar initial knowledge of members will work better than communities with highly polarized initial knowledge. This result is also in agreement with observed situations when fake news with political content are spreading on social media, and social media users are divided into partisan groups. In some cases, it may be impossible to reach the phase transition and to get the entire community to agree to deny the fake news.

From Figs. 5.9, 5.12, and 5.13, it can be observed that increasing the persuasiveness of the content by investing into $L = 1$ is an effective strategy in the initial stage of the simulation (before the phase transition towards maximal knowledge in the community). Producers need to persuade consumers who have low knowledge to accept information even if this information is truthful. This finding proves that Hypothesis 2 is not valid: increasing persuasiveness is not harmful for the community, especially in the stage when average knowledge is not high. In other words, *truth must still advertise*. This result also points out an effective strategy for combating fake news dissemination on social media: using a social media advertising campaign to spread the debunking information.

5.5.7 Community Robustness

In this section, the effect of the reputation system on strategies of dishonest producers is investigated again. This time, the setting differs, as the false information produced by dishonest producers has an impact on the credibility evaluations of consumers who accepted it. This scenario closely matches a situation when fake news are disseminated on social media by a group of malicious trolls or content providers who are paid to disseminate fake news.

In general, the more dishonest producers produce false information, the lower the average knowledge of the community will be. Because of this phenomenon, the Symmetric Credibility Game model may be more sensitive to the presence of dishonest producers.

The reputation system is using payoff-based reputation. The design of the reputation system is the same as described in Sect. 5.3.1.

In tested scenarios, the percentage of dishonest producers was varied (10%, 50%, and 90%). Other parameters were nearly the same as in previous scenarios (for clarity, initial look usage and initial knowledge were set to mean $= 0.3$).

The simulations clearly show the effectiveness of the reputation system. When reputation was used, the effect of the presence of 10% dishonest producers is almost unnoticeable. Comparing Fig. 5.14 with Fig. 5.9, it can be seen that although the initial conditions are slightly different, the stable state is the same and is also achieved in a similar number of simulation steps.

On the other hand, the effect of 50% dishonest producers is more pronounced. As shown in Fig. 5.15, achieving a stable state with maximum level of knowledge in the community takes more time. Also, there is a subtle but significant difference in the stable states of the scenario with 50% dishonest producers and scenarios with 10% dishonest producers or with 0% dishonest producers and no reputation system. Although the mean knowledge in the community is the same in both cases, in the first case the mean acceptance threshold (for signal values) is about 0.3, significantly higher than in the other two scenarios (0.2). This indicates that consumers have learned to be more critical of produced information (Figs. 5.16 and 5.17).

A percentage above 50% of dishonest producers in the community makes the reputation system increasingly ineffective. In the extreme case of 90% dishonest producers, the stable state is comparable to a scenario with the reputation system turned off (and 10% dishonest producers). All agents invest in presentation, decisions are based on signal with an extremely high acceptance threshold (for the scenario with 90% dishonest producers, the threshold is about 0.75, while for 10% dishonest producers with reputation system turned off the acceptance threshold

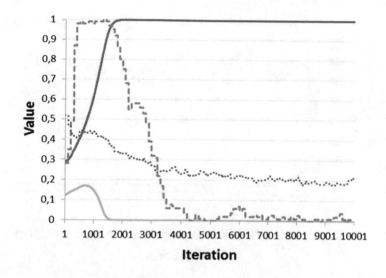

Fig. 5.14 Scenario with reputation on, 10% dishonest. Source: [93]

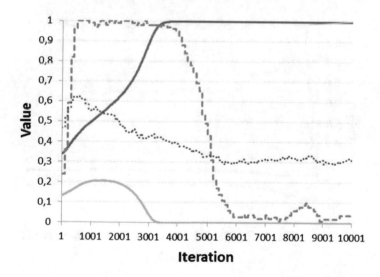

Fig. 5.15 Scenario with reputation on, 50% dishonest. Source: [93]

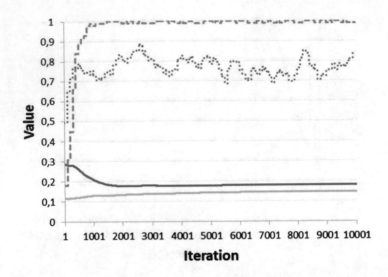

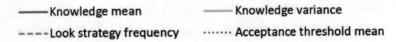

Fig. 5.16 Scenario with reputation on, 90% dishonest. Source: [93]

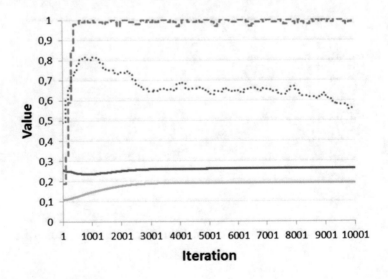

Fig. 5.17 Scenario with reputation off, 10% dishonest. Source: [93]

is slightly lower, about 0.65). This means that consumers will only rarely accept information, which is also usually incorrect ($TF = 0$) because of the extremely low mean knowledge (recall that an honest agent's knowledge is the probability that the agent will produce truthful information).

The simulation experiments described in this section demonstrate that a community that uses payoff-based reputation can tolerate up to 50% dishonest producers. Moreover, in such scenarios, the outcome was similar to the case when all producers were honest (and the reputation system was not used). The results clearly show the value of reputation for learning and credibility evaluation in knowledge communities. It should be stressed that current social media are not equipped with effective reputation mechanisms, which makes the combating of fake news dissemination by adversaries a challenging task.

5.6 Conclusions

This chapter has aimed to demonstrate the possibility of creating theoretical models of Web content credibility and using these models to explain several phenomena specific to credibility of content production and evaluation. Models of credibility can be extended towards specific systems and environments, such as Web 2.0 knowledge communities, or commercially motivated Web content production. Theoretical models can be simulated, enabling the study of various mechanisms for the improvement of Web content credibility evaluation (on the other hand, also of adversarial strategies). Moreover, signal models can also be fitted to experimental data, leading to the possibility of using behavioral data to drive simulations that would evaluate algorithmic effectiveness.

The models proposed in this chapter have indeed already been used to study algorithms and systems for Web content credibility evaluation support [107]. However, this is only the beginning. This chapter has attempted to lay down a theoretical framework for researchers wishing to study effects and phenomena related to information credibility evaluation. Such a theoretical basis has been mostly lacking from research on credibility so far. Increased use of models may lead to a much better understanding of credibility and the role it plays in contemporary information systems in the future. The models proposed in this chapter can also be used to understand fake news dissemination on social media and to study strategies that aim to counter fake news dissemination.

Chapter 6
Conclusions

Evaluation of Web content credibility is becoming increasingly significant. Our personal, political, work-related, medical, and health decisions (as well as many others) are frequently made on the basis of information on the Web. A recent, and quite concerning, example of the impact of information on the Internet is the 2016 American presidential election [4]. This important political decision has been influenced by numerous allegations and rumors circulating on the Internet, concerning both main candidates.

The increasing significance of the information on the Web is coupled with increasingly loud concerns about its credibility. This has led to the emergence of several voices that call for a rigid control of the Internet, sometimes in the form of government censorship.[1] This kind of control is in fact used in several countries, such as Singapore.[2]

If we wish to improve the decision making based on Web content, the only alternative to censorship is an increase in the education and awareness of Web users with regard to credibility evaluation, as well as an improvement of their ability to evaluate Web content credibility. Many existing services have emerged (and are described in this book) that try to address this need. Nevertheless, the technical and scientific knowledge in this area is still insufficient. The emerging research area of fake news detection [167] highlights the importance and immaturity of automatic solutions for Web content credibility evaluation support.

This book has attempted to review and synthesize the current state of the art in the area of Web content credibility evaluation support. Together with another recent review [49], this work documents hundreds of research papers on this subject, many

---

[1]https://en.wikipedia.org/wiki/Internet_censorship.

[2]https://en.wikipedia.org/wiki/Internet_censorship_in_Singapore.

of which report exciting and promising findings. Still, research results in this area have yet to reach technical maturity and become adopted by Internet users. I hope that this book will provide an incentive and basis for an accelerated research and development of Web content credibility evaluation support services.

References

1. K. Abramczuk, M. Kakol, A. Wierzbicki, How to support the lay users evaluations of medical information on the web?, in *International Conference on Human Interface and the Management of Information* (Springer, Cham, 2016), pp. 3–13
2. B.T. Adler, K. Chatterjee, L. de Alfaro, M. Faella, Assigning trust to Wikipedia content, in *WikiSym 2008: International Symposium on Wikis and Open Collaboration* (2008)
3. E. Agirre, M. Diab, D. Cer, A. Gonzalez-Agirre, Semeval-2012 task 6: a pilot on Semantic Textual Similarity, in *Proceedings of the First Joint Conference on Lexical and Computational Semantics-Volume 1: Proceedings of the Main Conference and the Shared Task, and Volume 2: Proceedings of the Sixth International Workshop on Semantic Evaluation* (Association for Computational Linguistics, Stroudsburg, 2012), pp. 385–393
4. H. Allcott, M. Gentzkow, Social media and fake news in the 2016 election. J. Econ. Perspect **31**(2), 211–236 (2017)
5. R. Axelrod, W.D. Hamilton, The evolution of cooperation. Science **211**(4489), 1390–1396 (1981)
6. D. Bär, C. Biemann, I. Gurevych, T. Zesch, Ukp: computing Semantic Textual Similarity by combining multiple content similarity measures, in *Proceedings of the First Joint Conference on Lexical and Computational Semantics-Volume 1: Proceedings of the Main Conference and the Shared Task, and Volume 2: Proceedings of the Sixth International Workshop on Semantic Evaluation* (Association for Computational Linguistics, Stroudsburg, 2012), pp. 435–440
7. B. Barber, *Logic and Limits of Trust* (Rutgers University Press, New Brunswick, 1983)
8. A. Barr, Trust and expected trustworthiness: an experimental investigation (No. 2001-12). Centre for the Study of African Economies, University of Oxford (2001)
9. J. Bian, Y. Liu, E. Agichtein, H. Zha, Finding the right facts in the crowd: factoid question answering over social media, in *Proceedings of the 17th International Conference on World Wide Web* (ACM, New York, 2008), pp. 467–476
10. R.P. Biuk-Aghai, C.-I. Pang, Y.-W. Si, Visualizing large-scale human collaboration in Wikipedia. Futur. Gener. Comput. Syst. **31**, 120–133 (2014)
11. D.M. Blei, A.Y. Ng, M.I. Jordan, Latent Dirichlet allocation. J. Mach. Learn. Res. **3**(Jan), 993–1022 (2003)
12. E. Borra, E. Weltevrede, P. Ciuccarelli, A. Kaltenbrunner, D. Laniado, G. Magni, M. Mauri, R. Rogers, T. Venturini, Societal controversies in Wikipedia articles, in *Proceedings of the 33rd Annual ACM Conference on Human Factors in Computing Systems, CHI '15* (ACM, New York, 2015), pp. 193–196

© Springer International Publishing AG, part of Springer Nature 2018
A. Wierzbicki, *Web Content Credibility*,
https://doi.org/10.1007/978-3-319-77794-8

13. P. Borzymek, M. Sydow, A. Wierzbicki, Enriching trust prediction model in social network with user rating similarity, in *International Conference on Computational Aspects of Social Networks, 2009. CASON'09* (IEEE, Washington, 2009), pp. 40–47

14. L. Buriol, C. Castillo, D. Donato, S. Leonardi, S. Millozzi, *Temporal Evolution of the Wikigraph* (IEEE CS Press, Washington, 2006), pp. 45–51

15. L. Cagnina, P. Rosso, Classification of deceptive opinions using a low dimensionality representation, in *Proceedings of the 6th Workshop on Computational Approaches to Subjectivity, Sentiment and Social Media Analysis* (2015), pp. 58–66

16. C. Castillo, M. Mendoza, B. Poblete, Information credibility on Twitter, in *Proceedings of the 20th International Conference on World Wide Web*, WWW '11 (ACM, New York, 2011), pp. 675–684

17. S. Chaiken, Heuristic versus systematic information processing and the use of source versus message cues in persuasion. J. Pers. Soc. Psychol. **39**(5), 752 (1980)

18. A. Chakraborty, B. Paranjape, S. Kakarla, N. Ganguly, Stop clickbait: detecting and preventing clickbaits in online news media, in *International Conference on Advances in Social Networks Analysis and Mining (ASONAM), 2016 IEEE/ACM* (IEEE, Washington, 2016), pp. 9–16

19. R. Chandy, Wikiganda: identifying propaganda through text analysis. Caltech Undergrad. Res. J. **9**(1), 6–11 (2008)

20. Y. Chen, N.J. Conroy, V.L. Rubin, Misleading online content: recognizing clickbait as false news, in *Proceedings of the 2015 ACM on Workshop on Multimodal Deception Detection* (ACM, New York, 2015), pp. 15–19

21. G.L. Ciampaglia, P. Shiralkar, L.M. Rocha, J. Bollen, F. Menczer, A. Flammini, Computational fact checking from knowledge networks. PLoS One **10**(6), e0128193 (2015)

22. N.J. Conroy, V.L. Rubin, Y. Chen, Automatic deception detection: methods for finding fake news. Proc. Assoc. Inf. Sci. Technol. **52**(1), 1–4 (2015)

23. A. Cusinato, V.D. Mea, F. Di Salvatore, S. Mizzaro, QuWi: quality control in Wikipedia, in *Proceedings of the 3rd Workshop on Information Credibility on the Web* (ACM, New York, 2009), pp. 27–34

24. A.P. Dawid, A.M. Skene, Maximum likelihood estimation of observer error-rates using the EM algorithm. Appl. Stat. **28**, 20–28 (1979)

25. L. Derczynski, K. Bontcheva, M. Liakata, R. Procter, G.W.S. Hoi, A. Zubiaga, SemEval-2017 Task 8: RumourEval: determining rumour veracity and support for rumours (2017). arXiv Preprint. arXiv:1704.05972

26. X. Dong, E. Gabrilovich, G. Heitz, W. Horn, N. Lao, K. Murphy, T. Strohmann, S. Sun, W. Zhang, Knowledge vault: a web-scale approach to probabilistic knowledge fusion, in *Proceedings of the 20th ACM SIGKDD International Conference on Knowledge Discovery and Data Mining* (ACM, New York, 2014), pp. 601–610

27. S. Dori-Hacohen, J. Allan, Detecting controversy on the web, in *Proceedings of the 22nd ACM International Conference on Information & Knowledge Management, CIKM '13* (ACM, New York, 2013), pp. 1845–1848

28. S. Dori-Hacohen, J. Allan, Automated controversy detection on the web, in *Advances in Information Retrieval* (Springer, Cham, 2015), pp. 423–434. https://doi.org/10.1007/978-3-319-16354-3_46

29. S. Dori-Hacohen, E. Yom-Tov, J. Allan, Navigating controversy as a complex search task, in *SCST@ ECIR* (2015)

30. J.R. Douceur, The sybil attack, in *International Workshop on Peer-to-Peer Systems* (Springer, Berlin, 2002), pp. 251–260

31. C. Eickhoff, A.P. de Vries, Increasing cheat robustness of Crowdsourcing tasks. Inf. Retr. **16**(2), 121–137 (2013)

32. E. Elgesem, Normative structures in trust management, in *Trust Management (iTrust 2006)*. Lecture Notes in Computer Science, vol. 3986 (Springer, Berlin, 2006)

33. R. Ennals, D. Byler, J.M. Agosta, B. Rosario, What is disputed on the web?, in *Proceedings of the 4th Workshop on Information Credibility, WICOW '10* (ACM, New York, 2010), pp. 67–74

34. R. Feldman, B. Rosenfeld, R. Bar-Haim, M. Fresko, The stock sonar—sentiment analysis of stocks based on a hybrid approach, in *Twenty-Third IAAI Conference* (2011)
35. V.W. Feng, G. Hirst, Detecting deceptive opinions with profile compatibility, in *Proceedings of the Sixth International Joint Conference on Natural Language Processing* (2013), pp. 338–346
36. S. Feng, R. Banerjee, Y. Choi, Syntactic stylometry for deception detection, in *Proceedings of the 50th Annual Meeting of the Association for Computational Linguistics: Short Papers-Volume 2* (Association for Computational Linguistics, Stroudsburg, 2012), pp. 171–175
37. O. Ferschke, I. Gurevych, Y. Chebotar, Behind the article: recognizing dialog acts in Wikipedia talk pages, in *Proceedings of the 13th Conference of the European Chapter of the Association for Computational Linguistics, EACL '12* (Association for Computational Linguistics, Stroudsburg, 2012), pp. 777–786
38. B.J. Fogg, H. Tseng, The elements of computer credibility, in *Proceedings of the SIGCHI Conference on Human Factors in Computing Systems, CHI '99* (ACM, New York, 1999), pp. 80–87
39. B.J. Fogg, J. Marshall, O. Laraki, A. Osipovich, C. Varma, N. Fang, J. Paul, A. Rangnekar, J. Shon, P. Swani, et al., What makes web sites credible?: a report on a large quantitative study, in *Proceedings of the SIGCHI Conference on Human Factors in Computing Systems* (ACM, New York, 2001), pp. 61–68
40. B.J. Fogg, C. Soohoo, D.R. Danielson, L. Marable, J. Stanford, E.R. Tauber, How do users evaluate the credibility of web sites?: a study with over 2500 participants, in *Proceedings of the 2003 Conference on Designing for User Experiences* (ACM, New York, 2003), pp. 1–15
41. B. Frénay, M. Verleysen, Classification in the presence of label noise: a survey. IEEE Trans. Neural Netw. Learn. Syst. **25**(5), 845–869 (2014)
42. M. Frické, D. Fallis, M. Jones, G.M. Luszko, Consumer health information on the Internet about carpal tunnel syndrome: indicators of accuracy. Am. J. Med. **118**(2), 168–174 (2005)
43. E. Friedman, P. Resnick, R. Sami, Manipulation-resistant reputation systems, in *Algorithmic Game Theory*, vol. 677 (Cambridge University Press, Cambridge, 2007)
44. D.H. Fusilier, M. Montes-y Gómez, P. Rosso, R.G. Cabrera, Detecting positive and negative deceptive opinions using PU-learning. Inf. Process. Manag. **51**(4), 433–443 (2015)
45. E. Gabrilovich, S. Markovitch, Computing semantic relatedness using Wikipedia-based explicit semantic analysis, in *IJcAI*, vol. 7 (2007), pp. 1606–1611
46. D. Gambetta, Can we trust trust?, in *Trust: Making and Breaking of Cooperative Relations*, ed. by D. Gambetta (Basil Blackwell, Oxford, 1988)
47. K. Garimella, G. De Francisci Morales, A. Gionis, M. Mathioudakis, Quantifying controversy in social media, in *Proceedings of the Ninth ACM International Conference on Web Search and Data Mining, WSDM '16* (ACM, New York, 2016), pp. 33–42
48. W.I. Gasarch, Guest column: the second P =?NP Poll. SIGACT News **43**(2), 53–77 (2012)
49. A.L. Ginsca, A. Popescu, M. Lupu, Credibility in information retrieval. Found. Trends Inf. Retr. **9**(5), 355–475 (2015)
50. J. Glazer, A. Rubinstein, A study in the pragmatics of persuasion: a game theoretical approach. Theor. Econ. **1**(4), 395–410 (2006)
51. M. Glenski, E. Ayton, D. Arendt, S. Volkova, Fishing for Clickbaits in social images and texts with linguistically-infused neural network models (2017). arXiv Preprint. arXiv:1710.06390
52. F.J. Gravetter, L.B. Wallnau, *Statistics for the Behavioral Sciences* (Cengage Learning, Boston, 2016)
53. M.S.A. Graziano, *God Soul Mind Brain: A Neuroscientist's Reflections on the Spirit World* (Leapfrog Press, New York, 2010)
54. K.M. Griffiths, T.T. Tang, D. Hawking, H. Christensen, Automated assessment of the quality of depression websites. J. Med. Internet Res. **7**(5), e59 (2005)
55. A. Gupta, P. Kumaraguru, Credibility ranking of tweets during high impact events, in *Proceedings of the 1st Workshop on Privacy and Security in Online Social Media* (ACM, New York, 2012), p. 8

56. A. Gupta, P. Kumaraguru, C. Castillo, P. Meier, TweetCred: real-time credibility assessment of content on twitter, in *6th International Conference, SocInfo 2014*. Lecture Notes in Computer Science (Springer, Berlin, 2014)

57. J.M. Guttman, The credibility game: reputation and rational cooperation in a changing population. J. Comp. Econ. **16**(4), 619–632 (1992)

58. A. Hanselowski, I. Gurevych, A framework for automated fact-checking for real-time validation of emerging claims on the web, in *NIPS Workshop on Prioritising Online Content (WPOC2017)* (Knowledge 4 All Foundation Ltd., 2017)

59. E. Hargittai, Beyond logs and surveys: in-depth measures of people's web use skills. J. Am. Soc. Inf. Sci. **53**(14), 1239–1244 (2002)

60. D. Harman, Overview of the first Text REtrieval Conference (TREC-1), in *Proceedings of the First Text REtrieval Conference (TREC-1)* (National Institute of Standards and Technology, Gaithersburg, 1992)

61. D. Harman, Overview of the second Text REtrieval Conference (TREC-2), in *Proceedings of the Second Text REtrieval Conference (TREC-2)* (National Institute of Standards and Technology, Gaithersburg , 1993)

62. N. Hassan, C. Li, M. Tremayne, Detecting check-worthy factual claims in presidential debates, in *Proceedings of the 24th ACM International on Conference on Information and Knowledge Management* (ACM, New York, 2015), pp. 1835–1838

63. N. Hassan, F. Arslan, C. Li, M. Tremayne, Toward automated fact-checking: detecting check-worthy factual claims by ClaimBuster, in *Proceedings of the 23rd ACM SIGKDD International Conference on Knowledge Discovery and Data Mining* (ACM, New York, 2017), pp. 1803–1812

64. A. Heydari, M.A. Tavakoli, N. Salim, Z. Heydari, Detection of review spam: a survey. Expert Syst. Appl. **42**(7), 3634–3642 (2015)

65. R.M. Hogarth, *Judgement and Choice: The Psychology of Decision* (Wiley, Hoboken, 1987)

66. B.D. Horne, S. Adali, This just in: fake news packs a lot in title, uses simpler, repetitive content in text body, more similar to satire than real news (2017). arXiv Preprint. arXiv:1703.09398

67. C.I. Hovland, W. Weiss, The influence of source credibility on communication effectiveness. Public Opin. Q. **15**(4), 635–650 (1951)

68. D. Hovy, T. Berg-Kirkpatrick, A. Vaswani, E.H. Hovy, Learning whom to trust with mace, in *HLT-NAACL* (2013), pp. 1120–1130

69. P.G. Ipeirotis, E. Gabrilovich, Quizz: targeted Crowdsourcing with a billion (potential) users, in *Proceedings of the 23rd International Conference on World Wide Web, WWW '14* (ACM, New York, 2014), pp. 143–154

70. P.G. Ipeirotis, F. Provost, V.S. Sheng, J. Wang, Repeated labeling using multiple noisy labelers. Data Min. Knowl. Disc. **28**(2), 402–441 (2014)

71. S. Jamieson et al., Likert scales: how to (ab) use them. Med. Educ. **38**(12), 1217–1218 (2004)

72. M. Jankowski-Lorek, R. Nielek, A. Wierzbicki, K. Zieliński, Predicting controversy of Wikipedia articles using the article feedback tool, in *Proceedings of the 2014 International Conference on Social Computing, SocialCom '14* (ACM, New York, 2014), pp. 22:1–22:7

73. J. Jeon, W.B. Croft, J.H. Lee, S. Park, A framework to predict the quality of answers with non-textual features, in *Proceedings of the 29th Annual International ACM SIGIR Conference on Research and Development in Information Retrieval* (ACM, New York, 2006), pp. 228–235

74. Z. Jin, J. Cao, Y. Zhang, J. Luo, News verification by exploiting conflicting social viewpoints in microblogs, in *AAAI* (2016), pp. 2972–2978

75. R. John, J.P. Cherian, J.J. Kizhakkethottam, A survey of techniques to prevent sybil attacks, in *2015 International Conference on Soft-Computing and Networks Security (ICSNS)*, February 2015, pp. 1–6

76. A. Josang, C. Keser, T. Dimitrakos, Can we manage trust? in *Trust Management (iTrust 2005)*. *Lecture Notes in Computer Science*, vol. 3477 (Springer, Berlin, 2005)

77. M. Juzwin, P. Adamska, M. Rafalak, B. Balcerzak, M. Kakol, A. Wierzbicki, Threats of using gamification for motivating web page quality evaluation, in *Proceedings of the 2014*

Mulitmedia, Interaction, Design and Innovation International Conference on Multimedia, Interaction, Design and Innovation (ACM, New York, 2014), pp. 1–8

78. D. Kahneman, *Thinking, Fast and Slow* (Macmillan, Basingstoke, 2011)

79. M. Kakol, M. Jankowski-Lorek, K. Abramczuk, A. Wierzbicki, M. Catasta, On the subjectivity and bias of web content credibility evaluations, in *Proceedings of the 22nd International Conference on World Wide Web Companion* (International World Wide Web Conferences Steering Committee, Geneva, 2013), pp. 1131–1136

80. M. Kakol, R. Nielek, A. Wierzbicki, Understanding and predicting web content credibility using the content credibility corpus. Inf. Process. Manag. **53**(5), 1043–1061 (2017)

81. R. Kaptein, M. Koolen, J. Kamps, Using Wikipedia categories for ad hoc search, in *Proceedings of the 32nd International ACM SIGIR Conference on Research and Development in Information Retrieval, SIGIR '09* (ACM, New York, 2009), pp. 824–825

82. T. Kaszuba, A. Hupa, A. Wierzbicki, Advanced feedback management for internet auction reputation systems. IEEE Internet Comput. **14**(5), 31–37 (2010)

83. T. Kawada, S. Akamine, D. Kawahara, Y. Kato, Y.I. Leon-Suematsu, K. Inui, S. Kurohashi, Y. Kidawara, Web information analysis for open-domain decision support: system design and user evaluation, in *Proceedings of the 2011 Joint WICOW/AIRWeb Workshop on Web Quality* (ACM, New York, 2011), pp. 13–18

84. D. Kawahara, K. Inui, S. Kurohashi, Identifying contradictory and contrastive relations between statements to outline web information on a given topic, in *Proceedings of the 23rd International Conference on Computational Linguistics: Posters, COLING '10* (Association for Computational Linguistics, Stroudsburg, 2010), pp. 534–542

85. Y. Kawai, Y. Fujita, T. Kumamoto, J. Jianwei, K. Tanaka, Using a sentiment map for visualizing credibility of news sites on the web, in *Proceedings of the 2nd ACM Workshop on Information Credibility on the Web, WICOW '08* (ACM, New York, 2008), pp. 53–58

86. E.F. Kelly, P.J. Stone, *Computer Recognition of English Word Senses*, vol. 13 (North-Holland, Amsterdam, 1975)

87. S. Kim, H. Chang, S. Lee, M. Yu, J. Kang, Deep semantic frame-based deceptive opinion spam analysis, in *Proceedings of the 24th ACM International on Conference on Information and Knowledge Management* (ACM, New York, 2015), pp. 1131–1140

88. A. Kittur, B. Suh, B.A. Pendleton, E.H. Chi, He says, she says: conflict and coordination in Wikipedia (ACM, New York, 2007), pp. 453–462

89. A. Kittur, E.H. Chi, B. Suh, Crowdsourcing user studies with mechanical Turk, in *Proceedings of the SIGCHI Conference on Human Factors in Computing Systems, CHI '08* (ACM, New York, 2008), pp. 453–456

90. A. Kittur, E.H. Chi, B. Suh, What's in Wikipedia?: mapping topics and conflict using socially annotated category structure, in *Proceedings of the SIGCHI Conference on Human Factors in Computing Systems, CHI '09* (ACM, New York, 2009), pp. 1509–1512

91. O. Kolomiyets, M.-F. Moens, A survey on question answering technology from an information retrieval perspective. Inf. Sci. **181**(24), 5412–5434 (2011)

92. V. Kostakos, Is the crowd's wisdom biased? A quantitative analysis of three online communities, in *International Conference on Computational Science and Engineering, 2009. CSE'09*, vol. 4 (IEEE, Washington, 2009), pp. 251–255

93. G. Kowalik, P. Adamska, R. Nielek, A. Wierzbicki, Simulations of credibility evaluation and learning in a web 2.0 community, in *International Conference on Artificial Intelligence and Soft Computing* (Springer, Cham, 2014), pp. 373–384

94. G. Kowalik, A. Wierzbicki, T. Borzyszkowski, W. Jaworski, Credibility as signal: predicting evaluations of credibility by a signal-based model (IEEE/WIC/ACM, Omaha, 2016)

95. R.E. Kraut, P. Resnick, Encouraging contribution to online communities, in *Building Successful Online Communities: Evidence-Based Social Design* (MIT Press, Cambridge, 2011), pp. 21–76

96. L.I. Kuncheva, C.J. Whitaker, C.A. Shipp, R.P.W. Duin, Limits on the majority vote accuracy in classifier fusion. Pattern. Anal. Appl. **6**(1), 22–31 (2003)

97. T.K. Landauer, P.W. Foltz, D. Laham, An introduction to latent semantic analysis. Discourse Process. **25**(2–3), 259–284 (1998)
98. D. Laniado, A. Kaltenbrunner, C. Castillo, M.F. Morell, Emotions and dialogue in a peer-production community: the case of Wikipedia, in *Proceedings of the Eighth Annual International Symposium on Wikis and Open Collaboration, WikiSym '12* (ACM, New York, 2012), pp. 9:1–9:10
99. N. Leibowitz, B. Baum, G. Enden, A. Karniel, The exponential learning equation as a function of successful trials results in sigmoid performance. J. Math. Psychol. **54**(3), 338–340 (2010)
100. R.K. Leik, A measure of ordinal consensus. Pac. Sociol. Rev. **9**(2), 85–90 (1966)
101. B.N. Levine, C. Shields, N.B. Margolin, *A Survey of Solutions to the Sybil Attack*, vol. 7 (University of Massachusetts Amherst, Amherst, 2006), p. 224
102. P. Levy, *Collective Intelligence* (Perseus Books, New York, 1997)
103. G. Lewis, Asymmetric information, adverse selection and online disclosure: the case of eBay motors. Am. Econ. Rev. **101**(4), 1535–1546 (2011)
104. J. Li, M. Ott, C. Cardie, E. Hovy, Towards a general rule for identifying deceptive opinion spam, in *Proceedings of the 52nd Annual Meeting of the Association for Computational Linguistics (Volume 1: Long Papers)*, vol. 1 (2014), pp. 1566–1576
105. H. Li, Z. Chen, A. Mukherjee, B. Liu, J. Shao, Analyzing and detecting opinion spam on a large-scale dataset via temporal and spatial patterns, in *ICWSM* (2015), pp. 634–637
106. L. Li, W. Ren, B. Qin, T. Liu, Learning document representation for deceptive opinion spam detection, in *Chinese Computational Linguistics and Natural Language Processing Based on Naturally Annotated Big Data* (Springer, Basel, 2015), pp. 393–404
107. X. Liu, R. Nielek, A. Wierzbicki, K. Aberer, Defending imitating attacks in web credibility evaluation systems, in *Proceedings of the 22nd International Conference on World Wide Web* (ACM, New York, 2013), pp. 1115–1122
108. M. Luca, G. Zervas, Fake it till you make it: reputation, competition, and yelp review fraud. Manag. Sci. **62**(12), 3412–3427 (2016)
109. R.D. Luce, The choice axiom after twenty years. J. Math. Psychol. **15**(3), 215–233 (1977)
110. A. Magdy, N. Wanas, Web-based statistical fact checking of textual documents, in *Proceedings of the 2nd International Workshop on Search and Mining User-Generated Contents* (ACM, New York, 2010), pp. 103–110
111. A. Malossini, E. Blanzieri, R.T. Ng, Detecting potential labeling errors in microarrays by data perturbation. Bioinformatics **22**(17), 2114–2121 (2006)
112. S.P. Marsh, Formalising trust as a computational concept, Ph.D. thesis, University of Stirling, April 1994
113. M. Mathioudakis, N. Koudas, Twittermonitor: trend detection over the Twitter stream, in *Proceedings of the 2010 ACM SIGMOD International Conference on Management of data* (ACM, New York, 2010), pp. 1155–1158
114. D. McFadden, Conditional logit analysis of qualitative choice behavior, in *Frontiers in Econometrics*, ed. by P. Zarembka (Wiley, New York, 1973)
115. O. Medelyan, D. Milne, C. Legg, I.H. Witten, Mining meaning from Wikipedia. Int. J. Hum. Comput. Stud. **67**(9), 716–754 (2009)
116. M. Mendoza, B. Poblete, C. Castillo, Twitter under crisis: can we trust what we RT?, in *Proceedings of the First Workshop on Social Media Analytics* (ACM, New York, 2010), pp. 71–79
117. M. Meola, *Computing Wikipedia's Authority* (2007), http://acrlog.org/2007/08/15/computing-wikipedias-authority/. Accessed 8 May 2018
118. M.J. Metzger, Making sense of credibility on the web: models for evaluating online information and recommendations for future research. J. Am. Soc. Inf. Sci. Technol. **58**(13), 2078–2091 (2007)
119. R. Mihalcea, C. Corley, C. Strapparava, Corpus-based and knowledge-based measures of text semantic similarity, in *AAAI*, vol. 6 (2006), pp. 775–780
120. N. Miller, P. Resnick, R. Zeckhauser, Eliciting informative feedback: the peer-prediction method. Manag. Sci. **51**(9), 1359–1373 (2005)

121. T. Mitra, E. Gilbert, CREDBANK: a large-scale social media corpus with associated credibility annotations, in *ICWSM* (2015), pp. 258–267

122. S. Mizzaro, Quality control in scholarly publishing: a new proposal. J. Am. Soc. Inf. Sci. Technol. **54**(11), 989–1005 (2003)

123. M. Morzy, A. Wierzbicki, The sound of silence: mining implicit feedbacks to compute reputation, in *International Workshop on Internet and Network Economics*, December 2006 (Springer, Berlin/Heidelberg, 2006), pp. 365–376

124. L. Mui, Computational models of trust and reputation: agents, evolutionary games, and social networks, Ph.D. thesis, Massachusetts Institute of Technology, December 2002

125. A. Mukherjee, V. Venkataraman, B. Liu, N. Glance, Fake review detection: classification and analysis of real and pseudo reviews, Technical report UIC-CS-2013-03, University of Illinois at Chicago, Tech. Rep., 2013

126. A. Mukherjee, V. Venkataraman, B. Liu, N.S. Glance, What yelp fake review filter might be doing? in *ICWSM* (2013)

127. K. Murakami, E. Nichols, S. Matsuyoshi, A. Sumida, S. Masuda, K. Inui, Y. Matumoto, Statement map: assisting information credibility analysis by visualizing arguments, in *Proceedings of the 3rd Workshop on Information Credibility on the Web, WICOW '09* (ACM, New York, 2009), pp. 43–50

128. V. Nastase, M. Strube, Decoding Wikipedia categories for knowledge acquisition, in *AAAI*, vol. 8 (2008), pp. 1219–1224

129. R. Nielek, A. Wawer, A. Wierzbicki, Spiral of hatred: social effects in Internet auctions. Between informativity and emotion. Electron. Commer. Res. **10**(3), 313–330 (2010)

130. R. Nielek, X. Liu, A. Wierzbicki, P. Adamska, K. Aberer, Towards a highly effective and robust web credibility evaluation system. Decis. Support. Syst. Electron. Commer. **79**, 99–108 (2015)

131. S. Nowak, S. Rüger, How reliable are annotations via Crowdsourcing: a study about inter-annotator agreement for multi-label image annotation, in *Proceedings of the International Conference on Multimedia Information Retrieval*, MIR '10 (ACM, New York, 2010), pp. 557–566

132. B. Nyhan, J. Reifler, When corrections fail: the persistence of political misperceptions. Polit. Behav. **32**(2), 303–330 (2010)

133. J. ODonovan, B. Kang, G. Meyer, T. Höllerer, S. Adalii, Credibility in context: an analysis of feature distributions in twitter, in *International Conference on Privacy, Security, Risk and Trust (PASSAT), 2012 and 2012 International Conference on Social Computing (SocialCom)* (IEEE, Washington, 2012), pp. 293–301

134. S. Oh, Y.J. Yi, A. Worrall, Quality of health answers in social Q&A. Proc. Am. Soc. Inf. Sci. Technol. **49**(1), 1–6 (2012)

135. C. Okoli, M. Mehdi, M. Mesgari, F.Å. Nielsen, A. Lanamäki, The people's encyclopedia under the gaze of the sages: a systematic review of scholarly research on Wikipedia. SSRN Scholarly Paper ID 2021326, Social Science Research Network, Rochester (2012)

136. A. Olteanu, S. Peshterliev, X. Liu, K. Aberer, Web credibility: features exploration and credibility prediction, in *Advances in Information Retrieval*, ed. by P. Serdyukov, P. Braslavski, S.O. Kuznetsov, J. Kamps, S. Rüger, E. Agichtein, I. Segalovich, E. Yilmaz. Lecture Notes in Computer Science, vol. 7814 (Springer, Berlin, 2013), pp. 557–568. https://doi.org/10.1007/978-3-642-36973-5_47

137. B. Orme, Scaling multiple items: monadic ratings versus paired comparisons, in *Sawtooth Software Conference Proceedings, Sequim* (2003), pp. 43–59

138. T.G. Papaioannou, K. Aberer, K. Abramczuk, P. Adamska, A. Wierzbicki, Game-theoretic models of web credibility, in *Proceedings of the 2nd Joint WICOW/AIRWeb Workshop on Web Quality* (ACM, New York, 2012), pp. 27–34

139. H. Azari, D. Parks, L. Xia, Random utility theory for social choice, in *Advances in Neural Information Processing Systems* (2012), pp. 126–134

140. D. Pelleg, E. Yom-Tov, Y. Maarek, Can you believe an anonymous contributor? On truthfulness in Yahoo! answers, in *International Conference on Privacy, Security, Risk and*

Trust (PASSAT), 2012 and 2012 International Conference on Social Computing (SocialCom) (2012), pp. 411–420

141. M. Pennacchiotti, A.-M. Popescu, Detecting controversies in Twitter: a first study, in *Proceedings of the NAACL HLT 2010 Workshop on Computational Linguistics in a World of Social Media, WSA '10* (Association for Computational Linguistics, Stroudsburg, 2010), pp. 31–32

142. R.E. Petty, J.T. Cacioppo, The elaboration likelihood model of persuasion, in *Communication and Persuasion* (Springer, New York, 1986), pp. 1–24

143. R.L. Plackett, The analysis of permutations. Appl. Stat. **24**, 193–202 (1975)

144. K. Popat, S. Mukherjee, J. Strötgen, G. Weikum, Where the truth lies: explaining the credibility of emerging claims on the web and social media, in *Proceedings of the 26th International Conference on World Wide Web Companion* (International World Wide Web Conferences Steering Committee, Geneva, 2017), pp. 1003–1012

145. M. Potthast, J. Kiesel, K. Reinartz, J. Bevendorff, B. Stein, A stylometric inquiry into hyperpartisan and fake news (2017). arXiv Preprint. arXiv:1702.05638

146. H.S. Rad, D. Barbosa, Identifying controversial articles in Wikipedia: a comparative study, in *Proceedings of the Eighth Annual International Symposium on Wikis and Open Collaboration, WikiSym '12* (ACM, New York, 2012), pp. 7:1–7:10

147. M. Rafalak, K. Abramczuk, A. Wierzbicki, Incredible: is (almost) all web content trustworthy? Analysis of psychological factors related to website credibility evaluation, in *Proceedings of the 23rd International Conference on World Wide Web* (ACM, New York, 2014), pp. 1117–1122

148. M. Rafalak, D. Deja, A. Wierzbicki, R. Nielek, M. Kakol, Web content classification using distributions of subjective quality evaluations. ACM Trans. Web **10**(4), 21 (2016)

149. Y. Ren, D. Ji, Neural networks for deceptive opinion spam detection: an empirical study. Inf. Sci. **385**, 213–224 (2017)

150. S.Y. Rieh, Judgment of information quality and cognitive authority in the web. J. Am. Soc. Inf. Sci. Technol. **53**(2), 145–161 (2002)

151. J.K. Rout, A. Dalmia, K.K.R. Choo, S. Bakshi, S.K. Jena, Revisiting semi-supervised learning for online deceptive review detection. IEEE Access **5**(1), 1319–1327 (2017)

152. V.L. Rubin, T. Lukoianova, Truth and deception at the rhetorical structure level. J. Assoc. Inf. Sci. Technol. **66**(5), 905–917 (2015)

153. V. Rubin, N. Conroy, Y. Chen, S. Cornwell, Fake news or truth? Using satirical cues to detect potentially misleading news, in *Proceedings of the Second Workshop on Computational Approaches to Deception Detection* (2016), pp. 7–17

154. Y. Rubner, C. Tomasi, L.J. Guibas, The earth mover's distance as a metric for image retrieval. Int. J. Comput. Vis. **40**(2), 99–121 (2000)

155. L. Samuelson, *Evolutionary Games and Equilibrium Selection*, vol. 1 (MIT Press, Cambridge, 1998)

156. E.T.K. Sang, J. Bos, Predicting the 2011 Dutch senate election results with Twitter, in *Proceedings of the Workshop on Semantic Analysis in Social Media* (Association for Computational Linguistics, Stroudsburg, 2012), pp. 53–60

157. R. Savolainen, The use of rhetorical strategies in Q&A discussion. J. Doc. **70**(1), 93–118 (2014)

158. P. Schönhofen, Identifying document topics using the Wikipedia category network. Web Intell. Agent Syst. Int. J. **7**(2), 195–207 (2009)

159. D.D.E.P. Schultz, Truth goggles: automatic incorporation of context and primary source for a critical media experience, Ph.D. thesis, Massachusetts Institute of Technology, 2012

160. J. Schwarz, M. Morris, Augmenting web pages and search results to support credibility assessment, in *Proceedings of the SIGCHI Conference on Human Factors in Computing Systems, CHI '11* (ACM, New York, 2011), pp. 1245–1254

161. C.E. Shannon, A mathematical theory of communication. SIGMOBILE Mob. Comput. Commun. Rev. **5**(1), 3–55 (2001)

162. C. Shao, G.L. Ciampaglia, A. Flammini, F. Menczer, Hoaxy: a platform for tracking online misinformation, in *Proceedings of the 25th International Conference Companion on World Wide Web* (International World Wide Web Conferences Steering Committee, 2016), pp. 745–750

163. S.M. Shariff, X. Zhang, M. Sanderson, User perception of information credibility of news on Twitter, in *European Conference on Information Retrieval* (Springer, Berlin, 2014), pp. 513–518

164. I. Sher, Credibility and determinism in a game of persuasion. Games Econ. Behav. **71**(2), 409–419 (2011)

165. B. Shi, T. Weninger, Fact checking in heterogeneous information networks, in *Proceedings of the 25th International Conference Companion on World Wide Web* (International World Wide Web Conferences Steering Committee, 2016), pp. 101–102

166. A. Shtok, G. Dror, Y. Maarek, I. Szpektor, Learning from the past: answering new questions with past answers, in *Proceedings of the 21st International Conference on World Wide Web* (ACM, New York, 2012), pp. 759–768

167. K. Shu, A. Sliva, S. Wang, J. Tang, H. Liu, Fake news detection on social media: a data mining perspective. ACM SIGKDD Explorations Newslett. **19**(1), 22–36 (2017)

168. K. Shu, S. Wang, H. Liu, Exploiting Tri-relationship for fake news detection (2017). arXiv Preprint. arXiv:1712.07709

169. S. Siegel, N. Castellan, *Nonparametric Statistics for the Behavioral Sciences* (McGraw-Hill, New York, 1981)

170. S. Sikdar, B. Kang, J. ODonovan, T. Höllerer, S. Adah, Understanding information credibility on Twitter, in *International Conference on Social Computing (SocialCom), 2013* (IEEE, Washington, 2013), pp. 19–24

171. S. Sikdar, S. Adali, M. Amin, T. Abdelzaher, K. Chan, J.-H. Cho, B. Kang, J. O'Donovan, Finding true and credible information on Twitter, in *2014 17th International Conference on Information Fusion (FUSION)* (2014), pp. 1–8

172. L.M. Smith, L. Zhu, K. Lerman, Z. Kozareva, The role of social media in the discussion of controversial topics, in *2013 International Conference on Social Computing*, September 2013, pp. 236–243

173. P. Smyth, U. Fayyad, M. Burl, P. Perona, P. Baldi, Inferring ground truth from subjective labelling of venus images. Adv. Neural Inf. Proces. Syst. **7**, 1085–1092 (1995)

174. R. Snow, B. O'Connor, D. Jurafsky, A.Y. Ng, Cheap and fast—but is it good?: evaluating non-expert annotations for natural language tasks, in *Proceedings of the Conference on Empirical Methods in Natural Language Processing, EMNLP '08* (Association for Computational Linguistics, Stroudsburg, 2008), pp. 254–263

175. A. Sorokin, D. Forsyth, Utility data annotation with Amazon mechanical Turk, in *2008 IEEE Computer Society Conference on Computer Vision and Pattern Recognition Workshops*, June 2008, pp. 1–8

176. H.A. Soufiani, H. Diao, Z. Lai, D.C. Parkes, Generalized random utility models with multiple types, in *Advances in Neural Information Processing Systems* (2013), pp. 73–81

177. M. Spence, Job market signaling. Q. J. Econ. **8**, 355–374 (1973)

178. P. Stone, D.C. Dunphy, M.S. Smith, D.M. Ogilvie, The general inquirer: a computer approach to content analysis. J. Reg. Sci. **8**(1), 113–116 (1968)

179. B. Stvilia, M.B. Twidale, L.C. Smith, L. Gasser, Assessing information quality of a community-based encyclopedia, in *IQ* (2005)

180. Q. Su, D. Pavlov, J.-H. Chow, W.C. Baker, Internet-scale collection of human-reviewed data, in *Proceedings of the 16th International Conference on World Wide Web* (ACM, New York, 2007), pp. 231–240

181. R. Sumi, T. Yasseri, A. Rung, A. Kornai, J. Kertész, Characterization and prediction of Wikipedia edit wars, in *Proceedings of the 3rd International ACM Conference on Web Science* (WebSci'2011), Koblenz, June 2011, pp. 1–3

182. R. Sumi, T. Yasseri, A. Rung, A. Kornai, J. Kertesz, Edit wars in Wikipedia, in *2011 IEEE Third International Conference on Privacy, Security, Risk and Trust and 2011 IEEE Third International Conference on Social Computing*, October 2011, pp. 724–727

183. S.S. Sundar, The MAIN model: a heuristic approach to understanding technology effects on credibility, in *Digital Media, Youth, and Credibility* (MIT Press, Cambridge, 2008), pp. 73–100
184. J. Surowiecki, *The Wisdom of Crowds* (Anchor, Hamburg, 2005)
185. P. Sztompka, *Trust: A Sociological Theory* (Cambridge University Press, Cambridge, 1999)
186. P. Sztompka, *Zaufanie. Fundament Społeczen'stwa (Trust. A Foundation of Society)* (Wydawnictwo Znak, Kraków, 2007)
187. E. Tacchini, G. Ballarin, M.L.D. Vedova, S. Moret, L. de Alfaro, Some like it hoax: automated fake news detection in social networks (2017). arXiv Preprint. arXiv:1704.07506
188. E.C. Tandoc Jr., Z.W. Lim, R. Ling, Defining "fake news" a typology of scholarly definitions. Digit. J. **6**, 1–17 (2017)
189. W.J. Tastle, M.J. Wierman, Consensus and dissention: a measure of ordinal dispersion. Int. J. Approx. Reason. **45**(3), 531–545 (2007)
190. L.L. Thurstone, A law of comparative judgment. Psychol. Rev. **34**(4), 273 (1927)
191. H. Toba, Z.-Y. Ming, M. Adriani, T.-S. Chua, Discovering high quality answers in community question answering archives using a hierarchy of classifiers. Inf. Sci. **261**, 101–115 (2014)
192. M. Tomasello, *A Natural History of Human Thinking* (Harvard University Press, Cambridge, 2014). Google-Books-ID: ksYXAgAAQBAJ
193. S. Tseng, B.J. Fogg, Credibility and computing technology. Commun. ACM **42**(5), 39–44 (1999)
194. M. Tsytsarau, T. Palpanas, K. Denecke, Scalable discovery of contradictions on the web, in *Proceedings of the 19th International Conference on World Wide Web, WWW '10* (ACM, New York, 2010), pp. 1195–1196
195. A. Tumasjan, T.O. Sprenger, P.G. Sandner, I.M. Welpe, Election forecasts with Twitter: how 140 characters reflect the political landscape. Soc. Sci. Comput. Rev. **29**(4), 402–418 (2011)
196. P. Turek, A. Wierzbicki, R. Nielek, A. Hupa, A. Datta, Learning about the quality of teamwork from wikiteams, in *International Conference on Social Computing (SocialCom), 2010 IEEE Second* (IEEE, Washington, 2010), pp. 17–24
197. U. Upadhyay, I. Valera, M. Gomez-Rodriguez, Uncovering the dynamics of crowdlearning and the value of knowledge (2016). arXiv Preprint. arXiv:1612.04831
198. C.Van der Eijk, Measuring agreement in ordered rating scales. Qual. Quant. **35**(3), 325–341 (2001)
199. F.B. Viégas, M. Wattenberg, K. Dave, Studying cooperation and conflict between authors with history flow visualizations, in *Proceedings of the SIGCHI Conference on Human Factors in Computing Systems* (ACM, New York, 2004), pp. 575–582
200. A. Vlachos, S. Riedel, Fact checking: task definition and dataset construction, in *Proceedings of the ACL 2014 Workshop on Language Technologies and Computational Social Science* (2014), pp. 18–22
201. E.M. Voorhees, D.M. Tice, Building a question answering test collection, in *Proceedings of the 23rd Annual International ACM SIGIR Conference on Research and Development in Information Retrieval* (ACM, New York, 2000), pp. 200–207
202. J. Voss, Collaborative thesaurus tagging the Wikipedia way, April 2006. arXiv:cs/0604036
203. L.H. Vu, J. Zhang, K. Aberer, Using identity premium for honesty enforcement and whitewashing prevention. Computational Intelligence, **30**(4), 771–797 (2014)
204. B.-Q. Vuong, E.-P. Lim, A. Sun, M.-T. Le, H.W. Lauw, K. Chang, On ranking controversies in Wikipedia: models and evaluation, in *WSDM 2008* (2008), pp. 171–182
205. W.Y. Wang, "Liar, liar pants on fire": a new benchmark dataset for fake news detection, May 2017. arXiv:1705.00648 [cs]
206. D. Wang, S. Zhu, T. Li, SumView: a web-based engine for summarizing product reviews and customer opinions. Expert Syst. Appl. **40**(1), 27–33 (2013)
207. C.N. Wathen, J. Burkell, Believe it or not: factors influencing credibility on the web. J. Am. Soc. Inf. Sci. Technol. **53**(2), 134–144 (2002)
208. A. Wawer, R. Nielek, Application of automated sentiment extraction from text to modeling of public opinion dynamics. Pol. J. Environ. Stud. **17**(3B), 508–513 (2008)

209. A. Wawer, R. Nielek, A. Wierzbicki, Predicting webpage credibility using linguistic features, in *Proceedings of the 23rd International Conference on World Wide Web* (ACM, New York, 2014), pp. 1135–1140

210. P. Welinder, S. Branson, S.J. Belongie, P. Perona, The multidimensional wisdom of crowds, in *NIPS*, vol. 23, 2010, pp. 2424–2432

211. J. Whitehill, T.-f. Wu, J. Bergsma, J.R. Movellan, P.L. Ruvolo, Whose vote should count more: optimal integration of labels from labelers of unknown expertise, in *Advances in Neural Information Processing Systems* (MIT Press, Cambridge, 2009), pp. 2035–2043

212. A. Wierzbicki, The case for fairness of trust management. Electron. Notes Theor. Comput. Sci. **197**(2), 73–89 (2008)

213. A. Wierzbicki, T. Kaszuba, R. Nielek, Trust and fairness management in P2p and grid systems, in *Handbook of Research on P2p and Grid Systems for Service-Oriented Computing: Models, Methodologies and Applications* (IGI Global, Hershey, 2010), pp. 748–773

214. A. Wierzbicki, P. Turek, R. Nielek, Learning about team collaboration from Wikipedia edit history, in *Proceedings of the 6th International Symposium on Wikis and Open Collaboration* (ACM, New York, 2010), p. 27

215. A. Wierzbicki, P. Adamska, K. Abramczuk, T. Papaioannou, K. Aberer, E. Rejmund, Studying web content credibility by social simulation. J. Artif. Soc. Soc. Simul. **17**(3), 6 (2014)

216. A.D. Williams, D. Tapscott, *Wikinomics* (Penguin Books, London, 2008)

217. J. Witkowski, Y. Bachrach, P. Key, D.C. Parkes, Dwelling on the negative: incentivizing effort in peer prediction, in *First AAAI Conference on Human Computation and Crowdsourcing* (2013)

218. L. Wu, H. Liu, Tracing fake-news footprints: characterizing social media messages by how they propagate, in *Proceedings of the 11th ACM International Conference on Web Search and Data Mining* (2018), pp. 637–645

219. L. Wu, H. Liu, Tracing fake-news footprints: characterizing social media messages by how they propagate (2018)

220. Y. Yamamoto, Disputed sentence suggestion towards credibility-oriented web search, in *Web Technologies and Applications*, ed. by Q.Z. Sheng, G. Wang, C.S. Jensen, G. Xu. Lecture Notes in Computer Science (Springer, Berlin, 2012), pp. 34–45. https://doi.org/10.1007/978-3-642-29253-8_4

221. Y. Yamamoto, S. Shimadam, Can disputed topic suggestion enhance user consideration of information credibility in web search? in *Proceedings of the 27th ACM Conference on Hypertext and Social Media, HT '16* (ACM, New York, 2016), pp. 169–177

222. Y. Yamamoto, K. Tanaka, Finding comparative facts and aspects for judging the credibility of uncertain facts, in *International Conference on Web Information Systems Engineering* (Springer, Berlin, 2009), pp. 291–305

223. Y. Yamamoto, K. Tanaka, Enhancing credibility judgment of web search results, in *Proceedings of the SIGCHI Conference on Human Factors in Computing Systems, CHI '11* (ACM, New York, 2011), pp. 1235–1244

224. Y. Yamamoto, K. Tanaka, ImageAlert: credibility analysis of text-image pairs on the web, in *Proceedings of the 2011 ACM Symposium on Applied Computing, SAC '11* (ACM, New York, 2011), pp. 1724–1731

225. Y. Yamamoto, T. Tezuka, A. Jatowt, K. Tanaka, Supporting judgment of fact trustworthiness considering temporal and sentimental aspects, in *International Conference on Web Information Systems Engineering* (Springer, Berlin, 2008), pp. 206–220

226. S. Yardi, D. Boyd, Dynamic debates: an analysis of group polarization over time on Twitter. Bull. Sci. Technol. Soc. **30**(5), 316–327 (2010)

227. T. Yasseri, R. Sumi, A. Rung, A. Kornai, J. Kertész, Dynamics of conflicts in Wikipedia. PLoS One **7**(6), e38869 (2012)

228. J. Yu, J.A. Thom, A. Tam, Ontology evaluation using Wikipedia categories for browsing, in *Proceedings of the Sixteenth ACM Conference on Conference on Information and Knowledge Management, CIKM '07* (ACM, New York, 2007), pp. 223–232

Index

© Springer International Publishing AG, part of Springer Nature 2018
A. Wierzbicki, *Web Content Credibility*,
https://doi.org/10.1007/978-3-319-77794-8

Printed in the United States
By Bookmasters